FREEBIRD PUBLISHERS
presents

M000240450

CELLPRENEUR

The Millionaire Prisoner's Guidebook

REVISED
2018

by

Josh Kruger
Author of The Millionaire Prisoner and Pen Pal Success

REVISED EDITION 2018
This publication has been revised to be in accordance with the Board Policy, 03.91, Uniform Offender Correspondence Rules and Regulations of the Texas Department of Criminal Justice.

Freebird Publishers
Box 541, North Dighton, MA 02764
Info@FreebirdPublishers.com
www.FreebirdPublishers.com

Copyright © 2017 Cellpreneur:
The Millionaire Prisoner's Guidebook By Josh Kruger

Publisher & Distributor: Freebird Publishers
Box 541 North Dighton, MA 02764
Web: FreebirdPublishers.com
E-Mail: diane@freebirdpublishers.com
Corrlinks: diane@freebirdpublishers.com
JPay: diane@freebirdpublishers.com
Toll-Free: 888-712-1987
Phone/Text: 774-406-8682
Send Letters to the Editor to the above address

All rights reserved. No part of this book may be reproduced in any form or by any means without the prior written consent of the Publisher, except in brief quotes used in reviews.

All Freebird Publishers titles, imprints and distributed lines are available at special quantity discounts for bulk purchases for sales promotions, premiums, fundraising educational or institutional use.

ISBN: 0-9913591-7-8

ISBN-13: 978-0-9913591-7-2

Printed in the United States of America

PRAISE FOR THE MILLIONAIRE PRISONER BOOKS

"I'm so impressed by Josh's work, I felt compelled to write and say I believe this book will help thousands of prisoners focus on a more positive and profitable life. I have seen a lot of submissions for publication, but Josh's is by far, the best I've seen."

George Kayer, original founding editor of *Inmate Shopper*, CEO of *Girls and Mags*

"The Millionaire Prisoner is a terrific guidebook for prisoners who desire to make something more of their life, even while in custody."
- Chris Zoukis, author of *College for Convicts*, Federal Prison Handbook: The Definitive guide to Surviving the Federal Bureau of Prisons, founder of *www.prisonlawblog.com* and *wwww.prisoneducation.com*.

"It is like a breath of fresh air to be working on a manuscript that is so positive and helpful to people who are in need of that kind of support. You will most surely be an inspiration to many who read your book. Your words have helped me also as I type."
- Jane Eichwald, *Ambler Document Processing*

"Millionaire Prisoner is a mandatory must have book for any prisoner that is tired of just going through the motions in prison. Millionaire Prisoner honestly changed my way of thinking. If you're tired of asking your family and friends for money and want to make your own, get this book and learn how to become a millionaire prisoner."
- Joshua "Butterbean" Snyder, IL. Prisoner

"Two thumbs up for this book. One would have to be a complete fool not to take advantage of the program that is shared in The Millionaire Prisoner."
- Jeremy Winsor, IL. Prisoner

"The Millionaire Prisoner is one of the best books a prisoner can read…a must-have in every prisoner's collection."
- Mike Enemigo, author, cellpreneur and CEO of *The Cell Block*

Praise for Pen Pal Success: The Ultimate Guide To Getting and Keeping Pen Pals. "Wow! You didn't leave anything out, a masterful presentation and tutorial on pen palling."
-George Kayer, *Girls and Mags*

"I recently had my mom purchase the Pen Pal Success book for me and I am 110% satisfied. Awesome!"
- Michael F., Nevada Prisoner

DEDICATION

This book is dedicated to my grandparents, Dorothy Mae and Walter Leon Barnett. They introduced me to small business with their antique store, "307 SHOP". The lessons I learned by watching my grandpa hustle out of the back rooms of his shop live on through me. Their legacy will continue to be honored. They are in heaven now, but they are never forgotten.

TABLE OF CONTENTS

WARNING-DISCLAIMER

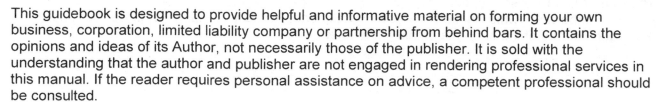

This guidebook is designed to provide helpful and informative material on forming your own business, corporation, limited liability company or partnership from behind bars. It contains the opinions and ideas of its Author, not necessarily those of the publisher. It is sold with the understanding that the author and publisher are not engaged in rendering professional services in this manual. If the reader requires personal assistance on advice, a competent professional should be consulted.

It's not the purpose of this guidebook to reprint every tip, tactic, and/or strategy that is available to a prisoner for starting a business. But instead to complement, amplify, and supplement on those books. You are urged to read all the available information and material, including the books listed throughout this book. Learn as much as you can and then develop your own strategies and implement your own plan. This guidebook is designed to provide accurate and authorative information on starting a business from prison. While every effort has been made to ensure factual accuracy, no warranties concerning such acts are made.

Having true business success is not some pie-in-the-sky get-rich-quick scheme. Any prisoner who wishes to have cellpreneur success must decide to invest a lot of time and effort into it. The advice and strategies contained in this guidebook may not be suitable for every situation. The purpose of this guide is to educate and entertain. While it was, the authors quest to make this guide as complete, up-to-date, and error free as possible. However, there will probably be errors, both typographical and in content. Because of this, it should be used as a guide, and not the be-all, end-all guide to starting a business from prison.

The fact that a website, business, organization, and/or association is listed or referred to in this guidebook as a citation and/or a potential source of further information does not mean the Author or Publisher endorses the Website, business, organization and/or association, or what those entities may offer. It should also be noted that the Internet Website listed, and other entities referred to may have, by the time you're reading this warning, changed, disappeared, closed and/or be dissolved.

Some terms mentioned in this guidebook are known to be or are suspected of being trademarks of different entities. Use of a term in this book should not be regarded to as affecting the validity of any trademark or service mark.

This guidebook should not be used as a substitute for competent legal advice from an attorney who specializes in business law. You should never automatically go against the advice of your attorney because of something you read in this guidebook. Even though the author is also a cellpreneur, he is not your attorney. Reading this guidebook doesn't create an attorney-client relationship or contract between you and him.

If, and to the extent that this book gives tax advice, the author-publisher is required by the Internal Revenue Service's Circular 230 (31 CFR Part 10) to advise you that such tax advice is not a formal legal opinion and was not intended or written to be used by you, and may not be used by you, (i) for the purpose of avoiding tax penalties that might be imposed on you or (ii) for promotion, marketing or recommending to another party any transaction or matter addressed herein.

Lastly, anyone who takes offense that the author uses he instead of the politically-correct "he or she, him or her" throughout this guidebook he apologizes ahead of time. He has done this because prison is still a male-dominated world, although women prisoners are the fastest growing segment in the prison-industrial complex of America. The author has tried to use "you" and "they" as much as he could, but some places he couldn't. If you're a transgender or female prisoner, he is speaking to you also. Don't let the fact that he may have used a male pronoun cause you to get dismayed. You can experience business success just as much, if not more, than male prisoners.

The Author and Publisher specifically disclaim any responsibility for any liability, loss, or risk, person or otherwise, which is incurred as a consequence, directly or indirectly, of the use and application of any of the contents of this guidebook.

INTRODUCTION

"The Author's character is read from title page to end."
- Henry David Thoreau

I have written this book, my third, with a single objective in mind: to help you form a business from behind bars. Why wait till you get out to get started when you can lay the groundwork now? Maybe you want to start a record label and become a music mogul? Maybe you want to start the next big Internet business? Maybe you want to open up a barbershop? No matter what your business hopes or dreams are, you now hold in your hands the answer you've been looking for.

What You'll Find In This Book

In his great book, *How To Write Simple Information for Fun and Profit*, author and copywriter Bob Bly says that there are three levels of "How-To" writing. These levels are:

1. At the first level: it tells you what to do.

2. At the next level: it tells you how to do it.

3. At the highest level: it does it for you.

Let's look at these levels in the sense of a how-to book for starting a business. A bad how-to book would only tell you what to do, i.e., "start a business and get paid." An okay how-to book would tell you how to do it, i.e., "Go down to your local chamber of commerce or courthouse and obtain the proper paperwork needed to start an LLC. Fill it out, file it, and you're in business." But the top of the line in how-to writings are those books that show you how to do it by including sample forms you can fill in and or copy for your own use. That way you can do it yourself. I've tried to do that in this book. Where it's possible I've included some fill-in-the-blank forms, so you can do it yourself. Not only will this save you time and money, but it will give you the results that you want.

WHO I AM AND MY ROLE IN YOUR LIFE

I am, by profession, a how-to writer of information that prisoners can use to make their lives better. I am, by captivity, a prisoner serving a life sentence for a felony murder conviction. I have over 26  years of experience in prisons across the Midwest. I do not write that to brag because it's not something to be boastful about, I tell you this to illustrate that I know what it's like to be kept behind bars. I know all about the bogus prison rules and regulations that are thrown at you. I understand the obstacles you face should you choose to journey down the cellpreneur path. How do I know? Because I've started two different businesses from behind bars. I have also formed partnerships and licenses with several other people as well. These entities have allowed me to make thousands of dollars legally. The truth is that I went from being a starving lifer to never missing a commissary. All because of a few simple ideas that I acted on. In this book, I'll show you how you can get started as well.

No B.S. business book author and marketing guru Dan S. Kennedy says that the test you put anyone through before you give them your money for business advice is this:

-   Have they been where you are and done what you hope to do?

-   Do they have real business battle scars?

-   Do they offer a guarantee?

Most people don't measure up to these standards. Test every so called cellpreneur you listen to within these four questions. If they don't measure up, don't pay too much attention to them. Go about your business. Save your time and money for those rare cellpreneurs who are about this life. I can name a few cellpreneurs off the top of my head who have real cellpreneur battle scars. George Kayer of *Inmate Shopper* fame, now *Girls and Mags*; Chris Zoukis of *PrisonEducation.com* and *PrisonLawBlog.com*; Mike Enemigo of *The Cell Block*; and former cellpreneur Paul Wright *of Prison Legal News*. These are some you can listen to. Others should be tested using Dan Kennedy's test.

That goes for me too. As you read this book pay attention. Put my words to the test. Read my other two books, The *Millionaire Prisoner* and *Pen Pal Success* and decide your verdict about me. I'm sure you'll see that I'm up to my neck in the cellpreneur niche. My business manager could show you the letters from prisoners all across the United States who are using my strategies or who say my books have changed their life. I hope this book will aide you in changing yours.

Before we get started on your cellpreneur journey, I need to make a few more valid points. First, this book is for both male and female prisoners. I don't use the terms "he" or "she" to intentionally exclude the other sex. I just write how I talk. I want our relationship to be as natural as it can be. So, I speak to you on these pages how I would if I was in your cell talking to you. Second: some of what is included throughout this book was also included in my first two books. This was done on purpose. Mainly because my whole *Millionaire Prisoner* philosophy is based on a set of ABCs of success that form the chapters of my first book. If you build on their foundations everything else will fall into place. I'm living proof of that. The other reason I repeat some stuff is because I work smart, not hard. Why write something all over again when I got it right the first time? Plus, I can't plagiarize myself!

HOW TO GET YOUR MONEY'S WORTH FROM THIS BOOK

Read this book carefully. Focus on the ideas offered. Follow the steps. And please don't just read this book once and forget about it. Come back to it. It's a conversation between anyone that has been inside. One of us has the answers to how you get where you want to go. So, keep a pen or highlighter handy. You'll find a wealth of knowledge that you may want to underline or highlight for emphasis.

I also invite you to stay in touch with us. The tips, tactics, and strategies throughout my books will need to be updated as better processes become available. I intend to learn those new processes and use them. Then share them with others if I see they work. If you find some cellpreneur success systems that a prisoner can use, or if you experience success using this book or my other books, feel free to write my business manager or publisher and tell us about it. I may just put you in the next edition of my *Millionaire Prisoner* products. Also, to congratulate you, not just for what you achieved, but for making the world a better place.

Your journey is just beginning. The Buddhist prisoners say that "a thousand-mile journey must start with a single footstep." Make sure that your first step is in the right direction. Why you? Why start now? Because right now you sit in a prison cell and have nothing to lose, but everything to gain.

> *"Some men see things as they are, and say 'Why?'*
> *I dream of things that never were, and say, 'Why not?'"*
> *- George Bernard Shaw*

Why not indeed?

This guide book can aid you on your quest to free yourself from the bondage of prison and unleash your power. You can start your journey by turning the page.

The Cell Block Presents TCB University

NEW NOW AVAILABLE IN BOOK FORMAT

Get Money

Self-Educate, Get Rich & Enjoy Life

3 Volume Series

Categories In Every Volume

- ✓ GET MONEY
- ✓ MAILBOX MONEY
- ✓ SURVIVING PRISON

Sections In Every Volume Filled With

- ✓ ALL NEW
- ✓ UP-TO-DATE
- ✓ IDEAS
- ✓ INSTRUCTIONS

ON HOW TO GET MONEY!

Each Book: Softcover, 6"x9", 125+ pages, B&W

Get Money
Self-Educate, Get Rich & Enjoy Life
Vol. 1
The Cell Block Presents TCB University

Get Money
Self-Educate, Get Rich & Enjoy Life
Vol. 2
The Cell Block Presents TCB University

Get Money
Self-Educate, Get Rich & Enjoy Life
Vol. 3
The Cell Block Presents TCB University

Over $70 Worth of Reports in Each Volume

These books are part of a three volume series that provide educational information to prisoners, street hustlers and anyone who wants to learn how to get money and win legally in their quest for wealth and prosperity. Each volume has three sections Get Money, Mailbox Money and How to Survive Prison. Every section is filled with new, up to date ideas and instructions on how to get money.

ORDER SEPARATELY or ORDER ALL 3 - SAVE

☐ GET MONEY: Self-Educate, Get Rich & Enjoy Life, Vol. 1… $15.99 plus $5 s/h
☐ GET MONEY: Self-Educate, Get Rich & Enjoy Life, Vol. 2… $15.99 plus $5 s/h
☐ GET MONEY: Self-Educate, Get Rich & Enjoy Life, Vol. 3… $15.99 plus $5 s/h
☐ VALUE PAK: 3 BOOK SET, GET MONEY: Vol. 1, 2 &3… $39.99 plus $7 s/h

WE ACCEPT ALL CHECKS & MONEY ORDERS
Payable to:
The Cell Block

To order, simply send the names of book volume(s) you want written clearly on paper, enclose the proper payment amount

The Cell Block, Dept. TCBU, Box 595, Seekonk, MA 02771
Also available Amazon & FreebirdPublishers.com & TheCellBlock.net

THE CELL BLOCK

CHAPTER 1
THE EDUCATION OF THE MILLIONAIRE PRISONER
"People don't realize how a man's whole life can be changed by one book."
- Malcolm X

THE EDUCATION OF THE MILLIONAIRE PRISONER

"You should write a book." I heard that a thousand times. All of my pen pals told me that. My family told me that. It seemed everyone wanted me to write a book. But the truth was, I didn't want to write a book. I just wanted to bet on sports and win money. Forget the hard stuff, I liked easy money. Then I lost the direct appeal on my criminal case, which caused a chain reaction of events. A lot of my pen pals became ghosts and the reality sank in with the fact that I just might be stuck in prison for a while since the judge had given me a natural life sentence. Playing around winning "zuzus" and "wham-whams" off the commissary doesn't seem so luxurious when you need $10,000 or more for a good post-conviction attorney. The thought occurred that maybe I should have written that book. But for me it didn't come easy. In this chapter, I tell you my story.

> *"It is by sitting down to write every*
> *morning that one becomes a writer."*
> *- Gerald Brennan*

I've been writing since I was thirteen years old. Only I wasn't writing books, but letters to pen pals. I'm a state-raised convict and I've been in and out of prison since I was a teenager. Way more in than out. I'm from a small town in Illinois and my uncle was a rogue cop on the town's police force and ended up in prison himself. So, prison is in my gene pool and I certainly carried along the family lineage of incarceration. One of the things that I did over the years to pass time was to read books. It didn't matter what it was, I would read it. I didn't care if I was locked down in segregation as long as I had some kind of book to read. Through books I could escape my incarceration. This foundation of knowledge has only helped me over the years to perfect my letter writing.

> *"First, we eat, then we beget;*
> *first we read, then we write. "*
> *- Ralph Waldo Emerson*

I began writing stories for my pen pals. I called them "scenarios". I was playing a game of "let's pretend" and would write out a story that was set in the future. The stars of the story would be me and whatever pen pal I was writing to. Depending on who I was writing to, the scenario could be an urban crime drama, a sex skit, or just a simple walk on the beach. I didn't know it at the time, but I was actually creating fictional short stories like any other author would. Except my payment was praise from whomever I was writing to instead of money. It wasn't until I got to maximum-security that I started to consider making writing my vocation.

Over the years, I had read numerous books composed by authors who have been in prison. Names like Doestoyevsky, Tolstoy, Edward Bunker, Malcolm X, Nelson Mandela, Rubin "Hurricane" Carter, and many others. If they could do it, why couldn't I? Why not use the solitude of a maximum-security prison cell to pen my masterpiece? It couldn't be that hard to write a book or get it published, could it? I was about to find out.

My first attempt at writing a book was a crime novel called *The Get-Back*. It was the story of a man who ends up in prison after being framed by rival gang members. While there, he plots his revenge and upon his release he takes down his rivals one by one. It was supposed to be my version of a modern day *The Count of Monte Cristo.* But I couldn't do it. I had a good plot and outline, but my writing sucked. I didn't like it and threw the half-written manuscript in the garbage. Then I went back to my comfort zone of writing pen pals. At least they worshiped my letters.

My next attempt at getting published was to enter a poetry contest. It was something I knew I could do well because I had been writing poetry to my pen pals for years. Shot Caller Press held the contest for their upcoming anthology, *Cellblock Poetry*. I entered my poem, *Isolation*, into the contest and waited. First, second, and third place all paid out a cash prize and I wanted to win. I didn't, but my poem was selected as an "honorable mention" and was included in the book. All of my family bought copies of that book and it made me feel proud. I was officially a published poet. I wasn't really happy because I didn't get paid for my work, someone else did. Still, it was nice to see my name listed as the author of that poem in a real book. Who doesn't like seeing their name in print? That success only made me hungry for more.

> *"Once you become a published*
> *author, your life will change. "*
> *- Dan Poynter*

Getting that poem published was a catalyst for me. It got me believing that maybe I could eke out a decent living from behind bars through writing. I checked out writing books from the prison library which led me to other books I read *How To Make $100,000 a Year as a Freelance Writer* and *How To Get Happily Published*. But the book that really got me seriously considering the craft was Stephen King's *On Writing*. Here was one of the most famous writers' ever telling how he started out by getting his short stories published in science fiction magazines. And he only got about $50 a pop. Heck, I would've been happy to get $40 for a short story. But, I didn't like science fiction and couldn't write fiction that good anyway. I had to find my genre. What I was reading at the time was mostly "How-To" nonfiction books. I read a lot of self-help and business books also. I started to get the reputation around the prison as the guy who had answers. Even if I didn't know off the top of my head, I could show you a book that could tell you want you needed to know. That's how I found my genre. I was going to write about what I knew…prison. And I was going to write for prisoners.

It was during one of my seg trips that the light bulb finally came on inside my head. In one of my business books, it talked about not working for someone else, but instead, to start your own business. I liked that idea because of my feelings towards Shot Caller Press when they got paid off my work and I didn't. Hey, they didn't do anything wrong, I was the one who signed on the dotted line. So, I started looking into how to open my own publishing company. I wrote to my mother and asked her to find me some books on starting your own publishing business. She sent me *The Self-Publishing Manual* by Dan Poynter; *How to Write and Sell Simple Information for Fun and Profit* by Robert Bly; and *The Well-Fed Self-Publisher* by Peter Bowerman. One of the lessons that I learned from these books is that you don't have to write a full-length book to make money with your writing. Once you know who your target audience is you can begin to write for them. After learning this, I decided to self-publish my own booklet.

> *"Everything you write doesn't*
> *have to be your magnum opus. "*
> *-Bob Bly*

My first booklet was How to Get Free Pen Pals. The process contained in that booklet was nothing ground breaking or new. Prisoners have been doing what I advocate in it for years. I was just the first prisoner that I know of to put it into salable form and profit from it. Here's how I did it. I hand wrote all the pages and then typed them up on my Swintec typewriter. I had a format of twenty pages, about five thousand words. I then paid a printing company in Wisconsin $117 to take those twenty pages, put them into booklet form, and give me one hundred copies of the booklet. My plan was to sell each booklet for $9.95 or the equivalent in stamps. I would use the money to reinvest and get 500-1,000 more copies of the booklet and lower my unit cost. I got 1,000 more copies of the booklet printed for $300, or .30 cents per booklet. When I received my first booklet, it was an awesome feeling. I was holding something in my hands that I wrote, put together, and paid for all by myself from my maximum-security prison cell. Not only was I a published poet, but also a published author; albeit of a booklet. My How To Get Free Pen Pals booklet didn't look as good as I wanted it to because I didn't understand at the time that typed single-spaced pages using a prison typewriter don't look professional once printed out. Not in today's computer-generated products world. But I had a finished product and I could start marketing it and hopefully generate some income.

My next step was to start a publishing company with my mother. We named it O'Barnett Publishing after my grandfather and it cost less than $200 to set up. I decided to use a "bait" ad to market my booklet. Anyone who responded to the ad would get a copy of my mini-sales brochure. I placed a 2-month classified ad in Prison Legal News that cost me $60. Here is that ad:

How to Get Free Pen Pals!
For More info send SASE to:
O'Barnett Publishing
P.O. Box xxx
Catlin, IL 61817

My booklet wasn't the only product I planned on selling. Because I had continued to read business books I was familiar with mail-order success secrets. I had the habit of reading mail-order ad sheets and catalogs to see what I could find. I saw an ad that said, "Become an Instant Publisher." I sent off for the information and found out that I could buy a CD-ROM that contained over 600 special reports that I could resell for profit. The CD-ROM was $50. I had my mom buy it for me as a birthday present. My plan was to take these reports and rewrite them to appeal to a prisoner because that's who my target audience was. I knew I could sell my booklet, but I wanted to offer other products so that I could make more money and establish myself as "the expert on having success from your prison cell."

My next idea was to put together some pen pal lists. Over the years, I had paid for numerous pen pal lists and was either disappointed because of the few numbers of actual people on the lists or the few number of replies that I got from my letters. I put together several lists: *100 Wealthy Women*, *100 Chicagoland Women*, and *100 Pen Pals*. Then I did an additional thirty pen pal addresses that I offered as a bonus for those who bought my *How To Get Free Pen Pals* booklet. My mother didn't want to sell the *100 Wealthy Women* list but agreed to sell my other lists. Next, I typed up the sales brochure in my cell. I then sent it to a friend in the free world who typeset it on his computer, so it looked more professional. Thus, my first product line was born. Little did I know the problems that would come.

After O'Barnett Publishing was up and running I began to work on another booklet, *How to Win Your Football Pool*. I was also working on my manuscript for The *Millionaire Prisoner*. I would get up at 7:00 A.M. when my cellmate would go to work, eat breakfast, and then get to work. I'd write, then type up my handwritten pages. Somedays I would skip lunch and just keep typing. My cellmate would come back to the cell at 2:30 P.M. and I'd still be typing. My manuscript quickly ballooned to over six hundred pages, but I didn't have any deadlines, so I could take my time and

get it right. But shortly after I started my typing job, a guard at Menard Correctional Center in Southern Illinois got stabbed by a prisoner wielding a shank made from the metal piece in the typewriter. This isolated incident caused an overreaction by the Illinois Department of Corrections administration and they deemed typewriters to be contraband in all maximum-security prisons. Starting in Menard, they used the "Orange Crush" tactical unit to confiscate all personal typewriters that prisoners had in their cells. Panic set in and I thought, "What am I going to do now?" At that time, I didn't have the money to pay someone in the free world to type up my handwritten pages. So, I did the only thing that made sense, I went into hyperdrive and typed for twelve to thirteen hours a day. I watched out my window as the Orange Crush rolled into my prison at 6:00 A.M. to hit the cellhouse next to mine. Luckily for me, they went to another cellhouse before they came back to the one I was housed in. By the time, they did come back I was done typing. Hillbilly guards assembled from prisons across the state herded us prisoners into the chow hall like cattle while another group of guards ransacked our cells in so-called "shakedown." When the dust settled and we were returned to our cells, my typewriter was gone. For the first few days after losing my typewriter, I was in a funk. I didn't want to do anything. Even my cellmate commented that his afternoon nap wasn't the same because he missed the soothing pitter-patter sound of my typing. I wrote to one of my writing mentors in the free world complaining about the fact that I lost my typewriter. She sent me an article about other prisoners who wrote books in the past. The lesson that she got me to see was that these famous authors didn't have typewriters. So, if they did it without one, I could also. I would just have to find a way to keep going no matter what. Life does go on.

> *"I'm all in favor of keeping dangerous weapons*
> *out of the hands of fools. Let's start with typewriters."*
> *-Frank Lloyd Wright*

Business was booming at O'Barnett Publishing and my pen pal booklet and pen pal lists were selling like hotcakes. I was even selling some of those prewritten reports off the CD-ROM. I went back to finishing my next booklet, *How To Win Your Football Pool*. Once I had my twenty handwritten pages, I paid a typist $50 to professionally type it up using MS-Word on her computer. I was more than pleased with the results. Finally, something I created looked professional. Then I drew up a front cover and sent it and my new manual/booklet home, so it would be safe. My next step was to design a one-page 8x12 flyer that I was going to use to sell the football pool booklet. It looked okay when I was done, but not professional. So, I found a graphic designer in Hawaii who took my "mechanical" ad and professionally typeset it for $25. When she sent the ad/flyer back to me, she sent some extra copies and a little note that said, "Josh, I hope you sell some football pools." That's when all hell broke loose.

A guard, who was on punishment detail, was sorting the mail in the prison mail room and saw my flyer and turned the whole thing over to the Internal Affairs department. At 7:30 A.M., on a Monday, two guards from the prison's Internal Affairs goon squad banged into my cell, removed all of my property and walked me to segregation under "investigation." I had no idea what I did wrong and when I asked I was only told, "You'll hear from us." I had heard stories of other prisoners being persecuted for getting their writing published, but I couldn't believe it was happening to me. I know most prison systems preach rehabilitation, but in reality, they don't want you to do anything unsupervised, i.e., censored. After two weeks of sitting in seg, I was called to the Internal Affairs office and interrogated about my business and my writing. I was told it was illegal to sell products to other prisoners under IDOC Rules and Regulations. Also, it was against the rules to run a business without getting prior approval from the warden. I told the IA guard that they could throw me in segregation for the rest of my life for all I cared because I wasn't going to stop writing. All I really cared about was my manuscript for The Millionaire Prisoner. I told IA that if they didn't return that, then I was going to sue them. I was given a disciplinary ticket for "running an unauthorized business venture and "gambling". All of my property was returned to me except three of Robert Greene's books, *The 48 Laws of Power*, *The Art of Seduction*, and *The 33 Strategies of War*. Those books are on IDOC's banned book list and considered contraband. After 30 days in segregation, I was released back into general population.

Luckily, IDOC has a rule that prisoners can write manuscripts for profit, so I was safe. What I did wrong was talk way too much on the phone with my mother about business related matters. The Internal Affairs guard conducting the investigation went back and reviewed all my phone conversations and used excerpts of them as evidence of wrong doing in the disciplinary ticket. For me, the time I did in seg didn't bother me. I'm a lifer and seg is just another aspect of prison that I accept as inevitable. Plus, I was honored to be in seg for doing something productive for once instead of a stupid act like cursing out a guard or some other minor disciplinary infraction. I was fine and on top of my little prison world. I was still in business and raking in the money. What I couldn't have fathomed was the toll all of this was taking on my mother's health.

Our post office box was receiving thousands of inquiries from the ad in *Prison Legal News.* So much that my mother had shoe boxes stuffed with envelopes all across her kitchen table and floor. Then she became sick. I do believe that this was partly my doing. I put too much stress on her by calling collect and asking a thousand questions about the business, she was already working part time and on top of that, trying to deal with my demands. Because she got physically sick, she fell behind on orders and then started worrying thinking she was letting  me down. Some of the prisoners who wrote were very demeaning and abusive and my mom would take this to heart. All she wanted to do was help me and other prisoners out. But she had no idea what it was going to be like. The seg trip was the last straw for her and she shut O'Barnett Publishing down. Below is the final ad she placed. I had to make a decision about what I was going to do about my reports and booklets. I knew I wasn't going to give up because I had a profitable venture going. I just had to find someone else to take over the publishing end of things.

BARNETT PUBLISHING CLOSED!
Why-Health issues & Prison Rules
Will fill all current orders BUT
No NEW orders & no pen pal lists
Sorry prisoners We really tried.

When I thought about my situation, I realized I had the perfect partner already. I had a friend who was in mail-order and who I had a profitable partnership with in the past. I wrote him a letter and explained everything that had happened. I offered him 50% of the rights to my special reports and booklets. He would be the publisher of record and I would just be the author and collect a royalty off each unit sold. He agreed to the deal, except he didn't want to sell any pen pal lists. We had been getting way too many complaints about the lists. Selling pen pal lists wasn't something I wanted to be known for, so leaving them alone was an easy thing to do. Doing this deal has worked for the best over the years. Not having to worry about the day to day operation of a publishing company has left me

with the free time to concentrate on writing and creating new products for prisoners. The downside is that the profit margin for me is not as large as it used to be. But slow money is better than no money.

"Everything you need is already in your life
merely awaiting your recognition of it."
-Dr. Mike Murdock

I wish I could say that IDOC left me alone, but I still get harassed from time to time. When Orange Crush hits a cellhouse on a special shakedown, my cell is on the target list. Internal Affairs has come back and torn up my cell on several occasions. It's just a way for them to let me know I'm on their radar. I've had my Millionaire Prisoner Newsletter banned. I got another disciplinary ticket for discussing my publishing stuff with Mike Werth of The Cell Block. They gave me another month in seg for that. That's okay with me, I expect it. I just roll with it, because no matter what, my words are in print and in the marketplace. They can't stop that, and they will never stop me from writing. I don't regret anything, only that I didn't start writing earlier.

"I persevered because I recognized that writing was my
sole choice of creating something, of climbing from
the dark pit, fulfilling the dream, and resting in the sun."
- Edward Bunker

After everything that has happened, I still went on to publish three books, start a newsletter, and legally and legibly, build my own publishing company from behind bars of several different maximum-security prisons. I did it with no access to a computer. Only pen, paper and the telephone. In this book, I show you how you can do it also. As you can tell from my story it won't be easy. But I guarantee that if you choose to journey down the cellpreneur path, it will be worth it. You can begin your journey by turning the page.

THE CELL BLOCK

PRESENTS

THE **MILLIONAIRE** PRISONER SPECIAL TCB EDITION

JOSHUA KRUGER

FORWARD BY MIKE ENEMIGO

HOW TO GET <u>REAL</u> MONEY <u>LEGALLY!</u>

ORDER NOW!

ONLY $19.99

+ $7.00 SHIPPING & HANDLING

ATTENTION: THIS BOOK IS A PRISONER MUST-HAVE!

Why wait until you get out of prison to achieve your dreams? Here's a blue print that you can use to become successful!

The Millionaire Prisoner is your complete reference to overcoming any obstacles in prison. You won't be able to put it down! With this book you will discover the secrets to: Making money from your cell! Obtain FREE money for correspondence courses! Become an expert on any topic! Develop the habits of the rich! Network with celebrities! Set up your own website! Market your products, ideas and services! Successfully use prison pen pal websites! How to get FREE pen pals! All of this and much, much more! This book has enabled thousands of prisoners to succeed and it will show you the way also!

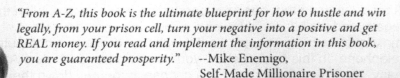

"From A-Z, this book is the ultimate blueprint for how to hustle and win legally, from your prison cell, turn your negative into a positive and get REAL money. If you read and implement the information in this book, you are guaranteed prosperity." --Mike Enemigo, Self-Made Millionaire Prisoner

THE CELL BLOCK
PO BOX 1025
RANCHO CORDOVA, CA 95741

CHAPTER 2
CELLPRENEURS AND THE LAW

"To say that laws are necessary to protect individuals sounds all right until you realize that most laws interfere with the freedom of individuals..."
– Robert Ringer

CELLPRENEURS AND THE LAW

Let's get something out of the way right now: *You do not have a constitutional right to run a business from prison. Stringer v. DeRobertis*, 541 F. Supp. 605 (n. D. ILL. 1982) The only exception to that restriction is that prisoners who have not yet been convicted (pre-trial detainees) have the right to do business as is accorded to all un-convicted citizens. *Tyler v. Ciccone*, 299 F. Supp. 684, 687 (W.D.1969)

But just because you don't have a constitutional right to run a business doesn't mean you should foreclose starting your own business. In this chapter, I'll explain what the law is in this arena and give you some tips and tactics about how to start your business. I'll also provide you with some Cellpreneur examples from the prison past (and present) as a source of inspiration. Be sure to check your own prison's (or jail's) rules and regulations before venturing down the Cellpreneur path.

UNITED STATES SUPREME COURT LAW

As a prisoner, you still have some First Amendment rights, although those rights may be curtailed in order to advance the legitimate penological objectives of the corrections system such as order, security, or rehabilitation. *Pell v. Procunier*, 417 U.S. 817, 822 (1974).

Most prisons have adopted regulations that outright ban you from running a business from prison, or at least force you to seek prior approval before you do so. But the Supreme Court has said that "when a prison regulation impinges on inmates' constitutional rights, the regulation is valid if it is reasonably related to legitimate penological interests..." *Turner v. Safley*, 482 U.S. 78, 89 (1987).

There are several factors known as the *Turner* standard that you need to examine to decide if your prison's regulation is reasonable. They are:

- Whether there is a valid, rational connection between the prison regulation and the legitimate governmental interest put forward to justify it.

- Whether there are alternative means of exercising the right that remain open to prison inmates.

- The impact of accommodating the right on other inmates, guards, and the allocation of prison resources generally.

- Whether alternatives exist that fully accommodate the prisoner's rights at de minimis cost to valid penological interests.

These four standards can be found at *Turner v. Safely*, 482 U.S. at 89-91.

It's hard for us prisoners to get over these standards in prison litigation. The problem is that prison officials get deferential treatment by the courts. *Shaw v. Murphy*, 532 U.S. 223, 229 (2001). But it's not an impossible standard to get over. *See, e.g., Beard v. Banks*, 548 U.S. 521, 535-36 (2006).

With these guidelines in mind, we can examine a few case studies from cellpreneurs who have gotten over the Turner standard. And some that have not. This will give you an idea of what is possible and what is not.

INFO-CELLPRENEURSHIP

Most of the cellpreneurs who have been successful in challenging prison regulations were info-cellpreneurs. They were authors who were persecuted for their work. Prison administrators used the "no business" rule to try to force them to quit. Most often, it didn't work. One of the more famous info cellpreneurs is Mumia Abu-Jamal.

Mumia was convicted of murdering a police officer and until recently, spent most of his time on death row. While there, Mumia continued to write books, do radio commentaries, and report on the injustices of the system. But Pennsylvania prison authorities don't like Mumia speaking the truth and tried to use a DOC Rule forbidding prisoner from "engaging in business or profession" while in prison. Mumia sued the Pennsylvania DOC and won an injunction banning prison officials from enforcing the business rule against him. *Abu-Jamal v. Price*, 154 F.3d 128(3d cir.1998).

Victor Martin is a critically acclaimed North Carolina prison author. Some of his books are Nude Awakening and The Game of Deception. Prison officials searched his cell and seized a manuscript and other materials. Martin kept getting disciplinary reports pertaining to his writing. Officials were alleging that he was conducting a business. Eventually the North Carolina chapter of the ACLU intervened on his behalf and filed a lawsuit. In 2010, the NCDOC settled out of court for $10,000 in damages. They also changed their policy. Now prisoners in NCDOC can submit manuscripts for publication and sign power of attorney over to someone else to handle the business side of publishing. *See Martin v. Keller*, USDC E.D. NC, Case ND. 5:09-cv-0044.

Mart Jordan was an ADX-Florance prisoner who was disciplined for publishing articles. The BOP tried to use their business rule to discipline him on several occasions. Mr. Jordan sued prison officials saying that the prison regulations in question were unconstitutional. After a bench trial on the merits, he won. The court ruled that the rule prohibiting prisoners from publishing under a byline violated the First Amendment. *Jordan v. Pugh*, 504 F. Supp. 2d 1109 (D.Colo.2007).

Pelican Bay state prisoner Dale Bretches wrote and published *Dog O War*, a book about attack-dog breeding, dog mauling death and subsequent criminal prosecution. He used *iUniverse* to publish his book in return for a 20% royalty. California prison officials punished Bretches because some of the content in his book was inflammatory, and that he participated in the crime, even though he was never charged. California prison regulation Title 15, Section 3024 allows prisoners to earn money by writing or artwork for a business or publication, if not owned or run by the prisoner. So Bretches filed grievances and then sued prison officials for violating his First Amendment Rights for banning his book. The district court dismissed his claim, but it was reinstated by the Appellate Court. *Bretches v. Kirkland*, 335 Fed.Appx.675 (9th Cir. 2009).

James L. Valentine drafted a form letter offering to sell seven "Special Reports". One report, "How to Have Local Businessman Give You $400,000 in Addition to Receiving $35,000 and a New Car", sold for $100. Other reports were offered at $25 and $500. Prison officials disciplined him and seized his property and mail. He sued and got an injunction, so officials couldn't seize mail and magazines like *Forbes* and *Business Week*, that weren't related to his info-cellpreneur business. But he lost on his other issues. *Valentine v. Gray*, 410 F. Supp. 1394 (S.D. Ohio 1975).

Jose Medina was a prisoner at the Curran-Fromhold Correctional Facility in Pennsylvania. He was working on a manuscript about the Latin Kings organization. Prison officials searched his cell on two separate occasions and seized his manuscripts. Prison officials justified the seizure of his manuscripts by saying they were "gang related". The court did not accept that view. But the court granted the prison officials qualified immunity, with a cautionary quote relevant to our discussion:

"Let there be no question, however, of this Court's deep concern that the confiscation of a prisoner's writings raises grave questions regarding when First Amendment Rights must give way to legitimate penological interests and the appropriate role of prison official and the courts in making that determination. Prison regulations limiting prisoner's First Amendment freedoms should be drafted and applied carefully and with due deference to the values the First Amendment was designed to protect, especially when such regulations impinge on a prisoner's possession of personal writings within the confines of his cell, as such acts tread dangerously close to regulation of the prisoner's thoughts themselves."

See *Medina v. City of Philadelphia*, 2004 WL 1126007 (USDC E.D.-PA, May 19, 2004).

It should be noted that Medina didn't ask for declaratory nor injunctive relief in his suit. If he would have, that would've foreclosed the finding of qualified immunity. *Hydrick v. Hunter*, 449 F.3d 978, 992 (9th Cir. 2006). So, if you have to sue to enforce your rights, always ask for declaratory and injunctive relief along with your damages claim.

Being an info-cellpreneur isn't just about publishing books. Florida prisoner David Ruetter wrote articles for *Prison Legal News* in the early 2000's and was paid for his work. He was disciplined for violating Florida DOC Rules that restrict prisoners from being compensated for their work. He sued and lost. The court said he could still write for free. *Prison Legal News v. McDonough*, 200 Fed. Appx. 873 (11th Cir. 2006)

Do not let prison officials tell you that because your work is being sold for profit it should not be given the protection of the First Amendment. The Supreme Court has said that's not the case: "That books, newspapers, and magazines are published and sold for profit does not prevent them from being a form of expression whose liberty is safeguarded by the First Amendment." *Joseph Burstyn, Inc. v. Wilson*, 343 U.S. 495, 501-02 (1952).

Another member of the info-cellpreneur hall of fame is Eddie Bunker. He is one of the most famous writers to come out of prison. Inspired by Caryl Chessman's book, *Cell 2455, Death Row*, Bunker taught himself how to type in San Quentin. He would handwrite his manuscripts with a no. 2 pencil at night while using a "*stolen*" flashlight for illumination, then type them up in the morning.

Bunker wrote a famous article for *Haper's* magazine which detailed racism in prison. Two of his novels were made into movies: *No Beast So Fierce* into *Straight Time* starring Dustin Hoffman, and *The Animal Factory* into a movie of the same name. Bunker also played "Mr. Blue" in the cult classic *Reservoir Dogs*. Although known for his novels, I recommend all prisoners who want to write for a living read his memoir, *Education of a Felon*.

> *"I used to think those prison writers who occasionally get published had it easy. All they have to do is sit in their cells and type away while other people wash their clothes and feed them. Then I realized prisons were even noisier than my house, so there went my plans to get arrested."*
> *- JoAnn Ross*

But info-cellprenuership isn't the only business that prisoners try to conduct from behind bars. Here's some others.

Jailhouse Lawyers Business

In 1985, Illinois prisoner Thomas Smith placed the following ad in Chicago Lawyer magazine:

"Do you have a client who is incarcerated at Menard Prison? Does this client have problems with the prison administration? Thomas W. Smith, a jailhouse lawyer, does expert grievances at a reasonable price. For more information, contact: Thomas W Smith…"

IDOC legal staff began investigating Smith for possible unauthorized practice of law. He was given a disciplinary report for failing to get permission from the Warden before engaging in a business venture. After he admitted he placed the ad he was given 30 days in segregation. Smith sued prison officials in federal court and lost. The court stated that he had no right to operate a business, get paid for helping other prisoners with legal work, and he didn't seek prior approval of the Warden. *Smith v. Umdenstock*, 962 F.2d 11 (7th Cir. 1992).

Jason Nicholas earned a degree while inside prison and concentrated on being a jailhouse lawyer. In 1995, he requested to form the Prisoners' Legal Defense Center in New York. Prison officials denied his request. He ended up getting a reversal of the district court's dismissal of his complaint. *Nicholas v. Miller*, 189 F.3d 191 (2d cir.1999)

Author Rico Stringer and Rabb Ra Chaka, two prisoners who were incarcerated at Statesville in Joliet, Illinois, formed a legal non-profit organization called the Jailhouse Lawyer's and Prisoner's Defense Foundation, Inc., in 1980. With the consent of the Warden, Richard DeRobertis, they ordered $900 worth of membership applications, cards, stationary, and copies of the corporation's constitution and by-laws. But when the free-world coordinator tried to deliver the printed materials to Stringer it never got there. They sued and lost because they didn't file grievances or request prior formal approval from the Warden. *Stringer v. DeRobertis*, 541 F. Supp. 605 (1982).

Natural Food Distributor

Wilfred Roy French was a prisoner at the Massachusetts State prison in Walpole. He tried to become a distributor of Erewhon Natural food products within the prison, and only wanted a low profit margin of 2%. The prison Superintendent turned his proposal down. He sued and lost because the court stated he had no "recognized right to conduct a business while incarcerated." It should be noted that French had signatures and support from hundreds of prisoners on his proposal. The Superintendent did put the natural foods on the commissary, but at a higher cost and to use the profits to benefit guards and the security of the prison rather than the prisoners. French v. Butterworth, 614F.2d 23 (1980).

Arts and Crafts

Gary Garland and another Iowa prisoner started a company called, "G and K Leather Goods." They applied for and received an Employer Identification Number from the IRS and a Retail Sales Permit from the state of Iowa. They received orders and their business began to prosper. But their vigorous cellpreneurship was beyond the scope of what the prison wanted to allow and shut it down. Prison administrators went too far when they transferred Garland to a maximum-security prison because he had the nerve to file a lawsuit about the forced closure of the leather goods business. *Garland v. Polley*, 594 F.2d 1220 (1979).

Intellectual Property Holding Company

New Jersey State prisoner Walter Tormasi formed an "intellectual-property holding company" called Advanced Data Solutions Corporation (ADS). He was the sole shareholder and authorized agent. In 2008, Tormasi was successful in getting a patent in which he was listed as the assignee. New Jersey prison officials confiscated an unfiled patent application for a "Geometric Optical Apparatus Featuring Antiglare Properties." He sued alleging that the confiscation of his patent application interfered with his statutory right to file to apply for a patent and violated his right to free speech. Prison officials based their seizure on the fact that New Jersey has a rule that prisoners can't operate a business without prior approval of the Warden. The court stated, "While we generally agree that the submission of a patent application does not involve a business activity in all circumstances." ... "Tormasi alleged that he was unable to directly or indirectly benefit from his intellectually-property assets, either by selling all or part of ADS...or by engaging in other monetization transactions involving ADS or its intellectual-property assets." The court concluded he was trying to run a business and affirmed the dismissal of his lawsuit. *Tormasi v. Hayman*, 443 Fed. Appx. 742 (3d Cir.2011).

There was one other note from the *Tormasi* decision relevant to our guidebook. A corporation must be represented by licensed counsel in federal court. So, you as a *pro se* prisoner cannot represent your corporation in federal court. *See Rowland v. California Men's Colony*, 506 U.S. 194, 202 (1993).

RESOURCE BOX

If you're interested in developing and protecting ideas and products, you'll want to grab copies of the following books:

- *The complete Patent Book*
- *Profit from Intellectual Property*
- *From Concept to Market*
- *How to License Your Million Dollar Idea*
- *The Anatomy of an Invention*

Books can be ordered from our Bookstore on page 224 or online. Contact Freebird Publishers about ordering if you don't have anyone to help you.

Prison Mail-Order Business

South Dakota prisoner John Nachtigall started a mail order business. As is common in most prisons, his outgoing mail was stamped with notice that it was being sent from the South Dakota State Penitentiary. He sued prison officials because he claimed that the stamp will hurt his mail order business because no one would seriously consider doing business with a prisoner. The court ruled that this policy did not violate any of his rights because he could not "claim that his mail order business constitutes employment because he has no constitutional right to engage in a business enterprise through the use of the United States mails while he is lawfully incarcerated by the state." *Nachtigall v. Board of Charities and Corrections*, 590 F. Supp. 1223, 1225 (S.D.S.D.1984)

Copyrights and Constitutional Law

Bernard Carter Jerry-El is a Pennsylvania prisoner who self-published a children's book through Author House. In 2008, while in the prison library, Jerry-El made copies of his book, *Pinky Pigg*, so that he could submit them to the Library of Congress to get full copyright privileges. The prison librarian confiscated them because he believed Jerry-El was trying to harass the courts and prisons. The librarian wrote him a misconduct report and the hearing examiner concluded he was trying to engage in a business activity and found him guilty. Jerry-El filed grievances which were denied. He then sued in federal district court in Pennsylvania. The court then dismissed his claims and he appealed.

One of Jerry-El's claims was that the DO violated his statutory right to protect his copyright of *Pinky Pigg*. The Copyright Act of 1976 allows an author limited exclusive control over that work. This included the right to prevent others from commercially exploiting their work. *See A.V. ex rel. Vanderhye v. iParadigms, LLC.*, 562 F. 3d 630, 636(4th Cir. 2009). That right begins the moment the author puts the story on paper. *See 17 U.S.C.§ 302.* A copyright holder may also register their work with the Library of Congress to obtain additional protections against infringement. *17 U.S.C. § 407.* The court stated that "it does not appear that exercising this right necessarily constitutes engaging in a business activity." The Court then reversed the dismissal of Jerry-El's suit because he could possibly state a claim for interfering with his ability to protect his copyright. *See Jerry-El v. Beard*, 419 Fed. Appx. 260 (3rd Cir. 2011).

RESOURCE BOX

If you would like to learn how you can register your own copyright; or more about the law for writers; you'll want to grab copies of the following books:

- *How To Register Your Own Copyright, 4th Edition*
- *Law (In Plain English) for Writers*
- *The Writer's Legal Guide, 4th Edition*
- *The Pocket Legal Companion to Copyright*

All of these books can be found online. Contact Freebird Publishers about ordering them if you don't have someone to help you.

Prison Visiting Business

Paul Dawson started the company VisitsTravel.com It was started to help combat the high prices that infiltrate the travel industry, especially those pertaining to prison visits. Mr. Dawson firmly believes that when a prisoner is in contact with family, friends, or a positive support system they have an incentive to strive for success. Vizits Travel believes that visitation is a benefit and contributes to good behavior while transitioning into other areas of a prisoner's life. Ultimately, they hope to reduce crime. For more about how Vizits Travel can help you contact Paul Dawson at visitstravel@gmail.com or (541)258-4075.

The Prior Approval Business Rule

I'm a prisoner in the Illinois Department of Corrections and IDOC has a business venture rule codified at Section 445.30. It states:

A) All committed persons are required to inform the Chief Administrative Officer of the following in writing before entering into any business venture:

    1) Type of business;

    2) Service or product to be provided;

    3) Anticipated mail volume (incoming and outgoing); and

    4) Date the business will begin.

B) The Chief Administrative Officer shall determine the facility's capability to handle any administrative burden generated by a business venture and shall specify reasons for denial of such a request in writing unless inappropriate because of safety or security considerations.

C) No committed person shall sell any property, product, or service, either individually or through a business entity in which he has a personal or economic interest, to any other committed person or employee, except as otherwise provided by 20. Ill. Adm. Code 120.50.

This IDOC rule has survived challenges over the years.

In one of those challenges, prisoner Joe Woods tried to establish a Universal Life Church (ULC) congregation at Statesville prison in Illinois. Prison officials stopped him from sending out ULC mail because they said he did not seek prior approval to run a business. Woods argued that the church was a tax-exempt organization and not a business. But the IRS had denied ULC tax-exempt status, so prison officials said it was a business. Woods was given a disciplinary ticket for trying to send out ULC mail. He then sued the Warden in federal court for an alleged violation of his First Amendment Rights. The Court found for prison officials because Woods never filed the business venture proposal nor suggested alternatives. *Woods v. O'Leary*, 890 F.2d 883 (7th Cir. 1989); *See also Smith v. Umbdenstock*, 962 F.2d 11 (7th cir.1992) (discussing IDOC's business rule).

There are several lessons that you can learn from these case studies and prisoner examples. First, learn your prison's rules and regulations regarding prisoner businesses. Research the law and any challenges to that rule in your circuit. Second, try and work with prison officials before you go to court. If you're in a prison system that has a "prior approval" rule, then submit your proposal. On the next few pages I share with you how I submitted my proposal. Use how I did it as a blueprint for your own plans.

If, and when, you have to go to court to challenge your prison's regulation it will be better if you had previously tried to submit a proposal of your business venture. Most courts let prison officials get away with the business rule. That doesn't mean that you should stop going after your dreams. And it can never stop you from owning a business, just running it from your cell.

There's another way to get around the "no business rule." Have someone else start it up in the free-world. Just make sure it's someone you trust 100%. I know that it's hard to find someone like that, so be careful before you sign over your idea to them. In later chapters, I'll give you some sample agreements that can help protect you in this regard. For now, here's how I submitted my proposal. Whatever you do, don't give up!

RESOURCE BOX

If you do feel that your rights have been violated, you should Shepardize® or KeyCite® the cases in this chapter to get the most up-to-date case law in your circuit. If you can afford to do so, you should also grab copies of the following books:

- *Prisoner's Self Help Litigation Manual, 4th Edition* by John Boston & Daniel Manville. from Prison Legal News, PO Box 1151, Lake Worth, FL 33460.

- *Battling the Administration: An Inmates Guide to a Successful Lawsuit* by David J. Meister. Available from Wynword Press, PO Box 557, Bonners Ferry, ID 83805.

Books can be ordered from our Bookstore on page 224 or online. Contact Freebird Publishers about ordering if you don't have anyone to help you.

To: Randy PFister   January 7, 2014
      Warden

FROM: Joshua Kruger   RE: Business Venture Proposal

Dear Warden PFister:

As a follow-up to our brief conversation today when you conducted the walk-through tour of the West Cellhouse I am submitting the enclosed "Business Venture" proposal. I am submitting this proposal to be in compliance with IDOC Rule 445.30 (Ill. Admin. Code tit. 20 Section 445.30 (1985) and *Woods v. O'Leary*, 890 F.2d 883 (7th Cir. 1989). This is the same proposal that I submitted to Asst. Warden Motteler in November via Counselor Simmons. In *Woods*, the Court stated: "The Regulation merely requires the filing of a proposal providing information on the anticipated mail volume." *890 F.3d at 886*. That's what I'm attempting to do.

Thank you in advance for your consideration of this letter and enclosed proposal. I look forward to hearing from you soon.

Respectfully Requested,

Joshua Kruger   Encl: 4-Page Proposal
                                     cc: File

Business Venture Proposal of Joshua Kruger

In accordance to IDOC Rules and Regulation 445.30 "Business Ventures" (Ill. Admin. Code tit. 20 Section 445.30 (1985)) and *Woods v. O'Leary*, 890 F.2d 883 (7th cir.1989), I, Joshua Kruger, a prisoner currently housed at Pontiac Correctional Center, hereby submit the following proposal:

Type of Business (Section 445:30(a)(1))

I am a freelance writer with published articles in newsletters, blogs, and poetry in a prison anthology. I've donated some and have been compensated for others. I have also published special reports and manuals. I just completed a full-length book, *The Millionaire Prisoner: How To Turn Your Prison Into A Stepping-Stone To Success*, ISBN: 978-0-9906154-4-6. I propose starting a publishing company to continue to publish my own written works.

The proposed entity will be operated as a sole proprietorship "doing business as" (DBA) Carceral Wealth Services, with an address of 3308 Route 940 Ste.104-3013, Mt. Pocono, PA 18344 (DBA #4288821).

Service or Product To be Provided (section 445.30(a)(2))

I will offer books, eBooks, articles, and special reports that I have written, both in print and online, for sale and for free through two websites that I currently own the URL's to: www.millionaireprisoner.com and www.carceralwealth.com and through Print On Demand (POD) entities like Lightning Source (www.lightningsource.com) and Amazon's POD arm CreateSpace (www.createspace.com). I will also sell these written works to other online outlets for publication. I will NOT sell any product or service from my cell or direct through the mail at the prison to any IDOC prisoner or employee. I will NOT publish other IDOC prisoners written works (either for free or for sale) or enter into any contract with an IDOC prisoner or employee to publish works on their behalf.

Anticipated Mail Volume (incoming and outgoing) (section 445.30(a)(3))

There will NOT be any influx of incoming mail to me at the prison nor outgoing mail from me to others. All business mail will go to the business address in Mt. Pocono, PA and through my Executive Assistant at Prisoner Assistant (www.prisonerassistant.com) 1-570-722-5800. My current Executive Assistant is Kim Sorrentino. She will check the company mailbox twice a week, process orders, answer mail, and send me a summary once a week. This will not burden the prison mail room in any way, nor will it create a security risk. (By rule, prison mail clerks already screen all incoming and outgoing mail. See 20 Ill. Admin. tit. Section 525. 120-140.)

Date the Business Will Begin (section 445.30(a)(4))

The business will begin operations on January 1, 2015 (the "DBA" was filed on July 7, 2014 and approved by the State of Pennsylvania on August 11, 2014.) (DBA Entity #4288821)

Additional Items for Consideration (section 445.30(c))

At no time will I personally sell any book, article, special report or any other product or service to any IDOC prisoner or employee from my cell or directly through the mail. Nor will my company, Carceral Wealth Services, sell any product or service to any IDOC prisoner or employee. I will NOT personally sell products or services to any other prisoner (State or Federal) from my cell or directly through the mail. All prisoner mail to me should be, and will be, rejected as it already is. (except from my brother, Joseph Kruger, who I'm approved to correspond with.) However, IDOC employees could possibly purchase my work online (through booksellers like Amazon) or at a bookstore in compliance with 20 Ill. Admin. Code tit. Section 120.50(a), but I will NOT seek to induce them to do so or even tell them about my books or work.

It should be further noted that I will NOT be running the day-to-day operation of the publishing company. That will be handled by my Executive Assistant, Kim Sorrentino at Prisoner Assistant. My only job and ask will be to write books, articles for newsletters and magazines, and to help write, create and review online content and marketing materials. The key to this is that this business will not be an "inmate ran business." While, technically I am, and will be, the owner of Carceral Wealth Services, I will have no direct hand in the day-to-day operations of this business entity.

Additional Legal Support

IDOC authorizes and Section 445.20 of the Code allows prisoners to submit manuscripts for publication. Also, IDOC and Pontiac C.C. periodically holds art, poetry, and essay contests through clinical staff as a creative outlet for its prisoners and to encourage rehabilitation.

The First Amendment of the U.S. Constitution guarantees the Right to freedom of expression to individuals and this encompasses the publication and dissemination of written material. See Jordan v. Pugh, 504 F.Supp.2d 1109, 1118 (D.Colo.2007) (Regulation prohibiting inmates from publishing under bylines violated First Amendment); Abu-Jamal v. Price, 154 F.3d 128(3d Cir. 1998) (DOC business or profession rule, as enforced against prisoner to restrict his writings, was not reasonably related to any legitimate interest).

Conclusion

I respectfully request that this proposal be granted so that I may continue to receive compensation for my written works without violating any IDOC Rules and Regulations.

Joshua Kruger

Date: 11-18-14

Illinois
Department of
Corrections

Bruce Rauner
Governor

S. A. Godinez
Acting Director

Pontiac Correctional Center
700 W. Lincoln Street, P.O. Box 99
Pontiac, IL 61764

Telephone: (815) 842-2816
TDD: (800) 526-0844

MEMORANDUM

DATE: January 21, 2015

TO: Joshua Kruger,

FROM: Randy Pfister, Warden

SUBJECT: BUSINESS VENTURE

I am in receipt of your letter dated January 9, 2015 relative to your business venture proposal. Please be advised, works of art, literature or handicraft produced by an offender may be sold to the public. If a particular work of art, literature, or handicraft or the sale of it raises or creates a security or administrative concern at the facility, it may be prohibited. A manuscript sent for publication which poses a threat to the safety and security of the facility will be withheld.

I trust this has been response to your concerns.

RP/mar

Xc: Master File
     File, Chron

20

CHAPTER 3
THE BIRTH OF CARCERAL WEALTH

"One good idea can enable a man to live like a king the rest of his life."
– Ross Perot

After we closed down O'Barnett Publishing I continued to put the finishing touches on my manuscript for The Millionaire Prisoner. I really did not want to take the time to find an agent, send my manuscript around to numerous publishers and wait to see what they said. The traditional publishing method didn't appeal to me because I'm a cellpreneur and wanted the lion's share of the profit. Plus, my whole idea behind O'Barnett Publishing was to become the owner of a successful company. So, I started looking for another way.

PRISONER ASSISTANT, INC.

During my search, I kept seeing ads in *Prison Legal News* for a company called Prisoner Assistant. I sent off for their catalog of services and saw that they were what I was looking for.

Prisoner Assistant was started by Michael Benanti. He was a former federal prisoner who did close to 20 years for bank robbery. Benanti left prison with an unsecured, open line of credit for $40,000, had a job lined up, an apartment, and a blueprint on how to jump start your life after prison. He started Prisoner Assistant to help other prisoners get the same head start he got.

Reading the Prisoner Assistant catalog was like Christmas for a cellpreneur like me. They offered everything I needed to get my company up and running. I'd have a Wells Fargo bank account and UPS mail box. All I'd have to do is sign Power of Attorney over to them. That was scary, but what other options did I have? The final push I received to go ahead and use Prisoner Assistant was on the day I asked my prison counselor how I could setup a free-world bank account, he handed me the Prisoner Assistant brochure. So, I signed on the dotted line and joined Prisoner Assistant.

But I didn't jump in head first, I slowly tested the Prisoner Assistant waters. I began with a basic "Silver" membership. Just enough to get me a UPS mailbox of my own and a Prisoner Assistant bank account and profile. (See next few pages). I started with $400. FYI: That $400 came from royalty checks from my booklet, *How To Get FREE Pen Pals*. When I was ready to move forward on my publishing company idea I started brainstorming names for my company. I got the idea for Carceral Wealth Services instead of Carceral Wealth Publishing out of Ty Hicks book, *How To Get Rich in Mail Order*. He said if you're going to offer more than just a product and also offer services then you might want to use "Services" in your name. I eventually wanted to provide some type of service for prisoners so I used "services." *Carceral Wealth* was easy. *Carceral* is the Latin word for "jail" and I knew I was going to write books about becoming prosperous so *Wealth* it was. That's how I came up with Carceral Wealth Services for my company's name.

Wells Fargo Business Online®

Account Activity

J. Kruger primary XXXXXX

Activity Summary

Ending Collected Balance as of 10/27/14	$820.59
Current Posted Balance	$820.59
Pending Withdrawals/ Debits	-$18.00
Pending Deposits/ Credits	$0.00
Available Balance	**$802.59**

The Available Balance shown above reflects the most up-to-date information available on your account. The balances shown below next to the last transaction o reflect any pending withdrawals or holds on deposited funds that may have been outstanding on your account when the transaction posted. If you had insufficien when the transaction posted to your account, fees may have been assessed.

Transactions

Show: for **Last 90 Days**

Date ↓	Description	Deposits / Credits	Withdrawals / Debits
Pending Transactions	Note: Debit card transaction amounts may change		
10/28/14	ONLINE MONEY TRANSFER		$18.00
Posted Transactions			
10/27/14	RECURRING TRANSFER FROM JOSHUA W KRUGER REF #OPE8H479TT BUSINESS MARKET RATE SAVINGMONTHLY TRANSFER	$150.00	
10/24/14	RECURRING TRANSFER TO JOSHUA W KRUGER REF #OPE5KZZXNS BUSINESS MARKET RATE SAVINGMONTHLY TRANSFER		$150.00
10/07/14	POS PURCHASE - USPS 4143680624 LAKE HARMONY PA 5709 00000000031498927		$3.50
10/06/14	TRANSFER TO ASSISTANT PRISONER REF #PPETV7Z9WL BOOK PUBLISHING		$44.31
09/30/14	BILL PAY Prisoner Assista RECURRINGxxxxx43772 ON 09-30		$18.00
09/30/14	CHECK CRD PURCHASE 09/30 AMAZON MKTPLACE PM AMZN.COM/BILL WA 474165XXXXXX5709 384271805393254 ?MCC=5942		$18.87
09/30/14	CHECK CRD PURCHASE 09/29 AMAZON MKTPLACE PM AMZN.COM/BILL WA 474165XXXXXX5709 304271805361547 ?MCC=5942		$8.20
09/29/14	POS PURCHASE - USPS 4143680624 LAKE HARMONY PA 5709 00000000751286121		$1.82
09/29/14	TRANSFER TO ASSISTANT PRISONER REF #PPEQY43NWJ INTERNET PURCHASE EMAIL MONITORING EMAILS		$41.16
09/29/14	CHECK CRD PURCHASE 09/28 AMAZON MKTPLACE PM AMZN.COM/BILL WA 474165XXXXXX5709 304271812514272 ?MCC=5942		$10.15
09/26/14	RECURRING TRANSFER FROM JOSHUA W KRUGER REF #OPETV4W2TX BUSINESS MARKET RATE SAVINGMONTHLY TRANSFER	$150.00	
09/24/14	RECURRING TRANSFER TO JOSHUA W KRUGER REF #OPE8GSFZHS BUSINESS MARKET RATE SAVINGMONTHLY TRANSFER		$150.00
09/11/14	POS PURCHASE - USPS 4143680624 LAKE HARMONY PA 5709 00000000551175294		$2.03
09/10/14	TRANSFER TO ASSISTANT PRISONER REF #PPEG8S2Y2F BANK MONEY ORDER AND EMAIL MONITORING		$16.07

SOME TIPS (AND TRICKS) ABOUT YOUR COMPANY'S NAME

Here are some tricks of the trade for getting your company's name right.

- Don't use your name in the title, e.g., John Smith Publishing. You can use your last name for certain business names: "Smith & Sons", etc.

- You can use "Company" in your name, but cannot use "Corp.", "Corporation", "Inc.", or "incorporated" unless you are forming a corporation.

- Search to see if the company's name is already taken? Use the trademark offices at both the federal and state levels. Search on Google®. Check the web domain name availability.

- In Dan Poynter's Self-Publishing Manual, he says this about using the word "enterprises" in your company's name." … the use of the word 'enterprises' is often the sign of a rank beginner and may give the impression that you don't know yet what your company is going to do."

- Think of one word that will make a good website domain and use that as your company's name. Like Amazon® and Google®, etc.

- You can make up a word for your company's name. One of my mentors did just that with his publishing company, Fanove®.

- You can also use three words and use an abbreviation. Think IBM® or International Business Machines; TCB or The Cell Block; EPS or Elite Paralegal Services. Of course, CWS or Carceral Wealth Services!

FILING YOUR "DBA" PAPERWORK

My next step was to file my "Doing Business As" fictitious name paperwork. It was pretty easy for me. I just told my personal assistant at Prisoner Assistant what my company's name was going to be and they took care of the rest. I just formed a sole proprietorship just to keep it simple until I got it up and running. Then I planned to form a LLC or Corporation later.

Because Prisoner Assistant's offices were in Pennsylvania and my UPS mailbox was in Pennsylvania I filed my paperwork in Pennsylvania. It cost $70 for filing. On the next few pages you'll see the paperwork for both my company and the mailbox.

As soon as you register your company's name you should get the domain name for your company also. You don't have to build a website right away. Just register the domain name. I did this with www.carceralwealth.com and www.millionaireprisoner.com. You'd hate to try and do it later and find out that someone else owns it. If that happens you'll have to buy it from them if you still want to use it. It only costs $9-15 to register a domain name for a year, so do it.

In Get Rich Click! Marc Ostrofsky says there are five ways you can profit from a domain name:

- Sell it outright for a profit.

- Rent the name to a firm willing to pay

- Put a website on it.

- Lease it out to a company.

- Park it so you get paid for clicks on the name.

"Domain Names and Websites are Internet Real Estate,
a good domain creates mindshare.
You can own it, lease it or put up a virtual shopping center."
-Marc Ostrofsky, GetRickClick.com

Department of State
Bureau of Corporations and Charitable Organizations
P.O. Box 8722
Harrisburg, PA 17105-8722
(717) 787-1057
Web site: www.dos.state.pa.us/corps

Instructions for Completion of Form:

A. Typewritten is preferred. If not, the form shall be completed in black or blue-black ink in order to permit reproduction. The filing fee for this form is $70 made payable to the Department of State.

B. Under 15 Pa.C.S. § 135(c) (relating to addresses) an actual street or rural route box number must be used as an address, and the Department of State is required to refuse to receive or file any document that sets forth only a post office box address.

C. The following, in addition to the filing fee, shall accompany this form:

(1) Any necessary copies of form DSCB:17.2.3 (Consent to Appropriation of Name).

(2) Any necessary governmental approvals.

D. For general instructions relating to fictitious name registration see 19 Pa. Code Subch. 17C (relating to fictitious names). These instructions relate to such matters as voluntary and mandatory registration, general restrictions on name availability, use of corporate designators, agent for effecting amendments, etc., execution, official advertising when an individual is a party to the registration, and effect of registration and non-registration.

E. The name of a commercial registered office provider may not be used in Paragraph 3 in lieu of an address.

F. Insert in Paragraph 5 for each entity which is not an individual the following information: (i) the name of the entity and a statement of its form of organization, e.g., corporation, general partnership, limited partnership, business trust, (ii) the name of the jurisdiction under the laws of which it is organized, (iii) the address, including street and number, if any, of its principal office under the laws of its domiciliary jurisdiction and (iv) the address, including street and number, if any, of its registered office, if any, in this Commonwealth. If any of the entities has an association which has designated the name of a commercial registered office provider in lieu of a registered office address as permitted by 15 Pa.C.S. § 109, the name of the provider and the venue county should be inserted in the last column.

G. Every individual whose name appears in Paragraph 4 of the form **must sign** the form exactly as the name is set forth in Paragraph 4. The name of every other entity listed in Paragraph 5 shall be signed on its behalf by an officer, trustee or other authorized person. See 19 Pa. Code § 13.8(b) (relating to execution), which permits execution pursuant to power of attorney. A copy of the underlying power of attorney or other authorization should not be submitted to, and will not be received by or filed in, the Department.

H. An entity (which includes an individual) that registers a fictitious name is required by 54 Pa.C.S. § 311(g) to advertise its intention to file or the filing of an application for registration of fictitious name. Proofs of publication of such advertising should not be submitted to the Department, and will not be received by or filed in the Department, but should be kept with the permanent records of the business.

I. This form and all accompanying documents shall be mailed to the address stated above.

PENNSYLVANIA DEPARTMENT OF STATE
BUREAU OF CORPORATIONS AND CHARITABLE ORGANIZATIONS

Application for Registration of Fictitious Name
54 Pa.C.S. § 311

Name _Joshua Kruger_

Address

. **Street Address**
/ **City, State and Zip Code**

Document will be returned to the name and address you enter to the left.

Fee: $70

In compliance with the requirements of 54 Pa.C.S. § 311 (relating to registration), the undersigned entity(ies) desiring to register a fictitious name under 54 Pa.C.S. Ch. 3 (relating to fictitious names), hereby state(s) that:

1. The fictitious name is: _Carceral Wealth Services_

2. A brief statement of the character or nature of the business or other activity to be carried on under or through the fictitious name is: _Publishing_

3. The address, including number and street, if any, of the principal place of business (P.O. Box alone is **not** acceptable):

Street Address, City, State and Zip Code

4. The name and address, including number and street, if any, of each individual interested in the business is:
   Name   Number and Street   City   State   Zip

   None

26

DSCB:54-311-2

5. Each entity, other than an individual, interested in such business is (are):

None
Name | Form of Organization | Organizing Jurisdiction

Principal Office Address

PA Registered Office, if any

Name | Form of Organization | Organizing Jurisdiction

Principal Office Address

PA Registered Office, if any

6. The applicant is familiar with the provisions of 54 Pa.C.S. § 332 (relating to effect of registration) and understands that filing under the Fictitious Names Act does not create any exclusive or other right in the fictitious name.

7. Optional): The name(s) of the agent(s), if any, any one of whom is authorized to execute amendments to, withdrawals from or cancellation of this registration in behalf of all then existing parties to the registration, is (are):

IN TESTIMONY WHEREOF, the undersigned have caused this Application for Registration of Fictitious Name to be executed this

_7_ day of _July_, _2014_.

_____ | _____
Individual Signature | Individual Signature

_____ | _____
Individual Signature | Individual Signature

_____ | _____
Entity Name | Entity Name

_____ | _____
Signature | Signature

_____ | _____
Title | Title

COMMONWEALTH OF PENNSYLVANIA
DEPARTMENT OF STATE
BUREAU OF CORPORATIONS AND CHARITABLE ORGANIZATIONS
401 NORTH STREET, ROOM 206
P.O. BOX 8722
HARRISBURG, PA 17105-8722
WWW.CORPORATIONS.STATE.PA.US/CORP

Carceral Wealth Services

THE BUREAU OF CORPORATIONS AND CHARITABLE ORGANIZATIONS IS HAPPY TO SEND YOU YOUR FILED DOCUMENT. THE BUREAU IS HERE TO SERVE YOU AND WANTS TO THANK YOU FOR DOING BUSINESS IN PENNSYLVANIA.

IF YOU HAVE ANY QUESTIONS PERTAINING TO THE BUREAU, PLEASE VISIT OUR WEB SITE LOCATED AT WWW.CORPORATIONS.STATE.PA.US/CORP OR PLEASE CALL OUR MAIN INFORMATION TELEPHONE NUMBER (717)787-1057. FOR ADDITIONAL INFORMATION REGARDING BUSINESS AND / OR UCC FILINGS, PLEASE VISIT OUR ONLINE "SEARCHABLE DATABASE" LOCATED ON OUR WEB SITE.

ENTITY NUMBER: 4288821

Kruger, Joshua

Entity #: 4288821
Date Filed: 08/11/2014
Carol Aichele
Secretary of the Commonwealth

PENNSYLVANIA DEPARTMENT OF STATE
BUREAU OF CORPORATIONS AND CHARITABLE ORGANIZATIONS

Application for Registration of Fictitious Name
54 Pa.C.S. § 311

Name
Joshua Kruger

Street Address
City, State and Zip Code

Document will be returned to the name and address you enter to the left.

Commonwealth of Pennsylvania
FICTITIOUS NAME 2 Page(s)

T1422560001

Fee: $70

In compliance with the requirements of 54 Pa.C.S. § 311 (relating to registration), the undersigned entity(ies) desiring to register a fictitious name under 54 Pa.C.S. Ch. 3 (relating to fictitious names), hereby state(s) that:

1. The fictitious name is:
Carceral Wealth Services

2. A brief statement of the character or nature of the business or other activity to be carried on under or through the fictitious name is:
Publishing

3. The address, including number and street, if any, of the principal place of business (P.O. Box alone is **not** ~~~~~~)

Number and street	City	State	Zip	County

4. The name and address, including number and street, if any, of each individual interested in the business is:

Name	Number and Street	City	State	Zip
Joshua Kruger				

PA DEPT. OF STATE

AUG 1 1 2014

DSCB:54-311-2

5. Each entity, other than an individual, interested in such business is (are):

None

| Name | Form of Organization | Organizing Jurisdiction |

Principal Office Address

PA Registered Office, if any

| Name | Form of Organization | Organizing Jurisdiction |

Principal Office Address

PA Registered Office, if any

6. The applicant is familiar with the provisions of 54 Pa.C.S. § 332 (relating to effect of registration) and understands that filing under the Fictitious Names Act does not create any exclusive or other right in the fictitious name.

7. Optional): The name(s) of the agent(s), if any, any one of whom is authorized to execute amendments to, withdrawals from or cancellation of this registration in behalf of all then existing parties to the registration, is (are):

IN TESTIMONY WHEREOF, the undersigned have caused this Application for Registration of Fictitious Name to be executed this

06   day of August   , 2014   .

Individual Signature

Individual Signature

Individual Signature

Entity Name

Entity Name

Signature

Signature

Title

Title

United States Postal Service
Application for Delivery of Mail Through Agent
See Privacy Act Statement on Reverse

1. Date
07/14/2014

In consideration of delivery of my or our (firm) mail to the agent named below, the addressee and agent agree: (1) the addressee or the agent must not file a change of address order with the Postal Service™ upon termination of the agency relationship; (2) the transfer of mail to another address is the responsibility of the addressee and the agent; (3) all mail delivered to the agency under this authorization must be prepaid with new postage when redeposited in the mails; (4) upon request the agent must provide to the Postal Service all addresses to which the agency transfers mail; and (5) when any information required on this form changes or becomes obsolete, the addressee(s) must file a revised application with the Commercial Mail Receiving Agency (CMRA).

NOTE: The applicant must execute this form in duplicate in the presence of the agent, his or her authorized employee, or a notary public

The agent provides the original completed signed PS Form 1583 to the Postal Service and retains a duplicate completed signed copy at the CMRA business location. The CMRA copy of PS Form PS 1583 must at all times be available for examination by the postmaster (or designee) and the Postal Inspection Service. The addressee and the agent agree to comply with all applicable Postal Service rules and regulations relative to delivery of mail through an agent. Failure to comply will subject the agency to withholding of mail from delivery until corrective action is taken.

This application may be subject to verification procedures by the Postal Service to confirm that the applicant resides or conducts business at the home or business address listed in boxes 7 or 10, and that the identification listed in box 8 is valid.

2. Name in Which Applicant's Mail Will Be Received for Delivery to Agent. (Complete a separate PS Form 1583 for EACH applicant. Spouses may complete and sign one PS Form 1583. Two items of valid identification apply to each spouse. Include dissimilar information for either spouse in appropriate box.)	3a. Address to be Used for Delivery (Include PMB or # sign.)		
	3b. City	3c. State	3d. Zip + 4
Joshua Kruger			

4. Applicant authorizes delivery to and in care of:	5. This authorization is extended to include restricted delivery mail for the undersigned(s):
a. Name	No
The UPS Store #5501	
b. Address (No., street, apt./ste. no.)	
3308 Route 940, Suite 104	

c. City	d. State	e. Zip + 4
Mt. Pocono	PA	18344

6. Name of Applicant	7a. Applicant Home Address (No., street, apt./ste.
Joshua Kruger	

8. Two types of identification are required. One must contain a photograph of the addressee(s). Social Security cards, credit cards, and birth certificates are unacceptable as identification. The agent must write in identifying information. Subject to verification.	7b. City	7c. State	7d. Zip + 4
	7e. Applicant Telephone Number (Include area code)		
a. Driver's License :	9. Name of Firm or Corporation		
	Carceral wealth services		
b. POA #on File	10a. Business Address (No., street, apt./ste. no.)		
	10b. City	10c. State	10d. Zip + 4
Acceptable identification includes: valid driver's license or state non-driver's identification card; armed forces, government, university, or recognized corporate identification card; passport, alien registration card or certificate of naturalization; current lease, mortgage or Deed of Trust; voter or vehicle registration card; or a home or vehicle insurance policy. A photocopy of your identification may be retained by agent for verification.	10e. Business Telephone Number (Include area code)		
	11. Type of Business		
	publishing		

12. If applicant is a firm, name each member whose mail is to be delivered. (All names listed must have verifiable identification. A guardian must list the names of minors receiving mail at their delivery address.)
Joshua Kruger

13. If a CORPORATION. Give Names and Addresses of Its Officers	14. If business name (corporation or trade name) has been registered, give name of county and state, and date of registration.
N/A	N/A

Warning: The furnishing of false or misleading information on this form or omission of material information may result in criminal sanctions (including fines and imprisonment) and/or civil sanctions (including multiple damages and civil enalties)

15. Signature of Agent/Notary Public	16. Signature of Applicant (If firm or corporation, application must be signed by officer. Show title.)

PS Form 1583 December 2004 (Page 1 of 2) (7530-01-000-9365)

Mailbox Service Agreement

any re-mailing that requires the filing of a Shipper's Export Declaration by the Center (i.e., any export transaction), in accordance with the laws and regulations of the United States. Customer further agrees to provide the Center with true, accurate, and complete information regarding the contents of any mail or packages to be re-mailed by the Center, whether during the term of the Agreement or after termination or cancellation.

9. The term of this Agreement shall be the initial period paid for by Customer and any renewal period paid for by Customer from time to time. Renewal of this Agreement for additional terms shall be at the Center's sole discretion.

10. Customer agrees that the Center may terminate or cancel this Agreement for good cause at any time by providing Customer with written notice. Good cause shall include but is not limited to: 1) Customer abandons the Mailbox; 2) Customer uses the Mailbox for unlawful, illegitimate, or fraudulent purposes; 3) Customer fails to pay monies owed the Center when due; 4) Customer receives an unreasonable volume of mail or packages; 5) Customer engages in offensive, abusive, or disruptive behavior toward other customers of the Center or the Center's employees; and 6) Customer violates any provision of this Agreement. Customer acknowledges that, for the purpose of determining good cause for termination of this Agreement as provided herein, the actions of any person authorized by Customer to use the Mailbox will be attributed to Customer.

11. Any written notice to Customer required or permitted under this Agreement shall be deemed delivered twenty-four (24) hours after placement of such notice in Customer's Mailbox or at the time personally delivered to Customer. In the event of a termination notice based upon abandonment of the Mailbox, notice shall be deemed delivered (a) on the next day after placing in the hands of a commercial carrier service or the United States Postal Service for next day delivery, or (b) five (5) days after placement in the United States Mail by Certified Mail, Return Receipt Requested, postage pre-paid, and addressed to Customer at Customer's address as set forth in Form 1583, or on the date of actual receipt, whichever is earlier.

12. As Customer's authorized agent for receipt of mail, the Center will accept all mail, including registered, insured, and certified items, and, if authorized on Form 1583, restricted mail (i.e., mail where the sender has paid a fee to direct delivery only to an individual addressee or addressee's authorized agent). Unless prior arrangements have been made, the Center shall only be obligated to accept mail or packages delivered by commercial carrier services, which require a signature from the Center as a condition of delivery. Customer must accept and sign for all mail and packages upon the request of the Center. Packages not picked up within __5__ days of notification will be subject to a storage fee of _$0.00_ per day per package, which must be paid before Customer receives the package. In the event Customer refuses to accept any mail or package, the Center may return the mail or package to the sender and Customer will be responsible for any postage or other fees associated with such return. C.O.D. items will be accepted ONLY if prior arrangements have been made and payment in advance is provided to the Center. In those states where the Center is required by law to act as Customer's agent for service of process, Customer hereby authorizes the Center to act as Customer's agent for service of process, and this authorization shall remain in effect for as long as this Agreement is in effect, or as long as required by state law, whichever is later. The Center agrees to follow its standard procedures for the timely placement of mail received at the Center and addressed to Customer into Customer's Mailbox, and agrees to protect, indemnify, defend, and hold harmless the Center from any and all liability that may arise at any time in connection with the Center's actions or status as Customer's agent for service of process.

13. Customer agrees to protect, indemnify, defend, and hold harmless the Center, MBE, and their respective affiliates, subsidiaries, parent corporations, franchisees, officers, directors, agents, and employees from and against any and all losses, damages, expenses, claims, demands, liabilities, judgments, settlement amounts, costs, and causes of action of every type and character arising out of or in connection with the use or possession of the Mailbox, including without limitation, any demands, claims, and causes of action for personal injury or property damage arising from such use or possession, from failure of the United States Postal Service or any commercial carrier service to deliver on time or otherwise deliver any items (mail, packages, etc.), from damage to or loss of any package or mail, or to the Mailbox contents by any cause whatsoever, from the Center's collection or remission of sales, use, or any other taxes, including, but not limited to, the Center's failure to refund any amounts that have been collected or remitted, from any penalties, fines, or other liabilities that arise out of, or in connection with, the Center's actions or status as Customer's agent with respect to export transactions, or the Center's completion and filing of any Shipper's Export Declaration on behalf of Customer, and from any violation by Customer of applicable federal, state, or local laws, or the laws of any foreign jurisdiction. In the event that the Center submits or processes any sales, use, or other tax refund claim on behalf of Customer, Customer agrees to cooperate fully with the Center, including, but not limited to, providing any and all information and documentation necessary to process or submit such a claim.

14. Customer acknowledges and agrees that the Center is an independently owned and operated franchise of MBE and that MBE is not responsible for any acts or omissions of its franchisees.

15. CUSTOMER HEREIN AGREES THAT THE TOTAL AMOUNT OF LIABILITY OF THE CENTER AND MBE, IF ANY, FOR ANY AND ALL CLAIMS ARISING OUT OF OR RELATED TO THIS AGREEMENT OR PERFORMANCE HEREUNDER SHALL NOT EXCEED $100.00 REGARDLESS OF THE NATURE OF THE CLAIM. (INITIAL: _JNS_)

16. Customer must use the exact mailing address for the Mailbox without modification as set forth in Section three (3) of Form 1583. The United States Postal Service will return mail without a proper address to the sender endorsed "Undeliverable as Addressed."

17. Delivery by commercial carrier services must be made to the Center street address only (and not to a P.O. Box). "P.O. Box" may be used only if it is part of Customer's "Caller Service" (arrangement for delivery of mail through Centers using a United States Postal Service address) address format.

18. Upon signing this Agreement, Customer shall provide two (2) forms of valid identification, one of which shall include a photograph. This Agreement may not be amended or modified, except in a writing signed by both parties.

Customer Signature:	Date:	7/14/2014

For Center Use Only		
Authorized Center Representative Signature:	Date:	7/14/2014
How did the customer hear about us?	Walk-In	
Comments:		

The UPS Store® Centers are independently owned and operated by licensed Franchisees of Mail Boxes Etc., Inc., an indirect subsidiary of United Parcel Service, Inc., a Delaware corporation. Services, prices, and hours of operation are subject to change and may vary by location. Copyright © 2009 Mail Boxes Etc., Inc. All rights reserved. • Last updated 02/18/09

32

THE DEATH OF PRISONER ASSISTANT, INC.

When I first wrote this book, I talked about Prisoner Assistant and Michael Benanti. I even wrote about him in articles for Inmate Shopper, and in my first book, The Millionaire Prisoner. After Freebird Publishers read my first draft, they sent me some news clippings, so I could see what really happened. Here's the real story behind the guy who wanted to be "God" to us cellpreneurs. Jamie Satterfield, of the Knoxville News Sentinel, (Jamie.Satterfield@knoxnews.com), did a great job of reporting on this. Much of what I write is adapted from her stories on the case.

Michael Benanti is a narcissist and had grandiose schemes. A lot of us cellpreneurs have a little bit of that in us. But, he took things to a new level. Benanti got locked up in the early 1990's for conspiracy to rob a bank. While he was in the federal prison at Lewisburg, PA, Benanti hatched together an elaborate plan to escape. He enlisted another prisoner, Brian Witham, to help out, but they were ratted out by a third guy. Because of the plan, they were sent to "super-max" prison in Florence, CO. Benanti would later say that he was revered as a "god" by other prisoners because he didn't "snitch" and did his time in ADX.

While he was inside his cell, Benanti did a lot of reading and planning. Some of the books he read were about how to disguise oneself. That would become useful once he was released. After Benanti got out in 2008, he started Prisoner Assistant, which he ran from his basement office in his Lake Harmony, PA home. Prisoner Assistant was a great company for us prisoners because it allowed us to have a real bank account with Wells Fargo and start building credit. You could have your mailbox through the UPS store and even run a business from your cell. In 2009, Benanti's girlfriend, Natasha Bogoev, joined Prisoner Assistant as its Chief Financial Officer. One of Prisoner Assistant's first clients was none other than Brian Witham, Benanti's rappy on the failed escaped attempt. Witham was able to build his credit score up to 660 by the time he was released in 2013. After he got out, he went to see Benanti in Atlantic City. Benanti told him that Prisoner Assistant was getting good publicity, but not making money. At least not enough to finance the lifestyle that he thought he should be living. Tape recordings of Benanti's calls reveal what he was thinking. He didn't want to work at Burger King and would be bored on a "12, 13-dollar an hour job." Instead of staying on the right path, he was "turning left." And as is now publicly known, he went so far left there wasn't any way to get back.

In 2014, the Wall Street Journal profiled Benanti and Prisoner Assistant and business started rolling in. I even joined Prisoner Assistant and started my publishing company, Cardinal Wealth Services, with their help. My first book, The Millionaire Prisoner, was published from my maximum-security prison cell using Prisoner Assistant's help. But, Wells Fargo shut all the Prisoner Assistant's accounts down. Why? There're two versions. One is because Wells Fargo had a conflict of interest as they hold lots of stock in private corporations. So, their ideals don't coincide with a company trying to help prisoners stay out. The other version is that Wells Fargo foresaw the client money mismanagement/embezzlement by Benanti and shut him down. No matter which version you believe, it was the beginning of the end for Benanti. He sent letters to clients telling us what happened with Wells Fargo and gave us the opportunity to rollover our money into a new company called Lifetime Liberty Group. He said he wanted to start a bank offshore. WTF? I said NO because it all seemed fishy. Lifetime Liberty Group's marketing materials all looked exactly like Prisoner Assistant's old stuff. Except whereas Prisoner Assistant had Benanti and Natasha's names all over the paperwork, Lifetime Liberty Group's was a mystery. I took my money and ran all the way across the country to Help From Outside in Washington. My intuition told me to flee. Other prisoners were not so lucky.

The truth was that Benanti wasn't a changed man, he was lying to everyone and stealing from his prisoner clients, the same guys he was once housed with. Because Benanti needed cash to fill up the Prisoner Assistant coffers, he turned to robbery. He enlisted his cohort and new employee, Brian Witham, to get some real money. Witham was broke and living with his mom, so he was down. They did little identity thefts and came up with a scheme called "deaf millionaire." It wouldn't pan out, so they bought some shotguns and in September 2014, they robbed a bank. They got $156,000. But, that was not enough. All Benanti wanted to do was get rich and he would do anything to achieve that goal. But, the people around him had no idea he was a criminal. They thought he was a successful businessman. Using the knowledge, he learned from the "disguise" books he read while inside, Benanti and Witham came up with different alias, so they could deceive everyone. They even pretended to be FBI agents. Still, they needed more money. The pair hit some jewelry stores in Connecticut. Now, they were addicted to the lifestyle. They started popping ecstasy and spending on strippers. Benanti continued to plan more elaborate bank robberies.

In December 2014, the bandits broke into a Fayetteville, NC car dealership. They were trying to steal a car to use in upcoming robberies. Police showed up and Witham ran away and wasn't captured. Benanti tried to run, but he was caught due to him being overweight. From jail, Benanti called his girlfriend and told her to pull money out of Prisoner Assistant to bond him out of jail. Using our money, he hired a big-time lawyer and got the charges dropped.

In February 2015, they targeted a credit union in New Britain, Connecticut. The plan was to use bank employees' family members as hostages while the manager would go inside to rob the bank. They taped a fake bomb to bank executive, Matthew Yassman and told him it would go off at a certain time if he didn't do as they said. Then they tied his 70-year-old mother up to the bed and said they put a bomb with her, so he should do what they said. Yassman got stopped by police on their way to the bank and Benanti and Witham fled to New York where they burnt their getaway car. They needed money, so they robbed a supermarket for a little over $10,000 which was just enough to plan their next caper. They would try three more times to kidnap bank employees and their families, even pointing guns at toddlers and infants. Only one of those robberies did they get their money.

Benanti and Witham had used money from Prisoner Assistant to purchase a luxury cabin in North Carolina. From that cabin, they planned their crimes and did all their surveillance. They used GoPro cameras around the house of Mark Zielger to spy on him. Ziegler was a bank executive with Y-12 Federal Credit Union in Oakridge, Tennessee. Benanti sent Witham to hide in a tree outside Ziegler's house. Witham did as he was told and used the bathroom in bottles and plastic bags, so he wouldn't leave any trace evidence. One morning, in elaborate disguises to try and fool police, they drove to Ziegler's house. They handcuffed Ziegler then tied up his family. They told Zielger to rob the credit union or they would cut off his wife's fingers for every minute he was late. Then, they would start on his daughter. Ziegler believed them and was able to get over $200,000, but police stopped him and the bandits fled again. They next hit a loan officer in Knoxville for $195,000 by holding his wife and infant child hostage. They used some of that money to fund Prisoner Assistant and the rest on personal stuff like their stripper mistresses.

In September 2015, North Carolina highway patrolmen chased Benanti and Witham in an SUV. Witham tried to elude police but crashed into another vehicle. Both jumped out of the SUV with large, dark duffle bags. Police were scared to follow thinking the bags were filled with guns and they might be ambushed. Using a GPS device that the bandits had left behind in the SUV, police were able to locate the rental cabin and began to close the net on the two ex-cons.

Police showed up at Benanti's Lake Harmony, PA home looking for Witham. Benanti wasn't there but his girlfriend was. Natasha told them he wasn't there then acted funny the police said. She called Benanti and frantically told him what happened. Witham said she began asking Benanti questions about why he was gone for long periods of time. He told her he was meeting with investors for Prisoner Assistant, but she knew better because she was CFO of the company. What happened next is still a mystery. Police say she knew about Benanti stealing the prisoners' money and about the robberies. A few days later, she was found dead in a nearby hotel with a gunshot wound, Benanti showed police an alleged suicide note and had her body cremated. He then spread her ashes out over the water in the Bahamas. Benanti has never been charged and officially it was ruled a suicide.

Eventually, in November, after another car chase, the bandits were arrested. A search of the cabin and Benanti's office turned up FBI ID cards and other incriminating evidence including a mask with Benanti's DNA. He told police, "there are two types of people—those who go in harm's way and do things and those who plan." From jail, Benanti called Prisoner Assistant offices and told them, "I want you to take all the money from the all the accounts and put into my personal account...I need the best Tennessee lawyer there is." When the FBI agents came to talk to Benanti in jail, he tried to make a deal with the "feds" for immunity. He wanted to turn over to the "feds" all of Prisoner Assistant/Lifetime Liberty Group accounts and information. He said the FBI could use it as an information gathering tool on the high-ranking gang members who used his business. On tape, he told agents to "google" him that he was somebody "big." Benanti even offered to wear a wire and be a snitch for six months, so he could get his life back. After that didn't work, he tried to slice his wrists and neck with a jail razor, so he could get outside and possibly escape. That didn't work because all he got was surgery and a nasty scar on his neck.

Brian Witham plead guilty and agreed to testify against Benanti for a 42-year-sentence. Benanti would go to trial in February 2017. He was forced to wear a "stun-belt" because he made threats about Witham and the prosecutors dying on phone calls since he was locked up. Benanti's lawyers argued that Witham was lying. But, the jury believed him. Benanti was convicted on twenty-three charges including carjacking, extortion, and kidnapping. He will never get out of prison again and the "feds" will probably send him back to ADX. We'll see if he's treated like a "god" now.

Freebird Publishers

Presents A New Self-Help Reentry Book

LIFE WITH A RECORD

Reenter Society, Finish Supervision and Live Successfully

Anthony Tinsman
Foreward by Sue Kastensen

Freebird Publishers

INSIDE COMPLETE REENTRY RESOURCE LISTINGS

INSIDE COMPLETE REENTRY RESOURCE LISTINGS

Hundreds of complete, up-to-date entries at your fingertips.

Life With A Record
Only $25.99
Plus $7 S/H with tracking
Softcover, 8" x 10", B&W, 360 pages

NEW RULES FOR A NEW YOU

Things don't magically change after you get kicked out of prison. Life starts all over again but there's a catch, having a record impacts almost every part of your life. With this book you'll find out how to prepare for life as an ex-offender. Filled with insights, advice, contacts, and exercises the information strikes legal, personal and professional levels. A real world guide for minimizing disruptions and maximizing success.

Life With A Record helps make sense of the major challenges facing ex-offenders today. Ten hard hitting chapters outline the purpose of making a Strategic Reentry Plan and making peace with supervisors, family, your community and your future. Written by well-known reentry technician Anthony Tinsman, it packs an amazing amount of material into its pages and gives you a quick, easy to follow, full spectrum of instruction.

Inside You Will Find:

- ☑ How to rebuild your credit and begin financial recovery
- ☑ Halfway house rules and supervision terms
- ☑ Special grants and loans to finance education, job training, or starting a business
- ☑ Legal tips for dealing with discrimination in employment, housing and collegiate settings
- ☑ Discussion of success stories, best practices, reuniting families, plus much more
- ☑ Directory with hundreds of reentry contacts
- ☑ Sample forms and documents that cut through red tape
- ☑ How to regain your civil and political rights

Life With a Record explores the most commonly confronted issues and attitudes that sabotage reentry. It provides tools that cut across functions of discrimination, in corporations, political life and throughout society. It opens the door to empowerment, reminding ex-offenders that change and long term freedom begins with a commitment to daily growth. Addressing the whole reentry process, Life With a Record is "must" reading for anyone preparing to leave prison and face the world. It's an ideal book for ex-offenders with decades of experience as well as first time prisoners who need help jump starting their new life.

NO ORDER FORM NEEDED CLEARLY WRITE ON PAPER & SEND PAYMENT TO:

Freebird Publishers Box 541, North Dighton, MA 02764

Diane@FreebirdPublishers.com   www.FreebirdPublishers.com

Toll Free: 888-712-1987   Text/Phone: 774-406-8682

MoneyGram

PayPal   VISA   DISCOVER   BANK

CHAPTER 4
INCORPORATING FROM PRISON

*"A criminal is a person with predatory instincts who has
not sufficient capital to form a corporation."*
- Howard Scott

There are several reasons why you should consider incorporating your business from prison. They are:

1) To protect your assets from lawsuits; and

2) To lower your tax bill and increase your profits.

Let's look at each reason more in-depth.

PROTECTION FROM LAWSUITS

America is a very litigation heavy society. I know firsthand because I'm currently involved in three lawsuits in federal court, another one in small claims court, and finally an appeal from another lawsuit dismissal in state court. That's partly because the IDOC administration is bogus and I'm trying to correct wrongs. But it's also partly due to the fact that I was raised in America where it's deemed okay to sue to right past wrongs and get damages. You can be sued for anything. I remember some years ago a lady sued McDonalds® because she had a cup of coffee that she had just purchased between her legs while driving and said it was too hot when it spilled on her and burnt her. She didn't win, but she cost McDonalds time and legal fees defending the suit. As I write this I heard on the news that someone was suing Starbucks® because they served iced coffee? WTF? Don't order it is my answer. Pretty absurd, right? But the truth is that it happens every day. These examples prove that you can be sued at any time.

Extra caution should be used when setting up a business that will cater to prisoners. We can be an extremely impatient bunch and will complain. One company I used in the past was Tiff Services, LLC. I used them for email services and never had any problems. But there was a rumor that a prisoner sued her over a $50,000 dispute and she went out of a business on a mass scale. Another example of a prisoner being suit happy is that of Illinois prisoner James Turner-El. He filed over 3,500 petitions and lawsuits and was finally admonished by the courts to stop it. Think about the prisoners all around you who are filing lawsuits. For some of them it is their hustle. You wouldn't want them to sue you over a business decision and grab a piece of what you have worked for. A corporation can give you some protection from these lawsuits.

"If you want to protect your personal assets, set up a corporation, LLC or another protective entity to operate your business or professional practice. That's Cardinal Rule #1."

-Attorney Hillel Presser

LOWER TAX BILL MEANS MORE PROFITS

There's a reason why so many corporations seek out legal loopholes and international tax havens. It's their duty to the shareholders of their company to increase profits. If they can do this by following the tax laws already in place they should. So, should you. For instance, if your setup a S-Corp, you as the owner would only pay federal taxes on your salary. If you set up a LLC (see next chapter) you'll pay taxes on all profits, and state taxes may be lower for an S-Corp. That is why so many corporations have headquarters in Nevada. It has no state income tax and is very corporation friendly. There's no reason why you can't do what the rich are doing and incorporate yourself.

There has been a lot of stuff in the news lately about closing all these legal loopholes. It's typical of the masses of asses to complain when they see someone else doing something they wish they could do. But they could if they just exercised their right to choose another life. Thank God you have chosen a different path. Now that you have chosen the path of becoming a cellpreneur it's your duty to learn all that you can about the proper way to lower your tax bill. And by combining the two areas – asset protection and lower tax bracket – you can be on your way to becoming a Millionaire Prisoner.

Since the colonial days, Americans have been rebelling against paying taxes. Just like our founding fathers who organized the Boston Tea Party, the rich believe in their right to avoid taxes. But they don't have to start a revolution to do it because the law is on their side. It can be on yours also.

"The avoidance of taxes is the only intellectual pursuit that carries any reward."

John Maynard Keynes

RESOURCE BOX

For more information on how you can lower your tax bill and increase your profits you should check out the following books:

- Doing Business Tax Free: Perfectly Legal Techniques for Reducing or Eliminating Your Federal Business Taxes by Robert Cooke

- Tax Deductions For Professionals, 4th Edition by Stephen Fishman

- Lower Your Taxes–Big Time! By Sandy Botkin, C.P.A.

- 475 Tax Deduction For Businesses and Self-Employed Individuals by Bernard B. Kamoroff, C.P.A.

Books can be ordered from our Bookstore on page 224 or online. Contact Freebird Publishers about ordering if you don't have anyone to help you.

THE LAW ACCORDING TO CORPORATIONS

There are a bunch of rules for incorporating. Your corporation must have a Registered Office and a Registered Agent. Your agent can be an attorney. When Prisoner Assistant, Inc. was still operating they allowed (and preferred) you to incorporate in Pennsylvania. This is where their headquarters were and that allowed them to act as your agent. If you chose to incorporate in another state other than your prison's location, you will need a person to act as your agent. It can be a family member. Just make sure they are trustworthy. Here are some more rules regarding corporations:

- All corporations must have by-laws. I've included a sample set that you can fill in and file at the end of this chapter.

- Prior to opening a bank account, a corporation must obtain an Employer Identification Number (EIN).

- S-Corps must file IRS Form 2553 within 75 days of incorporating. That form, and instructions are included at the end of this chapter.

- Corporations must keep permanent records of its legal affairs. You can keep yours in a binder or legal envelope until you get out. Or you can order a specially prepared corporate kit. They can be ordered from the following:

Blumberg Excelsior
4435 Old Winter Garden Road
Orlando, FL 32811
(800)327-9220
www.blumberg.com

Corpkit Legal Services
46 Taft Avenue
Islip, NY 11751
(888) 888-9120
www.corpkit.com

Corpex
1440 Fifth Avenue
Bay Shore, NY 11706
(800) 221-8181
www.corpexnet.com

You can get your corporate seal from an office supply store. A simple rubber stamp will do. But unless you get someone to assist you, it may have to wait till you get out.

- A corporation must hold annual meetings. These don't have to be elaborate board meetings like you see on TV. A sole officer and director can hold these meetings in their mind, and a simple document can be filed representing this. I've included one at the end of this chapter.

- You must file an annual report with a fee each year. It can range from $20 to several hundred dollars. You must check with your state's business office for the costs.

Because the two most popular states to incorporate in are Nevada and Delaware I have included two sample fill-in-the-blank Articles of Incorporation. One for each state. They are similar, but slightly different. You should write your state's business office and ask for a corporate kit with the required forms and instructions. A sample letter you can use is included in this chapter.

Once you get out of prison you may want to change the corporate address and registered agent. I've included a form that you could file to do this. But it costs a small fee to do so. All of this will be included in your state's laws or the rules governing corporations.

RESOURCE BOX

For more about forming and operating a corporation you should get a copy of the following books:

- Ultimate Guide To Incorporating In Any State: Everything You Need To Know by Michael Spadaccini

- The Complete Book of Corporate Forms by Ted Nicholas

- Starting Your Subchapter "S" Corporation: How To Build A Business The Right Way by Arnold Goldstein

- Inc. Yourself: How To Profit By Setting Up Your Own Corporation by Judith McQuown

- Start Your Own Corporation by Garrett Sutton

Books can be ordered from our Bookstore on page 224 or online. Contact Freebird Publishers about ordering if you don't have anyone to help you.

To:_____   _____,20_____

       _____   Date

       _____

       _____

Dear Sir or Madam:

I would like your application and/or business package for forming a corporation in _____. Please provide any forms and instructions that I need to follow to properly file the Corporate documents.

Thank you in advance for your corporation in this matter. I look forward to hearing from you soon.

Respectfully Requested,

_____

_____

_____

_____

Sample Letter Requesting Corporation Forms

To:_____   _____,20_____
    _____   Date
    _____
    _____

Dear Sir or Madam:

Please find the enclosed documents for the corporate registration of
_____, along with a check
in the amount of $_____ for the filing fee and any other required costs.

Also, enclosed are photocopies of the corporate documents. Please return them to me with the filing date stamped on them. Thank you in advance for your cooperation in this matter.

Respectfully Requested,

    _____
    _____
    _____
    _____

Sample Letter to Include When Filing Forms

STATE OF NEVADA

ARTICLES OF INCORPORATION

_____

A BUSINESS CORPORATION

The Name of the Corporation is _____

_____.

The duration of the corporation is perpetual.

The corporation has been organized to transact any and all lawful business for which corporations may be incorporated in this state.

The aggregate number of shares which the corporation shall have the authority to issue is zero.

The number of directors constituting the initial board of directors of the corporation is two, and his/her names and addresses are: _____

_____

The location and street address of the initial registered office is _____

_____

The name and address of the incorporators are:

_____   _____

_____   _____

_____   _____

_____   _____

In witness thereof, the undersigned incorporator(s) have executed these articles of incorporation this _____day of _____,_____.

_____   _____
Witness   Incorporator

_____   _____
Witness   Incorporator

State of_____

County of _____

On _____, _____ the above persons appeared before me, a notary public and are personally known or proved to me to be the persons whose names are subscribed to the above instrument who acknowledge that they executed the instrument.

s/_____

(Notary Stamp or Seal)

Sample Articles of Incorporation for Nevada

State of Delaware
Articles of Incorporation
of _____,
A Business Corporation

The name of the corporation is _____.

The business and mailing address of the corporation is _____ _____

The duration of the corporation is perpetual.

The corporation has been organized to transact any and all lawful business for which corporations may be incorporated in this state.

The aggregate number of shares which the corporation shall have the authority to issue is _____ and the par value of each shall be no par value.

The amount of the total authorized capitalized stock of this corporation is _____dollars $(_____) divided into _____ shares, of _____dollars $(_____).

The number of directors constituting the initial board of directors of the corporation is _____, and their names and addresses are:

_____   _____   _____
_____   _____   _____
_____   _____   _____

The location and street address of the initial registered office is _____ _____

and the name of its initial registered agent at such address is _____.

The name and address of each incorporator are:

_____   _____
_____   _____
_____   _____

In witness thereof, the undersigned incorporator(s) have executed these articles of incorporation this _____day of _____,_____.

_____
Incorporator

_____
Incorporator

State of _____
County of _____

On _____, the above person(s) appeared before me, a notary public and are personally known or proved to me to be the person(s) whose name(s) are subscribed to the above instrument who acknowledged that he/she executed the instrument.

(Notary Stamp or Seal)

_____
Notary Public

Sample Articles of Incorporation for Delaware

BYLAWS OF

_____

A _____ CORPORATION

ARTICLE 1- OFFICES

The principal office of the Corporation shall be located in the City of _____ and the state of _____. The Corporation may also maintain offices at such other places as the Board of Directors may, from time to time, determine.

ARTICLE II – SHAREHOLDERS

Section 1 – Annual Meetings: The annual meeting of the shareholders of the corporation shall be held each year on _____ at _____ or, at the principal office of the Corporation or at such other places, within or without the state of _____, as the Board may authorize, for the purpose of electing directors, and transacting such other business as may properly come before the meeting.

Section 2 – Special Meetings: Special meetings of the shareholders may be called at any time by the Board, the President, or by the holders of twenty-five percent (25%) of the shares then outstanding and entitled to vote.

Section 3 – Place of Meetings: All meetings of shareholders shall be held at the principal office of the Corporation, or at such other places as the board shall designate in the notice of such meetings.

Section 4 – Notice of Meetings: Written or printed notice stating the place, day, and hour of the meeting and, in the case of a special meeting, the purpose of the meeting, shall be delivered personally or by mail not less than ten days, nor more than sixty days, before the date of the meeting. Notice shall be given to each member of record entitle to vote at the meeting. If mailed, such notice shall be deemed to have been delivered when deposited in the United States Mail with postage paid and addressed to the member at his or her address as it appears on the records of the Corporation.

Section 5 – Waiver of Notice: A written waiver of notice signed by a Member, whether before or after a meeting, shall be equivalent to the giving of such notice. Attendance of a member at a meeting shall constitute a waiver of notice of such meeting, except when the Member attends for the express purpose of objecting, at the beginning of the meeting, to the transaction of any business because the meeting is not lawfully called or convened.

Section 6 – Quorum: Except as otherwise provided by Statute, or the Articles of Incorporation, at all meetings of shareholders of the corporation, the presence at the commencement of such meetings in person or by proxy of shareholders of record holding a majority of the total number of shares of the corporation then issued and outstanding and entitled to vote, but in no event less than one-third of the shares entitled to vote at the meeting, shall constitute a quorum for the transaction of any business. If any shareholder leaves after the commencement of a meeting, this shall have no effect on the existence of quorum, after a quorum has been established at such meeting.

Despite the absence of a quorum at any annual or special meeting of shareholders, the shareholders, by a majority of the votes cast by the holders of shares entitled to vote thereon, may adjourn the meeting. At any such adjourned meeting at which a quorum is present, any business may be transacted at the meeting as originally called as if a quorum had been present.

Section 7 – Voting: Except as otherwise provided by Statute or by the Articles of Incorporation, any corporate action, other than the election of directors, to be taken by vote of the shareholders, shall be authorized by a majority of votes cast at a meeting of shareholders by the holders of shares entitled to vote thereon.

Except as otherwise provided by Statute or by the Articles of Incorporation, at each meeting of shareholders, each holder of record of stock of the Corporation entitled to vote shall be entitled to one vote for each share of stock registered in his or her name on the stock transfer books of the corporation.

Each shareholder entitled to vote may do so by proxy; provided, however, that the instrument authorizing such proxy to act shall have been executed in writing by the shareholder him – or herself. No proxy shall be valid after the expiration of eleven months from the date of its execution, unless the person executing it shall have specified therein, the length of time it is to continue in force. Such instrument shall be exhibited to the Secretary at the meeting and shall be filed with the records of the corporation.

Any registration in writing, singed by all of the shareholders entitled to vote thereon, shall be and constitute action by such shareholders to the effect therein expressed, with the same force and effect as if the same had been duly passed by unanimous vote at a duly called meeting of shareholders and such resolution so signed shall be inserted in the Minute Book of the Corporation under its proper date.

ARTICLE III – BOARD OF DIRECTORS

Section 1 – Number, Election and Term of Office: The number of the directors of the Corporation shall be (_____). This number may be increased or decreased by the amendment of the bylaws by the Board but shall in no case be less than _____ director(s). The members of the Board, who need not be shareholders, shall be elected by a majority of the votes cast at a meeting of shareholders entitled to vote in the election. Each director shall hold office until the annual meeting of the shareholders next succeeding his election, and until his successor Is elected and qualified, or until his prior death, resignation or removal.

Section 2 – Vacancies: Any vacancy in the Board shall be filled for the unexpired portion of the term by a majority vote of the remaining directors, through less than a quorum, at any regular meeting or special meeting of the Board called for that purpose. Any such director so elected may be replaced by the shareholders at the regular or special meeting of shareholders.

Section 3 – Duties and Powers: The Board shall be responsible for the control and management of the affairs, property and interests of the Corporation, and may exercise all powers of the Corporation, except as limited by statute.

Section 4 – Annual Meetings: An annual meeting of the Board shall be held immediately following the annual meeting of the shareholders, at the place of such annual meeting of shareholders. The Board from time to time, may provide by resolution for the holding of other meetings of the Board, and may fix the time and place thereof.

Section 5 – Special Meetings: Special meetings of the Board shall be held whenever called by the President or by one of the directors, at such time and place as may be specified in the respective notice or waivers of notice thereof.

Section 6 – Notice and Waiver: Notice of any special meeting shall be given at least five days prior thereto by written notice delivered personally, by mail, or by telegram to each Director at his or her address. If mailed, such notice shall be deemed to be delivered when deposited in the United States Mail with postage prepaid. If notice is given by telegram, such notice shall be deemed to be delivered when the telegram is delivered to the telegraph company.

Any Director may waive notice of any meeting, either before, at, or after such meeting, by signing a waiver of notice. The attendance of a Director at a meeting shall constitute a waiver of notice of such meeting and a waiver of any and all objections to the place of such meeting, or the manner in which it has been called or convened, except when a Director states at the beginning of the meeting any objection to the transaction of business because the meeting is not lawfully called or convened.

Section 7 – Chairman: The Board may, at its discretion, elect a chairman. At all meetings of the Board, the Chairman of the Board, if any and if present, shall preside. If there is no Chairman, or he or she is absent, then the President shall preside, and in his or her absence, a chairman chosen by the directors shall preside.

Section 8 – Quorum and Adjournments: At all meetings of the Board, the presence of a majority of the entire Board shall be necessary and sufficient to constitute a quorum for the transaction of business, except as otherwise provided by law, by the Articles of Incorporation, or by these bylaws. A majority of the directors' present at the time and place of any regular or special meeting, although less than a quorum, may adjourn the same from time to time without notice, until a quorum shall be present.

Section 9 – Board Action: At all meetings of the Board, each director present shall have one vote, irrespective of the number of shares of stock, if any, which he may hold. Except as otherwise provided by statute, the action of a majority of the directors' present at any meeting at which a quorum is present shall be the act of the Board. Any action authorized, in writing, by all of the Directors entitled to vote and filed with the minutes of the Corporation shall be the act of the Board with the same force and effect as if the same had been passed by unanimous vote at a duly called meeting of the writing by all members before or after the action is taken and if a record of such action is filed in the minute book.

Section 10 – Telephone Meetings: Directors may participate in meetings of the Board through use of a telephone if such can be arranged so that all Board Members can hear all other members. The use of a telephone for participation shall constitute presence in person.

Section 11 – Resignation and Removal: Any director may resign at any time by giving written notice to another board member, the President or the Secretary of the Corporation. Unless otherwise specified in such written notice, such resignation shall take effect upon Receipt thereof by the Board or by such officer, and the acceptance of such

Resignation shall not be necessary to make it effective. Any director may be removed with or without cause at any time by the affirmative vote of shareholders called for that purpose, and may be removed for cause by action of the Board.

Section 12 – Compensation: No stated salary shall be paid to directors, as such for their services, but by resolution of the Board a fixed sum and/or expenses of attendance, if any, may be allowed for attendance at each regular or special meeting of the Board. Nothing herein contained shall be construed to preclude any director from serving the Corporation in any other capacity and receiving compensation therefor.

ARTICLE IV – OFFICERS

Section 1 – Number, Qualification, Election and Term: The officers of the Corporation shall consist of a President, a Secretary, a Treasurer, and such other officers, as the Board may from time to time deep advisable. Any officer may be, but is not required to be, a director of the Corporation. The officers of the Corporation shall be elected by the Board at the regular annual meeting of the Board each officer shall hold office until the annual meeting of the Board next succeeding his or her election, and until his or her successor shall have been elected and qualified, or until his or her death, resignation, or removal.

Section 2 – Resignation and Removal: Any officer may resign at any time by giving written notice of such resignation to the President or the Secretary of the corporation or to a member of the Board. Unless otherwise specified in such written notice, such resignation shall take effect upon receipt thereof by the Board member or by such officer, and the acceptance of such resignation shall not be necessary to make it effective. Any officer may be removed, either with or without cause, and a successor elected by a majority vote of the Board at any time.

Section 3 – Vacancies: A vacancy in any office may at any time be filled for the unexpired portion of the term by a majority vote of the Board.

Section 4 – Duties of Officers: Officers of the Corporation shall, unless otherwise provided by the Board, each have such powers and duties as generally pertain to their respective offices as well as such powers and duties as may from time to time be specifically decided by the Board. The President shall be the chief executive officer of the Corporation.

Section 5 – Compensation: The officers of the Corporation shall be entitled to such compensation as the Board shall from time to time determine.

Section 6 – Delegation of Duties: In the absence or disability of any Officer of the Corporation or for any other reason deemed sufficient by the Board of Directors, the Board may delegate his or her powers or duties to any other Officer or to any other Director.

Section 7 – Shares of Other Corporations: Whenever the Corporation is the holder of shares of any other Corporation, any right or power of the Corporation as such shareholder (including the attendance, acting and voting at shareholders' meetings and execution of waivers, consents, proxies or other instruments) may be exercised on behalf of the Corporation by the President, any Vice President, or such other person as the Board may authorize.

ARTICLE V – COMMITTEES

The Board of Directors may, by resolution, designate an Executive Committee and one or more other committees. Such committees shall have such functions and may exercise such power of the Board of Directors as can be lawfully delegated, and to the extent provided in the Resolution of Resolutions creating such committee or committees. Meetings of committees may be held without notice of such time and at such place as shall from time to time be determined by the committees. The committees of the corporation shall keep regular minutes of their proceedings and report these minutes to the Board of Directors when required.

ARTICLE VI – BOOKS, RECORDS, AND REPORTS

Section 1 – Annual Report: The Corporation shall send an annual report to the Members of the Corporation not later than _____ months after the close of each fiscal year of the Corporation. Such report shall include a balance sheet as of the close of the fiscal year of the Corporation and Revenue and disbursement statement for the year ending on such closing date. Such financial statements shall be prepared from and in accordance with the books of the corporation, and in conformity with generally accepted accounting principles applied on a consistent basis.

Section 2 – Permanent Records: The Corporation shall keep current and correct records of the accounts, minute of the meetings and proceedings and membership records of the corporation. Such records shall be kept at the registered office or the principle place of business of the corporation. Any such records shall be in written form or in form capable of being converted into written form.

Section 3 – Inspection of Corporate Records: Any person who is a Voting Member of the Corporation shall have the right at any reasonable time, and on written demand stating the purpose thereof, to examine and make copies from the relevant books and records of accounts, minutes, and records of the Corporation. Upon the written request of any Voting Member, the Corporation shall mail to such Member a copy of the most recent balance sheet and revenue and disbursement statement.

ARTICLE VII – SHARES OF STOCK

Section 1 – Certificates: Each shareholder of the corporation shall be entitled to have a certificate representing all shares which he or she owns. The form of such certificate shall be adopted by a majority vote of the Board of Directors and shall be signed by the President and Secretary of the Corporation and Sealed with the seal of the Corporation. No certificate representing shares shall be issued until the full amount of consideration therefore has been paid.

Section 3 Stock Ledger: The Corporation shall maintain a ledger of the stock records of the corporation. Transfers of shares of the Corporation shall be made on the stock ledger of the Corporation only at the direction of the holder of record upon surrender of the outstanding certificate(s). The Corporation shall be entitled to treat the holder of record of any share or shares as the absolute owner thereof for all purposes and, accordingly, shall not be bound to recognize any legal, equitable or other claim to, or interest in, such share or shares on the part of any other person, whether or not it shall have express or other

Notice thereof, except as otherwise expressly provided by law.

ARTICLE VIII – DIVIDENDS

Upon approval by the Board of Directors the Corporation may pay dividends on its shares in the form of cash, property or additional shares at any time that the Corporation is solvent and if such dividends would not render the Corporation insolvent.

ARTICLE IX – FISCAL YEAR

The fiscal year of the Corporation shall be the period selected by the Board of Directors as the tax year of the Corporation for federal income tax purposes.

ARTICLE X – CORPORATE SEAL

The Board of Directors may adapt, use and modify a corporate seal. Failure to affix the seal to corporate documents shall not affect the validity of such document.

ARTICLE XI – AMENDMENTS

The Articles of Incorporation may be amended by the shareholders a provided by _____statutes. These Bylaws may be altered, amended, or replaced by the Board of Directors; provided, however, that any Bylaws or amendments thereto as adopted by the Board of Directors may be Altered, amended, or repealed by vote of the Shareholders. Bylaws adopted by the Members may not be amended or repealed by the Board.

ARTICLE XII – INDEMNIFICATION

Any officer, director or employee of the Corporation shall be indemnified to the full extent allowed by the laws of the State of _____.

Certified to be the Bylaws of the Corporation adopted by the Board of Directors on _____, 20 _____.

_____
                                        Secretary

50

MINUTES OF THE ORGANIZATIONAL MEETING OF
INCORPORATORS AND DIRECTORS OF

_____

The organization meeting of the above corporation was held on _____,
20, _____ at _____at _____o'clock ____m.

The following persons were present:

_____   _____

_____   _____

_____   _____

The Waiver of notice of this meeting was signed by all directors and incorporators named in the Articles of Incorporation and filed in the minute book.

The meeting was called to order by _____, an Incorporator named in the Articles of Incorporation. _____was nominated and elected chairman and acted as such until relieved by the president. _____was nominated and elected temporary secretary and acted as such until relived by the permeant secretary.

A copy of the Articles of Incorporation, which was filed with the Secretary of State of the State of _____on_____,20_____, was examined by the Directors and Incorporators and filed in the minute book.

The election of officers for the coming year was then held and the following were duly nominated and elected by the Board of Directors to be the officers of the corporation, to serve until such time as their successors are elected and qualified:

President:

Vice President:

Secretary:

Treasurer:

The proposed Bylaws for the corporation were then presented to the meeting and discussed. Upon motion duly made, seconded and carried, the Bylaws were adopted and added to the minute book.

A corporate seal for the corporation was then presented to the meeting and upon motion duly made, seconded and carried, it was adopted as the seal of the corporation. An impression thereof was then made in the margin of these minutes.

(SEAL)

The necessity of opening a bank account was then discussed and upon motion duly made, seconded, and carried, the following resolution was adopted:

RESOLVED that the corporation open bank accounts with _____ _____and that the officers of the corporation are authorized to take such action as is necessary to open such accounts; that the bank's printed form of resolution is hereby adopted and incorporated into these minutes by reference and shall be placed in the minute book; that any _____of the following persons shall have signature authority over the account:

_____   _____

_____   _____

_____   _____

_____   _____

Proposed stock certificates and stock transfer ledger were then presented to the meeting and examined. Upon motion duly made, seconded, and carried the stock certificates and ledger were adopted as the certificates and transfer book to be used by the corporation. A sample stock certificate marked "VOID" and the stock transfer ledger were then added to the minute book. Upon motion duly made, seconded, and carried, it was then resolved that the stock certificates, when issued, would be signed by the President and the Secretary of the Corporation.

The tax status of the corporation was then discussed, and it was moved, seconded, and carried that the stock of the corporation be issued under §1244 of the Internal Revenue Code and that the officers of the corporation take the necessary action to:

1. Obtain an employer tax number by filing form SS-4

2. ☐ Become an S corporation for tax purposes

    ☐ Become a C corporation for tax purposes

The expenses of organizing the corporation were then discussed and it was moved, seconded, and carried that the corporation pay in full of the corporate funds the expenses and reimburse any advances made by the incorporators upon proof of payment.

The Directors named in the Articles of Incorporation then tendered their resignations, effective upon the adjournment of this meeting. Upon motion duly made, seconded and carried, the following named persons were elected as Directors of the corporation, each to hold office until the first annual meeting of shareholders, and until a successor of each shall have been elected and qualified.

_____   _____

_____   _____

There were presented to the corporation, the following offer(s) to purchase shares of capital stock:

FROM   NUMBER OF SHARES   CONSIDERATION

_____   _____   _____
_____   _____   _____
_____   _____   _____
_____   _____   _____

The offers were discussed and after motion duly made, seconded, and carried were approved. It was further resolved that the Board of Directors has determined that the consideration was valued at least equal to the value of the shares to be issued and that upon tender of the consideration, fully paid non-assessable shares of the corporation be issued.

There being no further business before the meeting, on motion duly made, seconded, and carried, the meeting adjourned.

Dated: _____

_____
President

_____
Secretary

MINUTES OF THE ANNUAL MEETING OF
THE BOARD OF DIRECTORS OF

_____

The annual meeting of the Board of Directors of the Corporation was held on the date and time and place set forth in the written waiver of notice signed by the directors and attached to the minutes of this meeting.

The following were present, being all the directors of the Corporation:

_____   _____

_____   _____

The meeting was called to order and it was moved, seconded, and unanimously carried that _____act as Chairman and that _____act as Secretary.

The minutes of the last meeting of the Board of Directors, which was held on _____, 20 _____, were read and approved by the Board.

Upon motion duly made, seconded and carried, the following were elected officers for the following year and until their successors are elected and qualify:

President: _____

Vice President: _____

Secretary: _____

Treasurer: _____

There being no further business to come before the meeting, upon motion duly made, seconded, and unanimously carried, it was adjourned.

_____
Secretary

Directors:

_____

_____

_____

_____

Form **2553**

(Rev. December 2013)

Department of the Treasury
Internal Revenue Service

Election by a Small Business Corporation
(Under section 1362 of the Internal Revenue Code)

▶ See Parts II and III on page 3.
▶ You can fax this form to the IRS (see separate instructions).
▶ Information about Form 2553 and its separate instructions is at *www.irs.gov/form2553*.

OMB No. 1545-0123

Note. This election to be an S corporation can be accepted only if all the tests are met under *Who May Elect* in the instructions, all shareholders have signed the consent statement, an officer has signed below, and the exact name and address of the corporation (entity) and other required form information have been provided.

Part I	Election Information

Type or Print

Name (see instructions)

Number, street, and room or suite no. (If a P.O. box, see instructions.)

City or town, state, and ZIP code

A Employer identification number

B Date incorporated

C State of incorporation

D Check the applicable box(es) if the corporation (entity), after applying for the EIN shown above, changed its ☐ name or ☐ address

E Election is to be effective for tax year beginning (month, day, year) (see instructions) . . . . ▶
Caution. A corporation (entity) making the election for its first tax year in existence will usually enter the beginning date of a short tax year that begins on a date other than January 1.

F Selected tax year:
(1) ☐ Calendar year
(2) ☐ Fiscal year ending (month and day) ▶
(3) ☐ 52-53-week year ending with reference to the month of December
(4) ☐ 52-53-week year ending with reference to the month of
If box (2) or (4) is checked, complete Part II.

G If more than 100 shareholders are listed for item J (see page 2), check this box if treating members of a family as one shareholder results in no more than 100 shareholders (see test under *Who May Elect* in the instructions) ▶ ☐

H Name and title of officer or legal representative who the IRS may call for more information

I Telephone number of officer or legal representative

If this S corporation election is being filed late, I declare that I had reasonable cause for not filing Form 2553 timely, and if this late election is being made by an entity eligible to elect to be treated as a corporation, I declare that I also had reasonable cause for not filing an entity classification election timely and that the representations listed in Part IV are true. See below for my explanation of the reasons the election or elections were not made on time and a description of my diligent actions to correct the mistake upon its discovery (see instructions).

Sign Here

Under penalties of perjury, I declare that I have examined this election, including accompanying documents, and, to the best of my knowledge and belief, the election contains all the relevant facts relating to the election, and such facts are true, correct, and complete.

▶

Signature of officer | Title | Date

For Paperwork Reduction Act Notice, see separate instructions.

Cat. No. 18629R

Form **2553** (Rev. 12-2013)

55

| Part I | Election Information (continued) | Note. If you need more rows, use additional copies of page 2. |

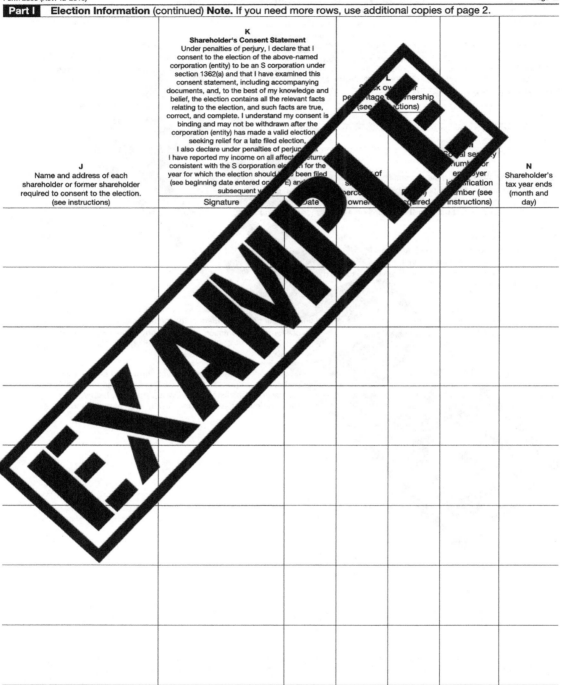

Form 2553 (Rev. 12-2013)   Page **3**

Part II **Selection of Fiscal Tax Year** (see instructions)

Note. All corporations using this part must complete item O and item P, Q, or R.

O Check the applicable box to indicate whether the corporation is:
  1. ☐ A new corporation **adopting** the tax year entered in item F, Part I.
  2. ☐ An existing corporation **retaining** the tax year entered in item F, Part I.
  3. ☐ An existing corporation **changing** to the tax year entered in item F, Part I.

P Complete item P if the corporation is using the automatic approval provisions of Rev. Proc. 2006-46, 2006-45 I.R.B. 859, to request **(1)** a natural business year (as defined in section 5.07 of Rev. Proc. 2006-46) or **(2)** a year that satisfies the ownership tax year test (as defined in section 5.08 of Rev. Proc. 2006-46). Check the applicable box below to indicate the representation statement the corporation is making.

  1. Natural Business Year ▶ ☐ I represent that the corporation is adopting, retaining, or changing to a tax year that qualifies as its natural business year (as defined in section 5.07 of Rev. Proc. 2006-46) and has attached a statement showing separately for each month the gross receipts for the most recent 47 months (see instructions). I also represent that the corporation is not precluded by section 4.01 of Rev. Proc. 2006-46 from obtaining automatic approval of such adoption, retention, or change in tax year.

  2. Ownership Tax Year ▶ ☐ I represent that shareholders (as described in section 5.08 of Rev. Proc. 2006-46) holding more than half of the shares of the stock (as of the first day of the tax year to which the request relates) of the corporation have the same tax year or are concurrently changing to the tax year that the corporation adopts, retains, or changes to per item F, Part I, and that such tax year satisfies the requirement of section 4.01(3) of Rev. Proc. 2006-46. I also represent that the corporation is not precluded by section 4.02 of Rev. Proc. 2006-46 from obtaining automatic approval of such adoption, retention, or change in tax year.

Note. If you do not use item P and the corporation wants a fiscal tax year, complete either item Q or R below. Item Q is used to request a fiscal tax year based on a business purpose and to make a back-up section 444 election. Item R is used to make a regular section 444 election.

Q Business Purpose—To request a fiscal tax year based on a business purpose, check box Q1. See instructions for details including payment of a user fee. You may also check box Q2 and/or box Q3.

  1. Check here ▶ ☐ if the fiscal year entered in item F, Part I, is requested under the prior approval provisions of Rev. Proc. 2002-39, 2002-22 I.R.B. 1046. Attach to Form 2553 a statement describing the relevant facts and circumstances and, if applicable, the gross receipts from sales and services necessary to establish a business purpose. See the instructions for details regarding the gross receipts from sales and services. If the IRS proposes to disapprove the requested fiscal year, do you want a conference with the IRS National Office?

  ☐ Yes ☐ No

  2. Check here ▶ ☐ to show that the corporation intends to make a back-up section 444 election in the event the corporation's business purpose request is not approved. (See instructions for more information.)

  3. Check here ▶ ☐ to show that the corporation agrees to adopt or change to a tax year ending December 31 if necessary for the IRS to accept this election for S corporation status in the event (1) the corporation's business purpose request is not approved and the corporation makes a back-up section 444 election, but is ultimately not qualified to make a section 444 election, or (2) the corporation's business purpose request is not approved and the corporation did not make a back-up section 444 election.

R Section 444 Election—To make a section 444 election, check box R1. You may also check box R2.

  1. Check here ▶ ☐ to show that the corporation will make, if qualified, a section 444 election to have the fiscal tax year shown in item F, Part I. To make the election, you must complete Form 8716, Election To Have a Tax Year Other Than a Required Tax Year, and either attach it to Form 2553 or file it separately.

  2. Check here ▶ ☐ to show that the corporation agrees to adopt or change to a tax year ending December 31 if necessary for the IRS to accept this election for S corporation status in the event the corporation is ultimately not qualified to make a section 444 election.

Part III **Qualified Subchapter S Trust (QSST) Election Under Section 1361(d)(2)***

Income beneficiary's name and address	Social security number
Trust's name and address	Employer identification number

Date on which stock of the corporation was transferred to the trust (month, day, year) . . . . ▶

In order for the trust named above to be a QSST and thus a qualifying shareholder of the S corporation for which this Form 2553 is filed, I hereby make the election under section 1361(d)(2). Under penalties of perjury, I certify that the trust meets the definitional requirements of section 1361(d)(3) and that all other information provided in Part III is true, correct, and complete.

Signature of income beneficiary or signature and title of legal representative or other qualified person making the election   Date

*Use Part III to make the QSST election only if stock of the corporation has been transferred to the trust on or before the date on which the corporation makes its election to be an S corporation. The QSST election must be made and filed separately if stock of the corporation is transferred to the trust **after** the date on which the corporation makes the S election.

Form **2553** (Rev. 12-2013)

Part IV   **Late Corporate Classification Election Representations** (see instructions)

If a late entity classification election was intended to be effective on the same date that the S corporation election was intended to be effective, relief for a late S corporation election must also include the following representations.

1   The requesting entity is an eligible entity as defined in Regulations section 301.7701-3(a);

2   The requesting entity intended to be classified as a corporation as of the effective date of the S corporation status;

3   The requesting entity fails to qualify as a corporation solely because Form 8832, Entity Classification Election, was not timely filed under Regulations section 301.7701-3(c)(1)(i), or Form 8832 was not deemed to have been filed under Regulations section 301.7701-3(c)(1)(v)(C);

4   The requesting entity fails to qualify as an S corporation on the effective date of the S corporation status solely because the S corporation election was not timely filed pursuant to section 1362(b); **and**

5a   The requesting entity timely filed all required federal tax returns and information returns consistent with its requested classification as an S corporation for all of the years the entity intended to be an S corporation and no inconsistent tax or information returns have been filed by or with respect to the entity during any of the tax years, **or**

b   The requesting entity has not filed a federal tax or information return for the first year in which the election was intended to be effective because the due date has not passed for that year's federal tax or information return.

Instructions for Form 2553
(Rev. December 2013)

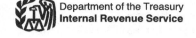
Department of the Treasury
Internal Revenue Service

Election by a Small Business Corporation

Section references are to the Internal Revenue Code unless otherwise noted.

Future Developments

For the latest information about developments related to Form 2553 and its instructions, such as legislation enacted after they were published, go to *www.irs.gov/form2553*.

What's New

New simplified methods for a corporation (entity) to request relief for a late S corporation election, ESBT election, QSST election, or corporate classification election are in effect. See *Relief for Late Elections*.

General Instructions

Purpose of Form

A corporation or other entity eligible to elect to be treated as a corporation must use Form 2553 to make an election under section 1362(a) to be an S corporation. An entity eligible to elect to be treated as a corporation that meets certain tests discussed below will be treated as a corporation as of the effective date of the S corporation election and does not need to file Form 8832, Entity Classification Election.

The income of an S corporation generally is taxed to the shareholders of the corporation rather than to the corporation itself. However, an S corporation may still owe tax on certain income. For details, see *Tax and Payments* in the Instructions for Form 1120S.

Who May Elect

A corporation or other entity eligible to elect to be treated as a corporation may elect to be an S corporation only if it meets all the following tests.

1. It is (a) a domestic corporation, or (b) a domestic entity eligible to elect to be treated as a corporation, that timely files Form 2553 and meets all the other tests listed below. If Form 2553 is not timely filed, see *Relief for Late Elections*, later.

2. It has no more than 100 shareholders. You can treat an individual and his or her spouse (and their estates) as one shareholder for this test. You can also treat all members of a family (as defined in section 1361(c)(1)(B)) and their estates as one shareholder for this test. For additional situations in which certain entities will be treated as members of a family, see Regulations section 1.1361-1(e)(3)(ii). All others are treated as separate shareholders. For details, see section 1361(c)(1).

3. Its only shareholders are individuals, estates, exempt organizations described in section 401(a) or 501(c)(3), or certain trusts described in section 1361(c)(2)(A).

For information about the section 1361(d)(2) election to be a qualified subchapter S trust (QSST), see the instructions for Part III. For information about the section 1361(e)(3) election to be an electing small business trust (ESBT), see Regulations section 1.1361-1(m). For guidance on how to convert a QSST to an ESBT, see Regulations section

1.1361-1(j)(12). If these elections were not timely made, see Rev. Proc. 2013-30, 2013-36 I.R.B. 173, available at *www.irs.gov/irb/2013-36_IRB/ar12.html*.

4. It has no nonresident alien shareholders.

5. It has only one class of stock (disregarding differences in voting rights). Generally, a corporation is treated as having only one class of stock if all outstanding shares of the corporation's stock confer identical rights to distribution and liquidation proceeds. See Regulations section 1.1361-1(l) for details.

6. It is not one of the following ineligible corporations.

a. A bank or thrift institution that uses the reserve method of accounting for bad debts under section 585.

b. An insurance company subject to tax under subchapter L of the Code.

c. A corporation that has elected to be treated as a possessions corporation under section 936.

d. A domestic international sales corporation (DISC) or former DISC.

7. It has or will adopt or change to one of the following tax years.

a. A tax year ending December 31.

b. A natural business year.

c. An ownership tax year.

d. A tax year elected under section 444.

e. A 52-53-week tax year ending with reference to a year listed above.

f. Any other tax year (including a 52-53-week tax year) for which the corporation establishes a business purpose.

For details on making a section 444 election or requesting a natural business, ownership, or other business purpose tax year, see the instructions for Part II.

8. Each shareholder consents as explained in the instructions for column K.

See sections 1361, 1362, and 1378, and their related regulations for additional information on the above tests.

A parent S corporation can elect to treat an eligible wholly owned subsidiary as a qualified subchapter S subsidiary. If the election is made, the subsidiary's assets, liabilities, and items of income, deduction, and credit generally are treated as those of the parent. For details, see Form 8869, Qualified Subchapter S Subsidiary Election.

When To Make the Election

Complete and file Form 2553:

• No more than two months and 15 days after the beginning of the tax year the election is to take effect, or

• At any time during the tax year preceding the tax year it is to take effect.

For this purpose, the 2-month period begins on the day of the month the tax year begins and ends with the close of the day before the numerically corresponding day of the second calendar month following that month. If there is no

Jan 24, 2014   Cat. No. 49978N

corresponding day, use the close of the last day of the calendar month.

Example 1. No prior tax year. A calendar year small business corporation begins its first tax year on January 7. The 2-month period ends March 6 and 15 days after that is March 21. To be an S corporation beginning with its first tax year, the corporation must file Form 2553 during the period that begins January 7 and ends March 21. Because the corporation had no prior tax year, an election made before January 7 will not be valid.

Example 2. Prior tax year. A calendar year small business corporation has been filing Form 1120 as a C corporation but wishes to make an S election for its next tax year beginning January 1. The 2-month period ends February 28 (29 in leap years) and 15 days after that is March 15. To be an S corporation beginning with its next tax year, the corporation must file Form 2553 during the period that begins the first day (January 1) of its last year as a C corporation and ends March 15th of the year it wishes to be an S corporation. Because the corporation had a prior tax year, it can make the election at any time during that prior tax year.

Example 3. Tax year less than 2 1/2 months. A calendar year small business corporation begins its first tax year on November 8. The 2-month period ends January 7 and 15 days after that is January 22. To be an S corporation beginning with its short tax year, the corporation must file Form 2553 during the period that begins November 8 and ends January 22. Because the corporation had no prior tax year, an election made before November 8 will not be valid.

Relief for Late Elections

The following two sections discuss relief for late S corporation elections and relief for late S corporation and entity classification elections for the same entity. For supplemental procedural requirements when seeking relief for multiple late elections, see Rev. Proc. 2013-30, section 4.04.

When filing Form 2553 for a **late** S corporation election, the corporation (entity) **must** write in the top margin of the first page of Form 2553 "FILED PURSUANT TO REV. PROC. 2013-30." Also, if the late election is made by attaching Form 2553 to Form 1120S, the corporation (entity) **must** write in the top margin of the first page of Form 1120S "INCLUDES LATE ELECTION(S) FILED PURSUANT TO REV. PROC. 2013-30."

The election can be filed with the current Form 1120S if all earlier Forms 1120S have been filed. The election can be attached to the first Form 1120S for the year including the effective date if filed simultaneously with any other delinquent Forms 1120S. Form 2553 can also be filed separately.

Relief for a Late S Corporation Election Filed by a Corporation

A late election to be an S corporation generally is effective for the tax year following the tax year beginning on the date entered on line E of Form 2553. However, relief for a late election may be available if the corporation can show that the failure to file on time was due to reasonable cause.

To request relief for a late election, a corporation that meets the following requirements can explain the reasonable cause in the designated space on page 1 of Form 2553.

1. The corporation intended to be classified as an S corporation as of the date entered on line E of Form 2553;

2. The corporation fails to qualify as an S corporation (see *Who May Elect*, earlier) on the effective date entered on line E of Form 2553 solely because Form 2553 was not filed by the due date (see *When To Make the Election*, earlier);

3. The corporation has reasonable cause for its failure to timely file Form 2553 and has acted diligently to correct the mistake upon discovery of its failure to timely file Form 2553;

4. Form 2553 will be filed within 3 years and 75 days of the date entered on line E of Form 2553; and

5. A corporation that meets requirements (1) through (4) must also be able to provide statements from all shareholders who were shareholders during the period between the date entered on line E of Form 2553 and the date the completed Form 2553 is filed stating that they have reported their income on all affected returns consistent with the S corporation election for the year the election should have been made and all subsequent years. Completion of Form 2553, Part I, column K, *Shareholder's Consent Statement* (or similar document attached to Form 2553), will meet this requirement; or

6. A corporation that meets requirements (1) through (3) but not requirement (4) can still request relief for a late election on Form 2553 if the following statements are true.

a. The corporation and all its shareholders reported their income consistent with S corporation status for the year the S corporation election should have been made, and for every subsequent tax year (if any);

b. At least 6 months have elapsed since the date on which the corporation filed its tax return for the first year the corporation intended to be an S corporation; and

c. Neither the corporation nor any of its shareholders was notified by the IRS of any problem regarding the S corporation status within 6 months of the date on which the Form 1120S for the first year was timely filed.

To request relief for a late election when the above requirements are not met, the corporation generally must request a private letter ruling and pay a user fee in accordance with Rev. Proc. 2014-1, 2014-1 I.R.B. 1 (or its successor).

Relief for a Late S Corporation Election Filed By an Entity Eligible To Elect To Be Treated as a Corporation

A late election to be an S corporation and a late entity classification election for the same entity may be available if the entity can show that the failure to file Form 2553 on time was due to reasonable cause. Relief must be requested within 3 years and 75 days of the effective date entered on line E of Form 2553.

To request relief for a late election, an entity that meets the following requirements can explain the reasonable cause in the designated space on page 1 of Form 2553.

1. The entity is an eligible entity as defined in Regulations section 301.7701-3(a) (see *Purpose of Form* in the Form 8832 instructions).

2. The entity intended to be classified as an S corporation as of the date entered on line E of Form 2553.

3. Form 2553 will be filed within 3 years and 75 days of the date entered on line E of Form 2553.

4. The entity failed to qualify as a corporation solely because Form 8832 was not timely filed under Regulations section 301.7701-3(c)(1)(i) (see *When To File* in the Form

-2-

8832 instructions), or Form 8832 was not deemed to have been filed under Regulations section 301.7701-3(c)(1)(v)(C) (see *Who Must File* in the Form 8832 instructions).

5. The entity fails to qualify as an S corporation (see *Who May Elect*, earlier) on the effective date entered on line E of Form 2553 because Form 2553 was not filed by the due date (see *When To Make the Election*, earlier).

6. The entity either:

a. Timely filed all Forms 1120S consistent with its requested classification as an S corporation, or

b. Did not file Form 1120S because the due date for the first year's Form 1120S has not passed.

7. The entity has reasonable cause for its failure to timely file Form 2553 and has acted diligently to correct the mistake upon discovery of its failure to timely file Form 2553.

8. The S corporation can provide statements from all shareholders who were shareholders during the period between the date entered on line E of Form 2553 and the date the completed Form 2553 is filed stating that they have reported their income on all affected returns consistent with the S corporation election for the year the election should have been made and all subsequent years. Completion of Form 2553, Part I, column K, *Shareholder's Consent Statement* (or similar document attached to Form 2553), will meet this requirement.

To request relief for a late election when the above requirements are not met, the entity generally must request a private letter ruling and pay a user fee in accordance with Rev. Proc. 2014-1, 2014-1 I.R.B. 1 (or its successor).

Where To File

Generally, send the original election (no photocopies) or fax it to the Internal Revenue Service Center listed below. If the corporation files this election by fax, keep the original Form 2553 with the corporation's permanent records. However, certain late elections can be filed attached to Form 1120S. See *Relief for Late Elections*, earlier.

For the latest mailing address of Form 2553, go to IRS.gov and enter "Where to file Form 2553" in the search box.

If the corporation's principal business, office, or agency is located in:	Use the following address or fax number:
Connecticut, Delaware, District of Columbia, Florida, Georgia, Illinois, Indiana, Kentucky, Maine, Maryland, Massachusetts, Michigan, New Hampshire, New Jersey, New York, North Carolina, Ohio, Pennsylvania, Rhode Island, South Carolina, Tennessee, Vermont, Virginia, West Virginia, Wisconsin	Department of the Treasury Internal Revenue Service Center Cincinnati, OH 45999 Fax: (859) 669-5748
Alabama, Alaska, Arizona, Arkansas, California, Colorado, Hawaii, Idaho, Iowa, Kansas, Louisiana, Minnesota, Mississippi, Missouri, Montana, Nebraska, Nevada, New Mexico, North Dakota, Oklahoma, Oregon, South Dakota, Texas, Utah, Washington, Wyoming	Department of the Treasury Internal Revenue Service Center Ogden, UT 84201 Fax: (801) 620-7116

Acceptance or Nonacceptance of Election

The service center will notify the corporation if its election is accepted and when it will take effect. The corporation will also be notified if its election is not accepted. The corporation should generally receive a determination on its election within 60 days after it has filed Form 2553. If box Q1 in Part II is checked, the corporation will receive a ruling letter from the IRS that either approves or denies the selected tax year. When box Q1 is checked, it will generally take an additional 90 days for the Form 2553 to be accepted.

Care should be exercised to ensure that the IRS receives the election. If the corporation is not notified of acceptance or nonacceptance of its election within 2 months of the date of filing (date faxed or mailed), or within 5 months if box Q1 is checked, take follow-up action by calling 1-800-829-4933.

If the IRS questions whether Form 2553 was filed, an acceptable proof of filing is:

• A certified or registered mail receipt (timely postmarked) from the U.S. Postal Service, or its equivalent from a designated private delivery service (see Notice 2004-83, 2004-52 I.R.B. 1030, available at *www.irs.gov/irb/2004-52_IRB/ar10.html* (or its successor));
• Form 2553 with an accepted stamp;
• Form 2553 with a stamped IRS received date; or
• An IRS letter stating that Form 2553 has been accepted.

 Do not file Form 1120S for any tax year before the year the election takes effect. If the corporation is now required to file Form 1120, U.S. Corporation Income Tax Return, or any other applicable tax return, continue filing it until the election takes effect.

End of Election

Once the election is made, it stays in effect until it is terminated or revoked. IRS consent generally is required for another election by the corporation (or a successor corporation) on Form 2553 for any tax year before the 5th tax year after the first tax year in which the termination or

-3-

revocation took effect. See Regulations section 1.1362-5 for details.

Specific Instructions

Part I

Name and Address

Enter the corporation's true name as stated in the corporate charter or other legal document creating it. If the corporation's mailing address is the same as someone else's, such as a shareholder's, enter "C/O" and this person's name following the name of the corporation. Include the suite, room, or other unit number after the street address. If the Post Office does not deliver to the street address and the corporation has a P.O. box, show the box number instead of the street address. If the corporation changed its name or address after applying for its employer identification number, be sure to check the box in item D of Part I.

Item A. Employer Identification Number (EIN)

Enter the corporation's EIN. If the corporation does not have an EIN, it must apply for one. An EIN can be applied for:
• Online–Click on the Employer ID Numbers (EINs) link at *www.irs.gov/businesses/small*. The EIN is issued immediately once the application information is validated.
• By telephone at 1-800-829-4933, or at 1-800-829-4059 for individuals who are deaf, hard of hearing, or have a speech disability and who have access to TTY/TDD equipment.
• By mailing or faxing Form SS-4, Application for Employer Identification Number.

If the corporation has not received its EIN by the time the return is due, enter "Applied For" and the date the corporation applied in the space for the EIN. For more details, see the Instructions for Form SS-4.

Item E. Effective Date of Election

 Form 2553 generally must be filed no later than 2 months and 15 days after the date entered for item E. For details and exceptions, see When To Make the Election, *earlier.*

A corporation (or entity eligible to elect to be treated as a corporation) making the election effective for its first tax year in existence should enter the earliest of the following dates:
• The date the corporation (entity) first had shareholders (owners),
• The date the corporation (entity) first had assets, or
• The date the corporation (entity) began doing business.

 When the corporation (entity) is making the election for its first tax year in existence, it will usually enter the beginning date of a tax year that begins on a date other than January 1.

A corporation (entity) not making the election for its first tax year in existence that is keeping its current tax year should enter the beginning date of the first tax year for which it wants the election to be effective.

A corporation (entity) not making the election for its first tax year in existence that is changing its tax year and wants to be an S corporation for the short tax year needed to switch tax years should enter the beginning date of the short tax year. If the corporation (entity) does not want to be an S corporation for this short tax year, it should enter the

beginning date of the tax year following this short tax year and file Form 1128, Application To Adopt, Change, or Retain a Tax Year. If this change qualifies as an automatic approval request (Form 1128, Part II), file Form 1128 as an attachment to Form 2553. If this change qualifies as a ruling request (Form 1128, Part III), file Form 1128 separately. If filing Form 1128, enter "Form 1128" on the dotted line to the left of the entry space for item E.

Item F

Check the box that corresponds with the S corporation's selected tax year. If box (2) or (4) is checked, provide the additional information about the tax year, and complete Part II of the form.

Signature

Form 2553 must be signed and dated by the president, vice president, treasurer, assistant treasurer, chief accounting officer, or any other corporate officer (such as tax officer) authorized to sign.

If Form 2553 is not signed, it will not be considered timely filed.

Column J

Enter the name and address of each shareholder or former shareholder required to consent to the election. If stock of the corporation is held by a nominee, guardian, custodian, or an agent, enter the name and address of the person for whom the stock is held. If a single member limited liability company (LLC) owns stock in the corporation, and the LLC is treated as a disregarded entity for federal income tax purposes, enter the owner's name and address. The owner must be eligible to be an S corporation shareholder.

For an election filed before the effective date entered for item E, only shareholders who own stock on the day the election is made need to consent to the election.

For an election filed on or after the effective date entered for item E, all shareholders or former shareholders who owned stock at any time during the period beginning on the effective date entered for item E and ending on the day the election is made must consent to the election.

If the corporation timely filed an election, but one or more shareholders did not timely file a consent, see Regulations section 1.1362-6(b)(3)(iii). If the shareholder was a community property spouse who was a shareholder solely because of a state community property law, see Rev. Proc. 2004-35, 2004-23 I.R.B. 1029, available at *www.irs.gov/irb/2004-23_IRB/ar11.html*.

Column K. Shareholder's Consent Statement

Each shareholder consents by signing and dating either in column K or on a separate consent statement. The following special rules apply in determining who must sign.
• If an individual and his or her spouse have a community interest in the stock or in the income from it, both must consent.
• Each tenant in common, joint tenant, and tenant by the entirety must consent.
• A minor's consent is made by the minor, legal representative of the minor, or a natural or adoptive parent of the minor if no legal representative has been appointed.
• The consent of an estate is made by the executor or administrator.

-4-

- The consent of an electing small business trust (ESBT) is made by the trustee and, if a grantor trust, the deemed owner. See Regulations section 1.1362-6(b)(2)(iv) for details.
- If the stock is owned by a qualified subchapter S trust (QSST), the deemed owner of the trust must consent.
- If the stock is owned by a trust (other than an ESBT or QSST), the person treated as the shareholder by section 1361(c)(2)(B) must consent.

Continuation sheet or separate consent statement. If you need a continuation sheet or use a separate consent statement, attach it to Form 2553. It must contain the name, address, and EIN of the corporation and the information requested in columns J through N of Part I.

Column L

Enter the number of shares of stock each shareholder owns on the date the election is filed and the date(s) the stock was acquired. Enter -0- for any former shareholders listed in column J. An entity without stock, such as a limited liability company (LLC), should enter the percentage of ownership and date(s) acquired.

Column M

Enter the social security number of each individual listed in column J. Enter the EIN of each estate, qualified trust, or exempt organization.

Column N

Enter the month and day that each shareholder's tax year ends. If a shareholder is changing his or her tax year, enter the tax year the shareholder is changing to, and attach an explanation indicating the present tax year and the basis for the change (for example, an automatic revenue procedure or a letter ruling request).

Part II

Complete Part II if you checked box (2) or (4) in Part I, Item F.

Note. Corporations cannot obtain automatic approval of a fiscal year under the natural business year (box P1) or ownership tax year (box P2) provisions if they are under examination, before an appeals (area) office, or before a federal court without meeting certain conditions and attaching a statement to the application. For details, see section 7.03 of Rev. Proc. 2006-46, 2006-45 I.R.B. 859, available at *www.irs.gov/irb/2006-45_IRB/ar14.html*.

Box P1

A corporation that does not have a 47-month period of gross receipts cannot automatically establish a natural business year.

Box Q1

For examples of an acceptable business purpose for requesting a fiscal tax year, see section 5.02 of Rev. Proc. 2002-39, 2002-22 I.R.B. 1046, and Rev. Rul. 87-57, 1987-2 C.B. 117.

Attach a statement showing the relevant facts and circumstances to establish a business purpose for the requested fiscal year. For details on what is sufficient to establish a business purpose, see section 5.02 of Rev. Proc. 2002-39.

If your business purpose is based on one of the natural business year tests provided in section 5.03 of Rev. Proc. 2002-39, identify which test you are using (the 25% gross receipts, annual business cycle, or seasonal business test). For the 25% gross receipts test, provide a schedule showing the amount of gross receipts for each month for the most recent 47 months. For either the annual business cycle or seasonal business test, provide the gross receipts from sales and services (and inventory costs, if applicable) for each month of the short period, if any, and the three immediately preceding tax years. If the corporation has been in existence for less than three tax years, submit figures for the period of existence.

If you check box Q1, you will be charged a user fee of $2,700 (subject to change by Rev. Proc. 2015-1 or its successor). Do not pay the fee when filing Form 2553. The service center will send Form 2553 to the IRS in Washington, DC, who, in turn, will notify the corporation that the fee is due.

Box Q2

If the corporation makes a back-up section 444 election for which it is qualified, then the section 444 election will take effect in the event the business purpose request is not approved. In some cases, the tax year requested under the back-up section 444 election may be different than the tax year requested under business purpose. See Form 8716, Election To Have a Tax Year Other Than a Required Tax Year, for details on making a back-up section 444 election.

Boxes Q3 and R2

If the corporation is not qualified to make the section 444 election after making the item Q2 back-up section 444 election or indicating its intention to make the election in item R1, and therefore it later files a calendar year return, it should write "Section 444 Election Not Made" in the top left corner of the first calendar year Form 1120S it files.

Part III

In Part III, the income beneficiary (or legal representative) of certain qualified subchapter S trusts (QSSTs) may make the QSST election required by section 1361(d)(2). Part III may be used to make the QSST election only if corporate stock has been transferred to the trust on or before the date on which the corporation makes its election to be an S corporation. However, a statement can be used instead of Part III to make the election. If there was an inadvertent failure to timely file a QSST election, see the relief provisions under Rev. Proc. 2013-30.

Note. Use Part III only if you make the election in Part I. Form 2553 cannot be filed with only Part III completed.

The deemed owner of the QSST must also consent to the S corporation election in column K of Form 2553.

Part IV

The representations listed in Part IV must be attached to a late corporate classification election intended to be effective on the same date that a late S corporation election was intended to be effective. For more information on making these late elections, see *Relief for a Late S Corporation Election Filed By an Entity Eligible To Elect To Be Treated as a Corporation*, earlier.

Paperwork Reduction Act Notice. We ask for the information on this form to carry out the Internal Revenue laws of the United States. You are required to give us the information. We need it to ensure that you are complying with these laws and to allow us to figure and collect the right amount of tax.

You are not required to provide the information requested on a form that is subject to the Paperwork Reduction Act unless the form displays a valid OMB control number. Books or records relating to a form or its instructions must be retained as long as their contents may become material in the administration of any Internal Revenue law. Generally, tax returns and return information are confidential, as required by section 6103.

The time needed to complete and file this form will depend on individual circumstances. The estimated average time is:

Recordkeeping	9 hr., 48 min.
Learning about the law or the form	2 hr., 33 min.
Preparing and sending the form to the IRS	4 hr., 1 min.

If you have comments concerning the accuracy of these time estimates or suggestions for making this form simpler, we would be happy to hear from you. You can write to the Internal Revenue Service, Tax Forms and Publications, SE:W:CAR:MP:TFP, 1111 Constitution Ave. NW, IR-6526, Washington, DC 20224. Do not send the form to this address. Instead, see *Where To File*, earlier.

Form SS-4
(Rev. January 2010)
Department of the Treasury
Internal Revenue Service

Application for Employer Identification Number

(For use by employers, corporations, partnerships, trusts, estates, churches, government agencies, Indian tribal entities, certain individuals, and others.)

► See separate instructions for each line.   ► Keep a copy for your records.

OMB No. 1545-0003

EIN

Type or print clearly.

1 Legal name of entity (or individual) for whom the EIN is being requested

2 Trade name of business (if different from name on line 1)

3 Executor, administrator, trustee, "care of" name

4a Mailing address (room, apt., suite no. and street, or P.O. box)

5a Street address (if different) (Do not enter a P.O. box.)

4b City, state, and ZIP code (if foreign, see instructions)

5b City, state, and ZIP code (if foreign, see instructions)

6 County and state where principal business is located

7a Name of responsible party

7b SSN, ITIN, or EIN

8a Is this application for a limited liability company (LLC) (or a foreign equivalent)? ☐ Yes ☐ No

8b If 8a is "Yes," enter the number of LLC members

8c If 8a is "Yes," was the LLC organized in the United States? ☐ Yes ☐ No

9a Type of entity (check only one box). Caution. If 8a is "Yes," see the instructions for the correct box to check.
☐ Sole proprietor (SSN)
☐ Partnership
☐ Corporation (enter form number to be filed)
☐ Personal service corporation
☐ Church or church-controlled organization
☐ Other nonprofit organization (specify)
☐ Other (specify) ►
☐ Estate (SSN of decedent)
☐ Plan administrator (TIN)
☐ Trust (TIN of grantor)
☐ National Guard ☐ State/local government
☐ Farmers' cooperative ☐ Federal government/military
☐ REMIC ☐ Indian tribal governments/enterprises
Group Exemption Number (GEN) if any ►

9b If a corporation, name the state or foreign country (if applicable) where incorporated
State   Foreign country

10 Reason for applying (check only one box)
☐ Started new business (specify type)
☐ Hired employees (Check the box and see line 13.)
☐ Compliance with IRS withholding regulations
☐ Other (specify)
☐ Banking purpose (specify purpose) ►
☐ Changed type of organization (specify new type) ►
☐ Purchased going business
☐ Created a trust (specify type) ►
☐ Created a pension plan (specify type) ►

11 Date business started or acquired (month, day, year). See instructions.

12 Closing month of accounting year

13 Highest number of employees expected in the next 12 months (enter -0- if none). If no employees expected, skip line 14.
Agricultural   Household   Other

14 If you expect your employment tax liability to be $1,000 or less in a full calendar year and want to file Form 944 annually instead of Forms 941 quarterly, check here. (Your employment tax liability generally will be $1,000 or less if you expect to pay $4,000 or less in total wages.) If you do not check this box, you must file Form 941 for every quarter. ☐

15 First date wages or annuities were paid (month, day, year). Note. If applicant is a withholding agent, enter date income will first be paid to nonresident alien (month, day, year).

16 Check one box that best describes the principal activity of your business.
☐ Construction ☐ Rental & leasing ☐ Transportation & warehousing
☐ Real estate ☐ Manufacturing ☐ Finance & insurance
☐ Health care & social assistance ☐ Wholesale-agent/broker
☐ Accommodation & food service ☐ Wholesale-other ☐ Retail
☐ Other (specify) ►

17 Indicate principal line of merchandise sold, specific construction work done, products produced, or services provided.

18 Has the applicant entity shown on line 1 ever applied for and received an EIN? ☐ Yes ☐ No
If "Yes," write previous EIN here ►

Third Party Designee
Complete this section only if you want to authorize the named individual to receive the entity's EIN and answer questions about the completion of this form.
Designee's name
Designee's telephone number (include area code)
Address and ZIP code
Designee's fax number (include area code)

Under penalties of perjury, I declare that I have examined this application, and to the best of my knowledge and belief, it is true, correct, and complete.
Name and title (type or print clearly) ►
Applicant's telephone number (include area code)
Applicant's fax number (include area code)

Signature ►   Date ►

For Privacy Act and Paperwork Reduction Act Notice, see separate instructions.   Cat. No. 16055N   Form **SS-4** (Rev. 1-2010)

EXAMPLE

Do I Need an EIN?

File Form SS-4 if the applicant entity does not already have an EIN but is required to show an EIN on any return, statement, or other document.[1] See also the separate instructions for each line on Form SS-4.

IF the applicant...	AND...	THEN...
Started a new business	Does not currently have (nor expect to have) employees	Complete lines 1, 2, 4a–8a, 8b–c (if applicable), 9a, 9b (if applicable), and 10–14 and 16–18.
Hired (or will hire) employees, including household employees	Does not already have an EIN	Complete lines 1, 2, 4a–6, 7a–b (if applicable), 8a, 8b–c (if applicable), 9a, 9b (if applicable), 10–18.
Opened a bank account	Needs an EIN for banking purposes only	Complete lines 1–5b, 7a–b (if applicable), 8a, 8b–c (if applicable), 9a, 9b (if applicable), 10, and 18.
Changed type of organization	Either the legal character of the organization or its ownership changed (for example, you incorporate a sole proprietorship or form a partnership)[2]	Complete lines 1–18 (as applicable).
Purchased a going business[3]	Does not already have an EIN	Complete lines 1–18 (as applicable).
Created a trust	The trust is other than a grantor trust or an IRA trust[4]	Complete lines 1–18 (as applicable).
Created a pension plan as a plan administrator[5]	Needs an EIN for reporting purposes	Complete lines 1, 3, 4a–5b, 9a, 10, and 18.
Is a foreign person needing an EIN to comply with IRS withholding regulations	Needs an EIN to complete a Form W-8 (other than Form W-8ECI), avoid withholding on portfolio assets, or claim tax treaty benefits[6]	Complete lines 1–5b, 7a–b (SSN or ITIN optional), 8a, 8b–c (if applicable), 9a, 9b (if applicable), 10, and 18.
Is administering an estate	Needs an EIN to report estate income on Form 1041	Complete lines 1–6, 9a, 10–12, 13–17 (if applicable), and 18.
Is a withholding agent for taxes on non-wage income paid to an alien (i.e., individual, corporation, or partnership, etc.)	Is an agent, broker, fiduciary, manager, tenant, or spouse who is required to file Form 1042, Annual Withholding Tax Return for U.S. Source Income of Foreign Persons	Complete lines 1, 2, 3 (if applicable), 4a–5b, 7a–b (if applicable), 8a, 8b–c (if applicable), 9a, 9b (if applicable), 10, and 18.
Is a state or local agency	Serves as a tax reporting agent for public assistance recipients under Rev. Proc. 80-4, 1980-1 C.B. 581[7]	Complete lines 1, 2, 4a–5b, 9a, 10, and 18.
Is a single-member LLC	Needs an EIN to file Form 8832, Classification Election, for filing employment tax returns and excise tax returns, or for state reporting purposes[8]	Complete lines 1–18 (as applicable).
Is an S corporation	Needs an EIN to file Form 2553, Election by a Small Business Corporation[9]	Complete lines 1–18 (as applicable).

[1] For example, a sole proprietorship or self-employed farmer who establishes a qualified retirement plan, or is required to file excise, employment, alcohol, tobacco, or firearms returns, must have an EIN. A partnership, corporation, REMIC (real estate mortgage investment conduit), nonprofit organization (church, club, etc.), or farmers' cooperative must use an EIN for any tax-related purpose even if the entity does not have employees.

[2] However, do not apply for a new EIN if the existing entity only (a) changed its business name, (b) elected on Form 8832 to change the way it is taxed (or is covered by the default rules), or (c) terminated its partnership status because at least 50% of the total interests in partnership capital and profits were sold or exchanged within a 12-month period. The EIN of the terminated partnership should continue to be used. See Regulations section 301.6109-1(d)(2)(iii).

[3] Do not use the EIN of the prior business unless you became the "owner" of a corporation by acquiring its stock.

[4] However, grantor trusts that do not file using Optional Method 1 and IRA trusts that are required to file Form 990-T, Exempt Organization Business Income Tax Return, must have an EIN. For more information on grantor trusts, see the Instructions for Form 1041.

[5] A plan administrator is the person or group of persons specified as the administrator by the instrument under which the plan is operated.

[6] Entities applying to be a Qualified Intermediary (QI) need a QI-EIN even if they already have an EIN. See Rev. Proc. 2000-12.

[7] See also *Household employer* on page 4 of the instructions. **Note.** State or local agencies may need an EIN for other reasons, for example, hired employees.

[8] See *Disregarded entities* on page 4 of the instructions for details on completing Form SS-4 for an LLC.

[9] An existing corporation that is electing or revoking S corporation status should use its previously-assigned EIN.

Instructions for Form SS-4
(Rev. February 2016)

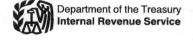

Department of the Treasury
Internal Revenue Service

Application for Employer Identification Number (EIN)
Use with Form SS-4 (Rev. January 2010)

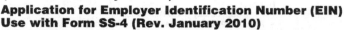

Section references are to the Internal Revenue Code unless otherwise noted.

General Instructions

Use these instructions to complete Form SS-4, Application for Employer Identification Number (EIN). Also see *Do I Need an EIN?* on page 2 of Form SS-4.

Future Developments

For the latest information related to Form SS-4 and its instructions, such as legislation enacted after they were published, go to *www.irs.gov/ss4*.

Purpose of Form

Use Form SS-4 to apply for an EIN. An EIN is a nine-digit number (for example, 12-3456789) assigned to sole proprietors, corporations, partnerships, estates, trusts, and other entities for tax filing and reporting purposes. The information you provide on this form will establish your business tax account.

 See Form SS-4PR (for Puerto Rico) for the Spanish-language version of Form SS-4.

 An EIN is for use in connection with your business activities only. Don't use your EIN in place of your social security number (SSN) or individual taxpayer identification number (ITIN).

Reminders

Apply for an EIN online. For applicants in the U.S. or U.S. possessions, you can apply for and receive an EIN free of charge on IRS.gov. See *How To Apply for an EIN*, later.

File only one Form SS-4. Generally, a sole proprietor should file only one Form SS-4 and needs only one EIN, regardless of the number of businesses operated as a sole proprietorship or trade names under which a business operates. However, if a sole proprietorship incorporates or enters into a partnership, a new EIN is required. Also, each corporation in an affiliated group must have its own EIN.

 For information about EINs and federal tax deposits, see Pub. 15, Pub. 51 and Pub. 80.

 To ensure fair and equitable treatment for all taxpayers, EIN issuances are limited to one per responsible party, per day. For trusts, the limitation is applied to the grantor, owner, or trustor. For estates, the limitation is applied to the decedent (decedent estate) or the debtor (bankruptcy estate). This limitation is applicable to all requests for EINs whether online, telephone, fax, or mail.

How To Apply for an EIN

You can apply for an EIN online (only for applicants in the U.S. or U.S. possessions), by telephone (only for applicants outside of the U.S. or U.S. possessions), by fax, or by mail, depending on how soon you need to use the EIN. Use only one method for each entity so you don't receive more than one EIN for an entity.

Apply for an EIN online. If you have a legal residence, principal place of business, or principal office or agency in the U.S. or U.S. possessions, you can receive an EIN online and use

it immediately to file a return or make a payment. Go to the IRS website at *www.irs.gov/businesses* and click on *Employer ID Numbers*.

The principal officer, general partner, grantor, owner, trustor, etc. must have a valid Taxpayer Identification Number (SSN, EIN, or ITIN) in order to use the online application. Taxpayers who apply online have an option to view, print, and save their EIN assignment notice at the end of the session. (Authorized third party designees will receive the EIN; however, the EIN assignment notice will be mailed to the applicant.)

 If you have NO legal residence, principal place of business, or principal office or agency in the U.S. or U.S. possessions, you can't use the online application to obtain an EIN. Please use one of the other methods to apply.

Apply by telephone—option available to international applicants only. If you have NO legal residence, principal place of business, or principal office or agency in the U.S. or U.S. possessions, you may call 267-941-1099 (not a toll-free number), 6:00 a.m. to 11:00 p.m. (Eastern time), Monday through Friday, to obtain an EIN.

The person making the call must be authorized to receive the EIN and answer questions concerning Form SS-4. Complete the Third Party Designee section only if you want to authorize the named individual to receive the entity's EIN and answer questions about the completion of Form SS-4. The designee's authority terminates at the time the EIN is assigned and released to the designee. You must complete the signature area for the authorization to be valid.

Note. It will be helpful to complete Form SS-4 before contacting the IRS. An IRS representative will use the information from Form SS-4 to establish your account and assign you an EIN. Write the number you're given on the upper right corner of the form and sign and date it. Keep this copy for your records.

If requested by an IRS representative, mail or fax the signed Form SS-4 (including any third party designee authorization) within 24 hours to the IRS address provided by the IRS representative.

 IRS no longer issues EINs by telephone for domestic taxpayers. Only international applicants can receive an EIN by telephone.

Apply by fax. Under the Fax-TIN program, you can receive your EIN by fax generally within 4 business days. Complete and fax Form SS-4 to the IRS using the appropriate fax number listed in *Where To File or Fax*, later. A long-distance charge to callers outside of the local calling area will apply. Fax-TIN numbers can only be used to apply for an EIN. The numbers may change without notice. Fax-TIN is available 24 hours a day, 7 days a week.

Be sure to provide your fax number so the IRS can fax the EIN back to you.

Apply by mail. Complete Form SS-4 at least 4 to 5 weeks before you will need an EIN. Sign and date the application and mail it to the appropriate address listed in *Where To File or Fax*, later. You will receive your EIN in the mail in approximately 4 weeks. Also see *Third Party Designee*, later.

Call 1-800-829-4933 to verify a number or to ask about the status of an application by mail.

Mar 16, 2016   Cat. No. 62736F

Form SS-4 downloaded from IRS.gov is a fillable form and, when completed, is suitable for faxing or mailing to the IRS.

Where To File or Fax

If you have a principal place of business, office or agency, or legal residence in the case of an individual, located in:	File or Fax to:
One of the 50 states or the District of Columbia	Internal Revenue Service Attn: EIN Operation Cincinnati, OH 45999 Fax: (859) 669-5760
If you have no legal residence, principal office or principal agency in any state or the District of Columbia (international/U.S. possessions)	Internal Revenue Service Attn: EIN International Operation Cincinnati, OH 45999 Fax: (859) 669-5987

How To Get Tax Help, Forms, and Publications

 Tax help for your business is available at www.irs.gov/businesses.

You can download or print all of the forms and publications you may need on www.irs.gov/formspubs. Otherwise, you can go to www.irs.gov/orderforms to place an order and have forms mailed to you. You should receive your order within 10 business days.

Related Forms and Publications

The following forms and instructions may be useful to filers of Form SS-4.
• Form 11-C, Occupational Tax and Registration Return for Wagering.
• Form 637, Application for Registration (For Certain Excise Tax Activities).
• Form 720, Quarterly Federal Excise Tax Return.
• Form 730, Monthly Tax Return for Wagers.
• Form 941, Employer's QUARTERLY Federal Tax Return.
• Form 944, Employer's ANNUAL Federal Tax Return.
• Form 990-T, Exempt Organization Business Income Tax Return.
• Instructions for Form 990-T.
• Form 1023, Application for Recognition of Exemption Under Section 501(c)(3) of the Internal Revenue Code.
• Form 1024, Application for Recognition of Exemption Under Section 501(a).
• Schedule C (Form 1040), Profit or Loss From Business (Sole Proprietorship).
• Schedule F (Form 1040), Profit or Loss From Farming.
• Instructions for Form 1041 and Schedules A, B, G, J, and K-1, U.S. Income Tax Return for Estates and Trusts.
• Form 1042, Annual Withholding Tax Return for U.S. Source Income of Foreign Persons.
• Form 1042-S, Foreign Person's U.S. Source Income Subject to Withholding.
• Instructions for Form 1065, U.S. Return of Partnership Income.
• Instructions for Form 1066, U.S. Real Estate Mortgage Investment Conduit (REMIC) Income Tax Return.
• Instructions for Form 1120, U.S. Corporation Income Tax Return.
• Form 1120S, U.S. Income Tax Return for an S Corporation.
• Form 2290, Heavy Highway Vehicle Use Tax Return.
• Form 2553, Election by a Small Business Corporation.

• Form 2848, Power of Attorney and Declaration of Representative.
• Form 8821, Tax Information Authorization.
• Form 8822-B, Change of Address or Responsible Party — Business.
• Form 8832, Entity Classification Election.
• Form 8849, Claim for Refund of Excise Taxes.

For more information about filing Form SS-4 and related issues, see:
• Pub. 15, Employer's Tax Guide.
• Pub. 51, Agricultural Employer's Tax Guide.
• Pub. 80, Federal Tax Guide for Employers in the U.S. Virgin Islands, Guam, American Samoa, and the Commonwealth of the Northern Mariana Islands.
• Pub. 538, Accounting Periods and Methods.
• Pub. 542, Corporations.
• Pub. 557, Tax-Exempt Status for Your Organization.
• Pub. 583, Starting a Business and Keeping Records.
• Pub. 966, Electronic Choices to Pay All Your Federal Taxes.
• Pub. 1635, Understanding Your EIN.

Specific Instructions

Follow the instructions for each line to expedite processing and to avoid unnecessary IRS requests for additional information. Enter "N/A" on the lines that don't apply.

Line 1. Legal name of entity (or individual) for whom the EIN is being requested. Enter the legal name of the entity (or individual) applying for the EIN exactly as it appears on the social security card, charter, or other applicable legal document. An entry is required.

Individuals. Enter your first name, middle initial, and last name. If you're a sole proprietor, enter your individual name, not your business name. Enter your business name on line 2. Don't use abbreviations or nicknames on line 1.

Trusts. Enter the name of the trust as it appears on the trust instrument.

Estate of a decedent. Enter the name of the estate. For an estate that has no legal name, enter the name of the decedent followed by "Estate."

Partnerships. Enter the legal name of the partnership as it appears in the partnership agreement.

Corporations. Enter the corporate name as it appears in the corporate charter or other legal document creating it.

Plan administrators. Enter the name of the plan administrator. A plan administrator who already has an EIN should use that number.

Line 2. Trade name of business. Enter the trade name of the business if different from the legal name. The trade name is the "doing business as" (DBA) name.

 Use the full legal name shown on line 1 on all tax returns filed for the entity. (However, if you enter a trade name on line 2 and choose to use the trade name instead of the legal name, enter the trade name on all returns you file.) To prevent processing delays and errors, use only the legal name (or the trade name) on all tax returns.

Line 3. Executor, administrator, trustee, "care of" name. For trusts, enter the name of the trustee. For estates, enter the name of the executor, administrator, or other fiduciary. If the entity applying has a designated person to receive tax information, enter that person's name as the "care of" person. Enter the individual's first name, middle initial, and last name.

Lines 4a–b. Mailing address. Enter the mailing address for the entity's correspondence. If the entity's address is outside the United States or its possessions, you must enter the city, province or state, postal code, and the name of the country. Don't abbreviate the country name. If line 3 is completed, enter the address for the executor, trustee, or "care of" person. Generally, this address will be used on all tax returns.

If the entity is filing the Form SS-4 only to obtain an EIN for the Form 8832, use the same address where you would like to have the acceptance or nonacceptance letter sent.

 TIP *File Form 8822-B to report any subsequent changes to the entity's mailing address.*

Lines 5a–b. Street address. Provide the entity's physical address only if different from its mailing address shown in lines 4a–b. Don't enter a P.O. box number here. If the entity's address is outside the United States or its possessions, you must enter the city, province or state, postal code, and the name of the country. Don't abbreviate the country name.

Line 6. County and state where principal business is located. Enter the entity's primary physical location.

Lines 7a–b. Name of responsible party. Enter the full name (first name, middle initial, last name, if applicable) and SSN, ITIN, or EIN of the entity's responsible party, as defined later.

Responsible party defined. For entities with shares or interests traded on a public exchange, or which are registered with the Securities and Exchange Commission, "responsible party" is (a) the principal officer, if the business is a corporation; (b) a general partner, if a partnership; (c) the owner of an entity that is disregarded as separate from its owner (disregarded entities owned by a corporation enter the corporation's name and EIN); or (d) a grantor, owner, or trustor, if a trust. For tax-exempt organizations, the "responsible party" is commonly the same as the "principal officer" as defined in the Form 990 instructions. For government entities, the "responsible party" is generally the individual in a position to legally bind the particular government entity.

For all other entities, "responsible party" is the individual who has a level of control over, or entitlement to, the funds or assets in the entity that, as a practical matter, enables the individual, directly or indirectly, to control, manage, or direct the entity and the disposition of its funds and assets. The ability to fund the entity or the entitlement to the property of the entity alone, however, without any corresponding authority to control, manage, or direct the entity (such as in the case of a minor child beneficiary), doesn't cause the individual to be a responsible party.

 TIP *File Form 8822-B to report any subsequent changes to responsible party information.*

If the responsible party is an alien individual with a previously assigned ITIN, enter the ITIN in the space provided and submit a copy of an official identifying document. If necessary, complete Form W-7, Application for IRS Individual Taxpayer Identification Number, to obtain an ITIN.

You must enter an SSN, ITIN, or EIN on line 7b unless the only reason you're applying for an EIN is to make an entity classification election (see Regulations sections 301.7701-1 through 301.7701-3) and you're a nonresident alien or other foreign entity with no effectively connected income from sources within the United States.

Lines 8a–c. Limited liability company (LLC) information. An LLC is an entity organized under the laws of a state or foreign country as a limited liability company. For federal tax purposes, an LLC may be treated as a partnership or corporation or be disregarded as an entity separate from its owner.

By default, a domestic LLC with only one member is disregarded as an entity separate from its owner and must include all of its income and expenses on the owner's tax return (for example, Schedule C (Form 1040)). For more information on single-member LLCs, see *Disregarded entities*, later.

Also by default, a domestic LLC with two or more members is treated as a partnership. A domestic LLC may file Form 8832 to

avoid either default classification and elect to be classified as an association taxable as a corporation. For more information on entity classifications (including the rules for foreign entities), see Form 8832 and its instructions.

If the answer to line 8a is "Yes," enter the number of LLC members. If the LLC is owned solely by an individual and his or her spouse in a community property state and they choose to treat the entity as a disregarded entity, enter "1" on line 8b.

 Don't file Form 8832 if the LLC accepts the default classifications above. If the LLC timely files Form 2553, it will be treated as a corporation as of the effective date of the S corporation election as long as it meets all other requirements to qualify as an S corporation. The LLC doesn't need to file Form 8832 in addition to Form 2553. See the Instructions for Form 2553.

Line 9a. Type of entity. Check the box that best describes the type of entity applying for the EIN. If you're an alien individual with an ITIN previously assigned to you, enter the ITIN in place of a requested SSN.

 This isn't an election for a tax classification of an entity. See Disregarded entities, later.

Sole proprietor. Check this box if you file Schedule C, or Schedule F (Form 1040) and have a qualified plan, or are required to file excise, employment, alcohol, tobacco, or firearms returns, or are a payer of gambling winnings. Enter your SSN or ITIN in the space provided. If you're a nonresident alien with no effectively connected income from sources within the United States, you don't need to enter an SSN or ITIN.

Corporation. This box is for any corporation other than a personal service corporation. If you check this box, enter the income tax form number to be filed by the entity in the space provided.

 If you entered "1120S" after the Corporation checkbox, the corporation must file Form 2553 no later than the 15th day of the 3rd month of the tax year the election to become an S corporation is to take effect. Until Form 2553 has been received and approved, you will be considered a Form 1120 filer. See the Instructions for Form 2553.

Personal service corporation. Check this box if the entity is a personal service corporation. An entity is a personal service corporation for a tax year only if:
• The principal activity of the entity during the testing period (generally the prior tax year) for the tax year is the performance of personal services substantially by employee-owners, and
• The employee-owners own at least 10% of the fair market value of the outstanding stock in the entity on the last day of the testing period.

Personal services include performance of services in such fields as accounting, actuarial science, architecture, consulting, engineering, health (including veterinary services), law, and the performing arts. For more information about personal service corporations, see the Instructions for Form 1120 and Pub. 542.

 If the corporation is recently formed, the testing period begins on the first day of its tax year and ends on the earlier of the last day of its tax year, or the last day of the calendar year in which its tax year begins.

Other nonprofit organization. Check the *Other nonprofit organization* box if the nonprofit organization is other than a church or church-controlled organization and specify the type of nonprofit organization (for example, an educational organization).

 If the organization also seeks tax-exempt status, you must file either Form 1023 (or Form 1023-EZ) or Form 1024. See Pub. 557 for more information.

Instr. for Form SS-4 (Rev. 2-2016) -3-

If the organization is covered by a group exemption letter, enter the four-digit group exemption number (GEN) in the last entry. (Don't confuse the GEN with the nine-digit EIN.) If you don't know the GEN, contact the parent organization. See Pub. 557 for more information about group exemption letters.

If the organization is a section 527 political organization, check the box for *Other nonprofit organization* and specify "Section 527 organization" in the space to the right. To be recognized as exempt from tax, a section 527 political organization must electronically file Form 8871, Political Organization Notice of Section 527 Status, within 24 hours of the date on which the organization was established. The organization may also have to file Form 8872, Political Organization Report of Contributions and Expenditures. Go to *www.irs.gov/polorgs* for more information.

Plan administrator. If the plan administrator is an individual, enter the plan administrator's taxpayer identification number (TIN) in the space provided.

REMIC. Check this box if the entity has elected to be treated as a real estate mortgage investment conduit (REMIC). See the Instructions for Form 1066 for more information.

State/local government. State and local governments generally have the characteristics of a government, such as powers of taxation, law enforcement, and civil authority. If you're unsure whether or not your organization is a government, search "Is My Entity a Government Entity?" at *www.irs.gov* for clarification.

Federal government/military. The federal government is made up of the Executive, Legislative, and Judicial branches, as well as independent federal agencies. Unions, VFW organizations, and political organizations aren't federal agencies.

Other. If not specifically listed, check the box for *Other*, enter the type of entity and the type of return, if any, that will be filed (for example, "Common trust fund, Form 1065" or "Created a pension plan"). Don't enter "N/A." If you're an alien individual applying for an EIN, see the instructions for *Lines 7a-b*.
- **Household employer.** If you're an individual that will employ someone to provide services in your household, check the box *Other* and enter "Household employer" and your SSN. If you're a trust that qualifies as a household employer, you don't need a separate EIN for reporting tax information relating to household employees; use the EIN of the trust.
- **Household employer agent.** If you're an agent of a household employer that is a disabled individual or other welfare recipient receiving home care services through a state or local program, check the box *Other* and enter "Household employer agent." For more information, see Rev. Proc. 84-33 and Rev. Proc. 2013-39. If you're a state or local government, also check the box for state/local government.
- **QSub.** For a qualified subchapter S subsidiary (QSub) check the box *Other* and specify "QSub."
- **Withholding agent.** If you're a withholding agent required to file Form 1042, check the box *Other* and enter "Withholding agent."

Disregarded entities. A disregarded entity is an eligible entity that is disregarded as separate from its owner for federal income tax purposes. Disregarded entities include single-member limited liability companies (LLCs) that are disregarded as separate from their owners, qualified subchapter S subsidiaries (qualified subsidiaries of an S corporation), and certain qualified foreign entities. See the Instructions for Form 8832 and Regulations section 301.7701-3 for more information on domestic and foreign disregarded entities.

The disregarded entity is required to use its name and EIN for reporting and payment of employment taxes. A disregarded entity is also required to use its name and EIN to register for excise tax activities on Form 637; pay and report excise taxes reported on Forms 720, 730, 2290, and 11-C; and claim any refunds, credits, and payments on Form 8849. See the instructions for the employment and excise tax returns for more information.

Complete Form SS-4 for disregarded entities as follows.
- If a disregarded entity is filing Form SS-4 to obtain an EIN because it is required to report and pay employment and excise taxes, or for non-federal purposes such as a state requirement, check the box *Other* for line 9a and write "Disregarded entity" (or "Disregarded entity-sole proprietorship" if the owner of the disregarded entity is an individual).
- If the disregarded entity is requesting an EIN for purposes of filing Form 8832 to elect classification as an association taxable as a corporation, or Form 2553 to elect S corporation status, check the box *Corporation* for line 9a and write "Single-member" and the form number of the return that will be filed (Form 1120 or 1120S).
- If the disregarded entity is requesting an EIN because it has acquired one or more additional owners and its classification has changed to partnership under the default rules of Regulations section 301.7701-3(f), check the box *Partnership* for line 9a.

Line 10. Reason for applying. Check only one box. Don't enter "N/A." A selection is required.

Started new business. Check this box if you're starting a new business that requires an EIN. If you check this box, enter the type of business being started. Don't apply if you already have an EIN and are only adding another place of business.

Hired employees. Check this box if the existing business is requesting an EIN because it has hired or is hiring employees and is therefore required to file employment tax returns. Don't apply if you already have an EIN and are only hiring employees. For information on employment taxes (for example, for family members), see Pub. 15, Pub. 51, or Pub. 80.

 You must make electronic deposits of all depository taxes (such as employment tax, excise tax, and corporate income tax) using EFTPS. See Pub. 15, Pub. 51, Pub. 80, and Pub. 966.

Banking purpose. Check this box if you're requesting an EIN for banking purposes only, and enter the banking purpose (for example, a bowling league for depositing dues or an investment club for dividend and interest reporting).

Changed type of organization. Check this box if the business is changing its type of organization. For example, the business was a sole proprietorship and has been incorporated or has become a partnership. If you check this box, specify in the space provided (including available space immediately below) the type of change made. For example, "From sole proprietorship to partnership."

Purchased going business. Check this box if you purchased an existing business. Don't use the former owner's EIN unless you became the "owner" of a corporation by acquiring its stock.

Created a trust. Check this box if you created a trust, and enter the type of trust created. For example, indicate if the trust is a nonexempt charitable trust or a split-interest trust.

Exception. Don't file this form for certain grantor-type trusts. The trustee doesn't need an EIN for the trust if the trustee furnishes the name and TIN of the grantor/owner and the address of the trust to all payers. However, grantor trusts that don't file using Optional Method 1 and IRA trusts that are required to file Form 990-T must have an EIN. For more information on grantor trusts, see the Instructions for Form 1041.

 Don't check this box if you're applying for a trust EIN when a new pension plan is established. Check the Created a pension plan box.

Created a pension plan. Check this box if you have created a pension plan and need an EIN for reporting purposes. Also, enter the type of plan in the space provided. For more information about pension plans, visit IRS.gov and enter "Types of retirement plans" in the search box.

TIP *Check this box if you're applying for a trust EIN when a new pension plan is established. In addition, check the Other box on line 9a and write "Created a pension plan" in the space provided.*

Other. Check this box if you're requesting an EIN for any other reason; and enter the reason. For example, a newly-formed state government entity should enter "Newly-formed state government entity" in the space provided.

Line 11. Date business started or acquired. If you're starting a new business, enter the starting date of the business. If the business you acquired is already operating, enter the date you acquired the business. For foreign applicants, this is the date you began or acquired a business in the United States. If you're changing the form of ownership of your business, enter the date the new ownership entity began. Trusts should enter the date the trust was funded or the date that the trust was required to obtain an EIN under Regulations section 301.6109-1(a)(2). Estates should enter the date of death of the decedent whose name appears on line 1 or the date when the estate was legally funded.

Line 12. Closing month of accounting year. Enter the last month of your accounting year or tax year. An accounting or tax year is usually 12 consecutive months, either a calendar year or a fiscal year (including a period of 52 or 53 weeks). A calendar year is 12 consecutive months ending on December 31. A fiscal year is either 12 consecutive months ending on the last day of any month other than December or a 52-53 week year. For more information on accounting periods, see Pub. 538.

   Individuals. Your tax year generally will be a calendar year.

   Partnerships. Partnerships must adopt one of the following tax years.
* The tax year of the majority of its partners.
* The tax year common to all of its principal partners.
* The tax year that results in the least aggregate deferral of income.
* In certain cases, some other tax year.

   See the Instructions for Form 1065 for more information.

   REMICs. REMICs must have a calendar year as their tax year.

   Personal service corporations. A personal service corporation generally must adopt a calendar year unless it meets one of the following requirements.
* It can establish a business purpose for having a different tax year.
* It elects under section 444 to have a tax year other than a calendar year.

   Trusts. Generally, a trust must adopt a calendar year except for the following trusts.
* Tax-exempt trusts.
* Charitable trusts.
* Grantor-owned trusts.

Line 13. Highest number of employees expected in the next 12 months. Complete each box by entering the number (including zero (-0-)) of *Agricultural, Household,* or *Other* employees expected by the applicant in the next 12 months.

   If no employees are expected, skip line 14.

Line 14. Do you want to file Form 944? If you expect your employment tax liability to be $1,000 or less in a full calendar year, you're eligible to file Form 944 annually (once each year) instead of filing Form 941 quarterly (every three months). Your employment tax liability generally will be $1,000 or less if you expect to pay $4,000 or less in total wages subject to social security and Medicare taxes and federal income tax withholding. If you qualify and want to file Form 944 instead of Forms 941, check the box on line 14. If you don't check the box, then you must file Form 941 for every quarter.

TIP *For employers in the U.S. possessions, generally, if you pay $6,536 or less in wages subject to social security and Medicare taxes, you're likely to pay $1,000 or less in employment taxes.*

   For more information on employment taxes, see Pub. 15, Pub. 51, or Pub. 80.

Line 15. First date wages or annuities were paid. If the business has employees, enter the date on which the business began to pay wages or annuities. For foreign applicants, this is the date you began to pay wages in the United States. If the business doesn't plan to have employees, enter "N/A."

   Withholding agent. Enter the date you began or will begin to pay income (including annuities) to a nonresident alien. This also applies to individuals who are required to file Form 1042 to report alimony paid to a nonresident alien. For foreign applicants, this is the date you began or will begin to pay income (including annuities) to a nonresident alien in the United States.

Line 16. Check the one box on line 16 that best describes the principal activity of the applicant's business. Check the box *Other* (and specify the applicant's principal activity) if none of the listed boxes applies. You must check a box.

   Construction. Check this box if the applicant is engaged in erecting buildings or engineering projects (for example, streets, highways, bridges, and tunnels). The term "construction" also includes special trade contractors (for example, plumbing, HVAC, electrical, carpentry, concrete, excavation, etc. contractors).

   Real estate. Check this box if the applicant is engaged in renting or leasing real estate to others; managing, selling, buying, or renting real estate for others; or providing related real estate services (for example, appraisal services). Also check this box for mortgage real estate investment trusts (REITs). Mortgage REITs are engaged in issuing shares of funds consisting primarily of portfolios of real estate mortgage assets with gross income of the trust solely derived from interest earned.

   Rental & leasing. Check this box if the applicant is engaged in providing tangible goods such as autos, computers, consumer goods, or industrial machinery and equipment to customers in return for a periodic rental or lease payment. Also check this box for equity real estate investment trusts (REITs). Equity REITs are engaged in issuing shares of funds consisting primarily of portfolios of real estate assets with gross income of the trust derived from renting real property.

   Manufacturing. Check this box if the applicant is engaged in the mechanical, physical, or chemical transformation of materials, substances, or components into new products. The assembling of component parts of manufactured products is also considered to be manufacturing.

   Transportation & warehousing. Check this box if the applicant provides transportation of passengers or cargo, warehousing or storage of goods; scenic or sight-seeing transportation, or support activities related to transportation.

   Finance & insurance. Check this box if the applicant is engaged in transactions involving the creation, liquidation, or change of ownership of financial assets and/or facilitating such financial transactions; underwriting annuities/insurance policies; facilitating such underwriting by selling insurance policies; or by providing other insurance or employee-benefit related services.

   Health care & social assistance. Check this box if the applicant is engaged in providing physical, medical, or psychiatric care; or providing social assistance activities such as youth centers, adoption agencies, individual/family services, temporary shelters, daycare, etc.

   Accommodation & food services. Check this box if the applicant is engaged in providing customers with lodging, meal preparation, snacks, or beverages for immediate consumption.

   Wholesale-agent/broker. Check this box if the applicant is engaged in arranging for the purchase or sale of goods owned by others or purchasing goods on a commission basis for goods traded in the wholesale market, usually between businesses.

Wholesale-other. Check this box if the applicant is engaged in selling goods in the wholesale market generally to other businesses for resale on their own account, goods used in production, or capital or durable nonconsumer goods.

Retail. Check this box if the applicant is engaged in selling merchandise to the general public from a fixed store; by direct, mail-order, or electronic sales; or by using vending machines.

Other. Check this box if the applicant is engaged in an activity not described above. Describe the applicant's principal business activity in the space provided.

Line 17. Use line 17 to describe the applicant's principal line of business in more detail. For example, if you checked the *Construction* box on line 16, enter additional detail such as "General contractor for residential buildings" on line 17. An entry is required. For mortgage REITs, indicate mortgage REIT; and for equity REITs, indicate what type of real property is the principal type (residential REIT, nonresidential REIT, miniwarehouse REIT).

Line 18. Check the applicable box to indicate whether or not the applicant entity applying for an EIN was issued one previously.

Third Party Designee. Complete this section only if you want to authorize the named individual to receive the entity's EIN and answer questions about the completion of Form SS-4. The designee's authority terminates at the time the EIN is assigned and released to the designee. You must complete the signature area for the authorization to be valid.

Signature. When required, the application must be signed by (a) the individual, if the applicant is an individual; (b) the president, vice president, or other principal officer, if the applicant is a corporation; (c) a responsible and duly authorized member or officer having knowledge of its affairs, if the applicant is a partnership, government entity, or other unincorporated organization; or (d) the fiduciary, if the applicant is a trust or an estate. Foreign applicants may have any duly-authorized person (for example, division manager) sign Form SS-4.

Privacy Act and Paperwork Reduction Act Notice. We ask for the information on this form to carry out the Internal Revenue laws of the United States. We need it to comply with section 6109 and the regulations thereunder, which generally require the inclusion of an employer identification number (EIN) on certain returns, statements, or other documents filed with the Internal Revenue Service. If your entity is required to obtain an EIN, you're required to provide all of the information requested on this form. Information on this form may be used to determine which federal tax returns you're required to file and to provide you with related forms and publications.

We disclose this form to the Social Security Administration (SSA) for their use in determining compliance with applicable laws. We may give this information to the Department of Justice for use in civil and/or criminal litigation, and to cities, states, the District of Columbia, and U.S. commonwealths and possessions for use in administering their tax laws. We may also disclose this information to other countries under a tax treaty, to federal and state agencies to enforce federal nontax criminal laws, and to federal law enforcement and intelligence agencies to combat terrorism.

We will be unable to issue an EIN to you unless you provide all of the requested information that applies to your entity. Providing false information could subject you to penalties.

You're not required to provide the information requested on a form that is subject to the Paperwork Reduction Act unless the form displays a valid OMB control number. Books or records relating to a form or its instructions must be retained as long as their contents may become material in the administration of any Internal Revenue law. Generally, tax returns and return information are confidential, as required by section 6103.

The time needed to complete and file this form will vary depending on individual circumstances. The estimated average time is:

Recordkeeping	8 hr., 36 min.
Learning about the law or the form	42 min.
Preparing, copying, assembling, and sending the form to the IRS	52 min.

If you have comments concerning the accuracy of these time estimates or suggestions for making this form simpler, we would be happy to hear from you. You can send your comments from *www.irs.gov/formspubs*. Click on *More Information* and then click on *Give us feedback*. Or you can write to the Internal Revenue Service, Tax Forms and Publications Division, 1111 Constitution Ave. NW, IR-6526, Washington, DC 20224. Don't send Form SS-4 to this address. Instead, see *Where To File or Fax*, earlier.

Instr. for Form SS-4 (Rev. 2-2016)

CHAPTER 5
LLC: LIMITED LIABILITY COMPANY

"Never be a minion, always be an owner."
– Cornelius Vanderbilt

CHANGE of Registered Agent and/or Registered Office

1. The name of the corporation is:

2. The street address of the current registered office is:

3. The new address of the registered office is to be:

4. The current registered agent is:

5. The new registered agent is:

6. The street address of the registered office and the street address of the business address of the registered agent are identical.

7. Such change was authorized by resolution duly adopted by the Board of Directors of the corporation or by an officer of the corporation so authorized by the board of directors.

_____
Secretary

Having been named as registered agent and to accept service of process for the above stated corporation at the place designated in this certificate, I hereby accept the appointment as registered agent and agree to act in this capacity. I further agree to comply with the provisions of all statutes relating to the proper and complete performance of my duties and am familiar with and accept the obligations of my position as registered agent.

_____
Registered Agent

THE BIRTH OF THE LLC

Limited Liability Company (LLC) was invented in 1977 by the state of Wyoming. Now every state in the U.S. has their own version of the LLC. In 1997, the IRS allowed LLCs to be operated by one person. But be sure to check your states laws before forming an LLC because you pay more in annual fees than an S Corporation.

An LLC is a legal person created under state law. It has certain rights and obligations. The main reason for forming an LLC is to limit personal risks financially. An LLC can have more than one member who are like stockholders in a corporation. Or it can have a manager who runs the LLC. I will not deal with those LLCs, but instead stick with a single person/owner LLC. If you're looking for

more information on having a manager run your LLC or want multiple members in your LLC you may want to order some of the books at the end of this chapter.

I personally like the LLC because it can continue on forever even after the owner's death should the heirs want it to. And you can transfer the LLC and all of its assets and accounts easily. But you can't with a sole proprietorship. With that you have to transfer each asset individually like I had to do with my intellectual property owned by my company *Carceral Wealth Services*. An LLC also has its own bank account and credit rating separate from its owners.

Sounds good, right? There are some roadblocks for prisoners to get over when forming an LLC. The main one being cost. When I formed *Carceral Wealth Services* as a sole proprietorship it cost me $70. But if I wanted to form it as a LLC it would cost me more. And I'd have to pay an annual fee. Each state has different costs and you can obtain the latest costs by writing your state's secretary of state business office. Those addresses will be provided along with a sample letter you can use.

You can take the easy route and just form a sole proprietorship then later on convert it to an LLC? That would be easier and save you money if your low on start-up funds? As I always caution my readers, do your research first before you jump into the cellpreneur world.

DIFFERENT TYPES OF LLCS

There are two main LLC: a domestic LLC or a foreign LLC. A domestic LLC is one that is set up and operated in your state. A foreign LLC is one that is formed in another state, like Delaware or Nevada, to do business in your state. When Prisoner Assistant, Inc. was doing business formation services for prisoners they offered Delaware and Nevada LLCs and Corporation start-up services. They were doing this because the two states offer friendly business tax laws and other advantages. A lot of major corporations use Delaware and Nevada as their states of choice. I personally prefer Nevada because it has no state income tax and does not share information with the IRS. But if you form your LLC in Nevada you have to have an agent or office in Nevada. You can already see how this can be more complicated and a lot more expensive for a prisoner. Maybe you're lucky and have family and friends who live in Nevada or Delaware? Then by all means use their help to form your LLC in one of those states. If not, you'll have to form it in your state, then transfer it when you get out of prison.

There is also a PLLC or "Professional Limited Liability Company." In some states, lawyers, doctors and chiropractors and other professional practitioners must form a PLLC. Most prisoners do not have to worry about this, so I will not go into any more about this type of LLC.

Lastly, as mentioned before, an LLC is either "membership controlled" or "management controlled." A one-person LLC operates as membership controlled and executes a "operating agreement." But if your LLC will have silent partners and have a manager you will declare it management controlled and use a "management operating agreement." I advocate you starting it on your own and being in control. If you want to explore the other route, check out the books at the end of this chapter.

FORMING YOUR LLC

The main forms you'll need to file will be as follows:

- Articles of Organization
- Membership Operating Agreement
- Tax Forms (SS-4 and 8832)

Other forms may be required by your state so be sure to check with them first before you file. And each state has its own rules about what records you must keep once your LLC is up and running. So be sure to check. Most states require you to produce an annual report.

Before I get into the actual documents you have to file here are some more ideas about LLCs.

- LLCs are great to protect personal assets

- Title your Real Estate to an LLC. In Delaware, you can do this in a "Series LLC." Each cell of the series LLC would be used to own each piece of property. This is a tactic Aristotle Onassis used to build his shipping empire. Each one of his ships was a separate entity. That if one went down it didn't bring the whole thing down. Plus, it offered many tax advantages. Learn from the masters.

- If you're an author or have other intellectual property (IP) you should title it to an LLC also. Preferably in a dominion that offers the best advantage for IP. An offshore LLC in Nevis or Cook Island would be great for this. Contact an IP lawyer before you do something like that though as it may be hard to run pro se from prison?

SAMPLE LLC DOCUMENTS

Once you have formed your LLC in your mind and have a company name that is not already taken you are ready to file your paperwork and legally form your LLC. The first thing you should do is write the business office of your state that deals with LLCs. You can find the address in chapter five and request a LLC application package and sample forms if they provide them? I have enclosed a sample letter you can use to form your request (see next page.)

After you get your state's business formation package (if it has one) you would fill them out and mail them in plus enclose a check for your filing fee or other costs. You should enclose a cover letter stating that you've enclosed the proper filing fee and correct documents to form your LLC.

Also request a date-stamped copy of your LLC formation and receipt for your filing fee. A sample letter has been provided in this chapter.

As mentioned before, in most states the main forms that are needed to file for a LLC formation are as follows:

- Articles of Organization
- Membership Operating Agreement
- Operating Minutes (some states only)

Those sample documents have been provided in this chapter.

If all of this is confusing, then you may want to hire an attorney to help you do all of this. In a later chapter, I'll provide you with some tips and tactics on hiring and working with your lawyer.

Just remember to check with your state's business office first before you decide to form your company. Do your research. Learn the rules and laws that govern your business. You may need to obtain special licenses to operate your business. This may require additional funds? Always remember, proper preparation prevents poor performance. I would say good luck, but "luck is the residue of design." May your new business bring you prosperity!

RESOURCE BOX

For more about forming and operating an LLC be sure to check out the following books:

- *Limited Liability Companies: A State by State Guide To Law and Practice* by William J. Callison and Maureen A. Sullivan.
- *Limited Liability Companies: Law, Practice and Forms* by Jeffery C. Rubenstein, et al.
- *How To Form A Limited Liability Company, 2nd Edition* by Mark Warda

Books can be ordered from our Bookstore on page 224 or online. Contact Freebird Publishers about ordering if you don't have anyone to help you.

To:_____   _____,20_____
                                                          Date
   _____
   _____
   _____

Dear Sir or Madam:

I would like your application and/or business package for forming a Limited Liability Company in _____. Please provide any forms and instructions that I need to follow to properly file the LLC documents.

Thank you in advance for your cooperation in this matter. I look forward to hearing from you soon.

Respectfully Requested,

_____
_____
_____
_____

Sample Letter Requesting LLC Forms

To:_____   _____,20_____
       _____   Date
       _____
       _____

Dear Sir or Madam:

Please find the enclosed original and _____ copies of articles of organization for the above referenced LLC along with a check for $_____. This check covers the filing fee and other costs as follows _____.

Please send acknowledgement of receipt and/or file-date stamped copy to:

                              _____
                              _____
                              _____
                              _____

Thank you in advance for your cooperation in this matter. I look forward to hearing from you soon.

Respectfully Requested

s/_____

Sample Letter to Include with LLC Filings

ARTICLES OF ORGANIZATION FOR A LIMITED LIABILITY COMPANY

ARTICLE I – Name:

The name of the Limited Liability Company is:

ARTICLE II - Purpose:

The purpose for which this limited liability company is organized is:

ARTICLE III – Duration:

The period of duration for the Limited Liability Company shall be:

ARTICLE IV – Registered (or Statutory) Agent and Address:

The name and address of the initial registered (statutory) agent is:

ARTICLE V – Management
(check the appropriate box and complete the statement)

☐ The Limited Liability Company is to be managed by a manager or managers and the name(s) and address(es) of such manager(s) who is/are to serve as manager(s) is/are:

☐ The Limited Liability Company is to be managed by the members and the name(s) and address(es) of the managing members is/are:

ARTICLE VI – Principle Place of Business
The initial principal place of business of the limited liability company is:

ARTICLE VII – Effective Date
The effective date of these articles is   ☐ Upon filing   ☐ on _____

ARTICLE VIII – Nonliability
The member and managers, if any, shall not be liable for any debts, obligations or liabilities of the limited liability company.

ARTICLE IX – MISCELLANEOUS

IN WITNESS WHEREOF the undersigned members executed these Articles of Organization this _____day of _____, _____.

_____
Member   Address:

_____
Member   Address:

_____
Member   Address:

_____
Member   Address:

Acceptance of Registered (statutory) agent

Having been named as registered agent and to accept service of process for the above stated limited liability company at the place designated in this certificate, I hereby accept the appointment as registered agent and agree to act in this capacity. I further agree to comply with the provisions of all statues relating to the proper and complete performance of my duties, and am familiar with and accept the obligations of my position as registered agent.

_____
Agent:

Limited Liability Company
Member-Managed Operating Agreement of

_____

THIS AGREEMENT is made effective as of _____, 20_____ among the member(s) and the company.

1. <u>Formation</u>. A limited liability company of the above name has been formed under the laws of the state of _____ by filing articles of organization with the secretary of state. The purpose of the business shall be to carry on any activity which is lawful under the jurisdiction in which it operates. The company may operate under a fictitious name or names as long as the company is in compliance with applicable fictitious name registration laws. The term of the company shall be perpetual or until dissolved as provided by law or by vote of the member(s) as provided in this agreement. Upon dissolution, the remaining members shall have the power to continue the operation of the company as long as necessary and allowable under state law until the winding up of the affairs of the business has been completed.

2. <u>Members</u>. The initial member(s) shall be listed on Schedule A, which shall accompany and be made a part of this Agreement. Additional members may be admitted to membership upon the unanimous consent of the current members. Transfer or pledge of member's interest may not be made except upon consent of all members.

3. <u>Contributions</u>. The initial capital contribution(s) shall be listed on Schedule A. No member shall be obligated to contribute any more than the amount set forth on Schedule A unless agreed to in writing by all of the members and no member shall have any personal liability for any debt, obligation or liability of the company other than for full payment of his or her capital contribution. No member shall be entitled to interest on the capital contribution. Member voting rights shall be in proportion to the amount of their contributions.

4. <u>Profit and loss</u>. The profits and losses of the business, and all other taxable or deductible items shall be allocated to the members according to the percentages on Schedule A. Distributions of profits can be made to the member(s) at any time and in any amount, except where prohibited by law.

5. <u>Distributions</u>. The company shall have the power to make distributions to its members in such amounts and at such intervals as a majority of the members deem appropriate according to law.

6. <u>Management</u>. The limited liability company shall be managed by its members listed on schedule A, which shall accompany and be made a part of this agreement. Any member may bind the company in all matters in the ordinary course of company business. In the event of a dispute between members, final determination shall be made with a vote by the member's votes being proportioned according to capital contributions.

7. <u>Registered Agent</u>. The company shall at all times have a registered agent and registered office. The initial registered agent and registered office shall be listed on Schedule A.

8. <u>Assets</u>. The assets of the company shall be registered in the legal name of the company and not in the names of the individual members.

9. <u>Records and Accounting</u>. The company shall keep an accurate accounting of its affairs using any method accounting allowed by law. All members shall have the power to hire such accountants as they deem necessary or desirable.

10. <u>Banking</u>. The members of the company shall be authorized to set up bank accounts as in their sole discretion are deemed necessary and are authorized to execute any banking resolutions provided by the institution in which the accounts are being set up.

11. <u>Taxes</u>. The company shall file such tax returns as required by law. The company shall elect to be taxed as a majority of the members decide is in their best interests. The "tax matters partner," as required by the Internal Revenue Code, shall be listed on Schedule A.

12. <u>Separate Entity</u>. The company is a legal entity separate from its members. No member shall have any separate liability for any debts, obligations or liability of the company except as provided in this agreement.

13. <u>Indemnity and Exculpation</u>. The limited liability company shall indemnify and hold harmless its members, managers, employees and agents to the fullest extent allowed by law for acts or omissions done as part of their duties to or for the company. Indemnification shall include all liabilities, expenses, attorney and accountant fees, and other costs reasonably expended. No member shall be liable to the company for acts done in good faith.

14. <u>Meetings</u>. The members shall have no obligation to hold annual or any other meeting but may hold such meetings if they deem them necessary or desirable.

15. <u>Amendment of this Agreement</u>. This agreement may not be amended except in writing signed by all of the members.

16. <u>Conflict of Interest</u>. No member shall be involved with any business or undertaking which competes with the interests of the company except upon agreement in writing by all of the members.

17. <u>Deadlock</u>. In the event that the members cannot come to an agreement on any matter the members agree to submit the issue to mediation to be paid for by the company. In the event the mediation is unsuccessful, they agree to seek arbitration under the rules of the American Arbitration Association.

18. <u>Dissociation</u>, of a member. A member shall have the right to discontinue membership upon giving thirty-day notice. A member shall cease to have the right to membership upon death, court-ordered incapacity, bankruptcy or expulsion. The company shall have the right to buy the interest of any dissociated member at fair market value.

19. <u>Dissolution.</u> The company shall dissolve upon the unanimous consent of all the members or upon any event requiring dissolution under state law. In the event of the death, bankruptcy, permanent incapacity, or withdrawal of a member the remaining members may elect to dissolve or to continue the operation of the company.

20. <u>General Provisions.</u> This agreement is intended to represent the entire agreement between the parties. In the event that any party of this agreement is held to be contrary to law or unenforceable, said party shall be considered amended to comply with the law and such holding shall not affect the enforceability of other terms of this agreement. This agreement shall be binding upon the heirs, successors and assigns of the members.

21. <u>Miscellaneous,</u>

_____
_____
_____
_____
_____
_____
_____

IN WITNESS whereof, the members of the limited liability company sign this agreement and adopt it as their operating agreement this _____day of _____, 20_____.

_____   _____

_____   _____

_____   _____

Form **SS-4**	**Application for Employer Identification Number**		OMB No. 1545-0003
(Rev. January 2010) Department of the Treasury Internal Revenue Service	(For use by employers, corporations, partnerships, trusts, estates, churches, government agencies, Indian tribal entities, certain individuals, and others.) ▶ See separate instructions for each line. ▶ Keep a copy for your records.		EIN

Type or print clearly.

1	Legal name of entity (or individual) for whom the EIN is being requested	
2	Trade name of business (if different from name on line 1)	3 Executor, administrator, trustee, "care of" name
4a	Mailing address (room, apt., suite no. and street, or P.O. box)	5a Street address (if different) (Do not enter a P.O. box.)
4b	City, state, and ZIP code (if foreign, see instructions)	5b City, state, and ZIP code (if foreign, see instructions)
6	County and state where principal business is located	
7a	Name of responsible party	7b SSN, ITIN, or EIN

8a	Is this application for a limited liability company (LLC) (or a foreign equivalent)? ☐ Yes ☐ No	8b If 8a is "Yes," enter the number of LLC members ▶
8c	If 8a is "Yes," was the LLC organized in the United States?	☐ Yes ☐ No

9a	**Type of entity** (check only one box). **Caution.** If 8a is "Yes," see the instructions for the correct box to check.	
	☐ Sole proprietor (SSN) _____	☐ Estate (SSN of decedent) _____
	☐ Partnership	☐ Plan administrator (TIN) _____
	☐ Corporation (enter form number to be filed) ▶	☐ Trust (TIN of grantor) _____
	☐ Personal service corporation	☐ National Guard ☐ State/local government
	☐ Church or church-controlled organization	☐ Farmers' cooperative ☐ Federal government/military
	☐ Other nonprofit organization (specify) ▶	☐ REMIC ☐ Indian tribal governments/enterprises
	☐ Other (specify) ▶	Group Exemption Number (GEN) if any ▶
9b	If a corporation, name the state or foreign country (if applicable) where incorporated	State _____ Foreign country _____

10	**Reason for applying** (check only one box)	☐ Banking purpose (specify purpose) ▶ _____
	☐ Started new business (specify type) ▶	☐ Changed type of organization (specify new type) ▶ _____
		☐ Purchased going business
	☐ Hired employees (check the box and see line 13)	☐ Created a trust (specify type) ▶ _____
	☐ Compliance with IRS withholding regulations	☐ Created a pension plan (specify type) ▶ _____
	☐ Other (specify) ▶	

11	Date business started or acquired (month, day, year). See instructions.	12 Closing month of accounting year
13	Highest number of employees expected in the next 12 months (enter -0- if none). If no employees expected, skip line 14. Agricultural ____ Household ____ Other ____	14 If you expect your employment tax liability to be $1,000 or less in a full calendar year **and** want to file Form 944 annually instead of Forms 941 quarterly, check here. (Your employment tax liability generally will be $1,000 or less if you expect to pay $4,000 or less in total wages.) If you do not check this box, you must file Form 941 for every quarter. ☐

15	First date wages or annuities were paid (month, day, year). **Note.** If applicant is a withholding agent, enter date income will first be paid to nonresident alien (month, day, year) ▶

16	Check one box that best describes the principal activity of your business.	☐ Health care & social assistance ☐ Wholesale-agent/broker
	☐ Construction ☐ Rental & leasing ☐ Transportation & warehousing	☐ Accommodation & food service ☐ Wholesale-other ☐ Retail
	☐ Real estate ☐ Manufacturing ☐ Finance & insurance	☐ Other (specify) ▶
17	Indicate principal line of merchandise sold, specific construction work done, products produced, or services provided.	

18	Has the applicant entity shown on line 1 ever applied for and received an EIN? ☐ Yes ☐ No If "Yes," write previous EIN here ▶

Third Party Designee	Complete this section **only** if you want to authorize the named individual to receive the entity's EIN and answer questions about the completion of this form.	
	Designee's name	Designee's telephone number (include area code)
	Address and ZIP code	Designee's fax number (include area code)

Under penalties of perjury, I declare that I have examined this application, and to the best of my knowledge and belief, it is true, correct, and complete.

Name and title (type or print clearly) ▶	Applicant's telephone number (include area code)
Signature ▶ Date ▶	Applicant's fax number (include area code)

For Privacy Act and Paperwork Reduction Act Notice, see separate instructions.   Cat. No. 16055N   Form **SS-4** (Rev. 1-2010)

EXAMPLE

Do I Need an EIN?

File Form SS-4 if the applicant entity does not already have an EIN but is required to show an EIN on any return, statement, or other document.[1] See also the separate instructions for each line on Form SS-4.

IF the applicant...	AND...	THEN...
Started a new business	Does not currently have (nor expect to have) employees	Complete lines 1, 2, 4a–8a, 8b–c (if applicable), 9a, 9b (if applicable), and 10–14 and 16–18.
Hired (or will hire) employees, including household employees	Does not already have an EIN	Complete lines 1, 2, 4a–6, 7a–b (if applicable), 8a, 8b–c (if applicable), 9a, 9b (if applicable), 10–18.
Opened a bank account	Needs an EIN for banking purposes only	Complete lines 1–5b, 7a–b (if applicable), 8a, 8b–c (if applicable), 9a, 9b (if applicable), 10, and 18.
Changed type of organization	Either the legal character of the organization or its ownership changed (for example, you incorporate a sole proprietorship or form a partnership)[2]	Complete lines 1–18 (as applicable).
Purchased a going business[3]	Does not already have an EIN	Complete lines 1–18 (as applicable).
Created a trust	The trust is other than a grantor trust or an IRA trust[4]	Complete lines 1–18 (as applicable).
Created a pension plan as a plan administrator[5]	Needs an EIN for reporting purposes	Complete lines 1, 3, 4a–5b, 9a, 10, and 18.
Is a foreign person needing an EIN to comply with IRS withholding regulations	Needs an EIN to complete a Form W-8 (other than Form W-8ECI), avoid withholding on portfolio assets, or claim tax treaty benefits[6]	Complete lines 1–5b, 7a–b (SSN or ITIN optional), 8a, 8b–c (if applicable), 9a, 9b (if applicable), 10, and 18.
Is administering an estate	Needs an EIN to report estate income on Form 1041	Complete lines 1–6, 9a, 10–12, 13–17 (if applicable), and 18.
Is a withholding agent for taxes on non-wage income paid to an alien (i.e., individual, corporation, or partnership, etc.)	Is an agent, broker, fiduciary, manager, tenant, or spouse who is required to file Form 1042, Annual Withholding Tax Return for U.S. Source Income of Foreign Persons	Complete lines 1, 2, 3 (if applicable), 4a–5b, 7a–b (if applicable), 8a, 8b–c (if applicable), 9a, 9b (if applicable), 10, and 18.
Is a state or local agency	Serves as a tax reporting agent for public assistance recipients under Rev. Proc. 80-4, 1980-1 C.B. 581[7]	Complete lines 1, 2, 4a–5b, 9a, 10, and 18.
Is a single-member LLC	Needs an EIN to file Form 8832, Classification Election, for filing employment tax returns and excise tax returns, or for state reporting purposes[8]	Complete lines 1–18 (as applicable).
Is an S corporation	Needs an EIN to file Form 2553, Election by a Small Business Corporation[9]	Complete lines 1–18 (as applicable).

[1] For example, a sole proprietorship or self-employed farmer who establishes a qualified retirement plan, or is required to file excise, employment, alcohol, tobacco, or firearms returns, must have an EIN. A partnership, corporation, REMIC (real estate mortgage investment conduit), nonprofit organization (church, club, etc.), or farmers' cooperative must use an EIN for any tax-related purpose even if the entity does not have employees.

[2] However, do not apply for a new EIN if the existing entity only (a) changed its business name, (b) elected on Form 8832 to change the way it is taxed (or is covered by the default rules), or (c) terminated its partnership status because at least 50% of the total interests in partnership capital and profits were sold or exchanged within a 12-month period. The EIN of the terminated partnership should continue to be used. See Regulations section 301.6109-1(d)(2)(iii).

[3] Do not use the EIN of the prior business unless you became the "owner" of a corporation by acquiring its stock.

[4] However, grantor trusts that do not file using Optional Method 1 and IRA trusts that are required to file Form 990-T, Exempt Organization Business Income Tax Return, must have an EIN. For more information on grantor trusts, see the Instructions for Form 1041.

[5] A plan administrator is the person or group of persons specified as the administrator by the instrument under which the plan is operated.

[6] Entities applying to be a Qualified Intermediary (QI) need a QI-EIN even if they already have an EIN. See Rev. Proc. 2000-12.

[7] See also *Household employer* on page 4 of the instructions. **Note.** State or local agencies may need an EIN for other reasons, for example, hired employees.

[8] See *Disregarded entities* on page 4 of the instructions for details on completing Form SS-4 for an LLC.

[9] An existing corporation that is electing or revoking S corporation status should use its previously-assigned EIN.

Instructions for Form SS-4

Department of the Treasury
Internal Revenue Service

(Rev. February 2016)

Application for Employer Identification Number (EIN)
Use with Form SS-4 (Rev. January 2010)

Section references are to the Internal Revenue Code unless otherwise noted.

General Instructions

Use these instructions to complete Form SS-4, Application for Employer Identification Number (EIN). Also see *Do I Need an EIN?* on page 2 of Form SS-4.

Future Developments

For the latest information related to Form SS-4 and its instructions, such as legislation enacted after they were published, go to *www.irs.gov/ss4*.

Purpose of Form

Use Form SS-4 to apply for an EIN. An EIN is a nine-digit number (for example, 12-3456789) assigned to sole proprietors, corporations, partnerships, estates, trusts, and other entities for tax filing and reporting purposes. The information you provide on this form will establish your business tax account.

See Form SS-4PR (for Puerto Rico) for the Spanish-language version of Form SS-4.

An EIN is for use in connection with your business activities only. Don't use your EIN in place of your social security number (SSN) or individual taxpayer identification number (ITIN).

Reminders

Apply for an EIN online. For applicants in the U.S. or U.S. possessions, you can apply for and receive an EIN free of charge on IRS.gov. See *How To Apply for an EIN*, later.

File only one Form SS-4. Generally, a sole proprietor should file only one Form SS-4 and needs only one EIN, regardless of the number of businesses operated as a sole proprietorship or trade names under which a business operates. However, if a sole proprietorship incorporates or enters into a partnership, a new EIN is required. Also, each corporation in an affiliated group must have its own EIN.

For information about EINs and federal tax deposits, see Pub. 15, Pub. 51 and Pub. 80.

To ensure fair and equitable treatment for all taxpayers, EIN issuances are limited to one per responsible party, per day. For trusts, the limitation is applied to the grantor, owner, or trustor. For estates, the limitation is applied to the decedent (decedent estate) or the debtor (bankruptcy estate). This limitation is applicable to all requests for EINs whether online, telephone, fax, or mail.

How To Apply for an EIN

You can apply for an EIN online (only for applicants in the U.S. or U.S. possessions), by telephone (only for applicants outside of the U.S. or U.S. possessions), by fax, or by mail, depending on how soon you need to use the EIN. Use only one method for each entity so you don't receive more than one EIN for an entity.

Apply for an EIN online. If you have a legal residence, principal place of business, or principal office or agency in the U.S. or U.S. possessions, you can receive an EIN online and use it immediately to file a return or make a payment. Go to the IRS website at *www.irs.gov/businesses* and click on *Employer ID Numbers*.

The principal officer, general partner, grantor, owner, trustor, etc. must have a valid Taxpayer Identification Number (SSN, EIN, or ITIN) in order to use the online application. Taxpayers who apply online have an option to view, print, and save their EIN assignment notice at the end of the session. (Authorized third party designees will receive the EIN; however, the EIN assignment notice will be mailed to the applicant.)

If you have NO legal residence, principal place of business, or principal office or agency in the U.S. or U.S. possessions, you can't use the online application to obtain an EIN. Please use one of the other methods to apply.

Apply by telephone—option available to international applicants only. If you have NO legal residence, principal place of business, or principal office or agency in the U.S. or U.S. possessions, you may call 267-941-1099 (not a toll-free number), 6:00 a.m. to 11:00 p.m. (Eastern time), Monday through Friday, to obtain an EIN.

The person making the call must be authorized to receive the EIN and answer questions concerning Form SS-4. Complete the Third Party Designee section only if you want to authorize the named individual to receive the entity's EIN and answer questions about the completion of Form SS-4. The designee's authority terminates at the time the EIN is assigned and released to the designee. You must complete the signature area for the authorization to be valid.

Note. It will be helpful to complete Form SS-4 before contacting the IRS. An IRS representative will use the information from Form SS-4 to establish your account and assign you an EIN. Write the number you're given on the upper right corner of the form and sign and date it. Keep this copy for your records.

If requested by an IRS representative, mail or fax the signed Form SS-4 (including any third party designee authorization) within 24 hours to the IRS address provided by the IRS representative.

IRS no longer issues EINs by telephone for domestic taxpayers. Only international applicants can receive an EIN by telephone.

Apply by fax. Under the Fax-TIN program, you can receive your EIN by fax generally within 4 business days. Complete and fax Form SS-4 to the IRS using the appropriate fax number listed in *Where To File or Fax*, later. A long-distance charge to callers outside of the local calling area will apply. Fax-TIN numbers can only be used to apply for an EIN. The numbers may change without notice. Fax-TIN is available 24 hours a day, 7 days a week.

Be sure to provide your fax number so the IRS can fax the EIN back to you.

Apply by mail. Complete Form SS-4 at least 4 to 5 weeks before you will need an EIN. Sign and date the application and mail it to the appropriate address listed in *Where To File or Fax*, later. You will receive your EIN in the mail in approximately 4 weeks. Also see *Third Party Designee*, later.

Call 1-800-829-4933 to verify a number or to ask about the status of an application by mail.

Mar 16, 2016

Cat. No. 62736F

Form SS-4 downloaded from IRS.gov is a fillable form and, when completed, is suitable for faxing or mailing to the IRS.

Where To File or Fax

If you have a principal place of business, office or agency, or legal residence in the case of an individual, located in:	File or Fax to:
One of the 50 states or the District of Columbia	Internal Revenue Service Attn: EIN Operation Cincinnati, OH 45999 Fax: (859) 669-5760
If you have no legal residence, principal office or principal agency in any state or the District of Columbia (international/U.S. possessions)	Internal Revenue Service Attn: EIN International Operation Cincinnati, OH 45999 Fax: (859) 669-5987

How To Get Tax Help, Forms, and Publications

 Tax help for your business is available at www.irs.gov/businesses.

You can download or print all of the forms and publications you may need on www.irs.gov/formspubs. Otherwise, you can go to www.irs.gov/orderforms to place an order and have forms mailed to you. You should receive your order within 10 business days.

Related Forms and Publications

The following forms and instructions may be useful to filers of Form SS-4.
• Form 11-C, Occupational Tax and Registration Return for Wagering.
• Form 637, Application for Registration (For Certain Excise Tax Activities).
• Form 720, Quarterly Federal Excise Tax Return.
• Form 730, Monthly Tax Return for Wagers.
• Form 941, Employer's QUARTERLY Federal Tax Return.
• Form 944, Employer's ANNUAL Federal Tax Return.
• Form 990-T, Exempt Organization Business Income Tax Return.
• Instructions for Form 990-T.
• Form 1023, Application for Recognition of Exemption Under Section 501(c)(3) of the Internal Revenue Code.
• Form 1024, Application for Recognition of Exemption Under Section 501(a).
• Schedule C (Form 1040), Profit or Loss From Business (Sole Proprietorship).
• Schedule F (Form 1040), Profit or Loss From Farming.
• Instructions for Form 1041 and Schedules A, B, G, J, and K-1, U.S. Income Tax Return for Estates and Trusts.
• Form 1042, Annual Withholding Tax Return for U.S. Source Income of Foreign Persons.
• Form 1042-S, Foreign Person's U.S. Source Income Subject to Withholding.
• Instructions for Form 1065, U.S. Return of Partnership Income.
• Instructions for Form 1066, U.S. Real Estate Mortgage Investment Conduit (REMIC) Income Tax Return.
• Instructions for Form 1120, U.S. Corporation Income Tax Return.
• Form 1120S, U.S. Income Tax Return for an S Corporation.
• Form 2290, Heavy Highway Vehicle Use Tax Return.
• Form 2553, Election by a Small Business Corporation.

• Form 2848, Power of Attorney and Declaration of Representative.
• Form 8821, Tax Information Authorization.
• Form 8822-B, Change of Address or Responsible Party — Business.
• Form 8832, Entity Classification Election.
• Form 8849, Claim for Refund of Excise Taxes.

For more information about filing Form SS-4 and related issues, see:
• Pub. 15, Employer's Tax Guide.
• Pub. 51, Agricultural Employer's Tax Guide.
• Pub. 80, Federal Tax Guide for Employers in the U.S. Virgin Islands, Guam, American Samoa, and the Commonwealth of the Northern Mariana Islands.
• Pub. 538, Accounting Periods and Methods.
• Pub. 542, Corporations.
• Pub. 557, Tax-Exempt Status for Your Organization.
• Pub. 583, Starting a Business and Keeping Records.
• Pub. 966, Electronic Choices to Pay All Your Federal Taxes.
• Pub. 1635, Understanding Your EIN.

Specific Instructions

Follow the instructions for each line to expedite processing and to avoid unnecessary IRS requests for additional information. Enter "N/A" on the lines that don't apply.

Line 1. Legal name of entity (or individual) for whom the EIN is being requested. Enter the legal name of the entity (or individual) applying for the EIN exactly as it appears on the social security card, charter, or other applicable legal document. An entry is required.

Individuals. Enter your first name, middle initial, and last name. If you're a sole proprietor, enter your individual name, not your business name. Enter your business name on line 2. Don't use abbreviations or nicknames on line 1.

Trusts. Enter the name of the trust as it appears on the trust instrument.

Estate of a decedent. Enter the name of the estate. For an estate that has no legal name, enter the name of the decedent followed by "Estate."

Partnerships. Enter the legal name of the partnership as it appears in the partnership agreement.

Corporations. Enter the corporate name as it appears in the corporate charter or other legal document creating it.

Plan administrators. Enter the name of the plan administrator. A plan administrator who already has an EIN should use that number.

Line 2. Trade name of business. Enter the trade name of the business if different from the legal name. The trade name is the "doing business as" (DBA) name.

 Use the full legal name shown on line 1 on all tax returns filed for the entity. (However, if you enter a trade name on line 2 and choose to use the trade name instead of the legal name, enter the trade name on all returns you file.) To prevent processing delays and errors, use only the legal name (or the trade name) on all tax returns.

Line 3. Executor, administrator, trustee, "care of" name. For trusts, enter the name of the trustee. For estates, enter the name of the executor, administrator, or other fiduciary. If the entity applying has a designated person to receive tax information, enter that person's name as the "care of" person. Enter the individual's first name, middle initial, and last name.

Lines 4a–b. Mailing address. Enter the mailing address for the entity's correspondence. If the entity's address is outside the United States or its possessions, you must enter the city, province or state, postal code, and the name of the country. Don't abbreviate the country name. If line 3 is completed, enter the address for the executor, trustee, or "care of" person. Generally, this address will be used on all tax returns.

If the entity is filing the Form SS-4 only to obtain an EIN for the Form 8832, use the same address where you would like to have the acceptance or nonacceptance letter sent.

 File Form 8822-B to report any subsequent changes to the entity's mailing address.

Lines 5a–b. Street address. Provide the entity's physical address only if different from its mailing address shown in lines 4a–b. Don't enter a P.O. box number here. If the entity's address is outside the United States or its possessions, you must enter the city, province or state, postal code, and the name of the country. Don't abbreviate the country name.

Line 6. County and state where principal business is located. Enter the entity's primary physical location.

Lines 7a–b. Name of responsible party. Enter the full name (first name, middle initial, last name, if applicable) and SSN, ITIN, or EIN of the entity's responsible party, as defined later.

Responsible party defined. For entities with shares or interests traded on a public exchange, or which are registered with the Securities and Exchange Commission, "responsible party" is (a) the principal officer, if the business is a corporation; (b) a general partner, if a partnership; (c) the owner of an entity that is disregarded as separate from its owner (disregarded entities owned by a corporation enter the corporation's name and EIN); or (d) a grantor, owner, or trustor, if a trust. For tax-exempt organizations, the "responsible party" is commonly the same as the "principal officer" as defined in the Form 990 instructions. For government entities, the "responsible party" is generally the individual in a position to legally bind the particular government entity.

For all other entities, "responsible party" is the individual who has a level of control over, or entitlement to, the funds or assets in the entity that, as a practical matter, enables the individual, directly or indirectly, to control, manage, or direct the entity and the disposition of its funds and assets. The ability to fund the entity or the entitlement to the property of the entity alone, however, without any corresponding authority to control, manage, or direct the entity (such as in the case of a minor child beneficiary), doesn't cause the individual to be a responsible party.

 File Form 8822-B to report any subsequent changes to responsible party information.

If the responsible party is an alien individual with a previously assigned ITIN, enter the ITIN in the space provided and submit a copy of an official identifying document. If necessary, complete Form W-7, Application for IRS Individual Taxpayer Identification Number, to obtain an ITIN.

You must enter an SSN, ITIN, or EIN on line 7b unless the only reason you're applying for an EIN is to make an entity classification election (see Regulations sections 301.7701-1 through 301.7701-3) and you're a nonresident alien or other foreign entity with no effectively connected income from sources within the United States.

Lines 8a–c. Limited liability company (LLC) information. An LLC is an entity organized under the laws of a state or foreign country as a limited liability company. For federal tax purposes, an LLC may be treated as a partnership or corporation or be disregarded as an entity separate from its owner.

By default, a domestic LLC with only one member is disregarded as an entity separate from its owner and must include all of its income and expenses on the owner's tax return (for example, Schedule C (Form 1040)). For more information on single-member LLCs, see *Disregarded entities*, later.

Also by default, a domestic LLC with two or more members is treated as a partnership. A domestic LLC may file Form 8832 to avoid either default classification and elect to be classified as an association taxable as a corporation. For more information on entity classifications (including the rules for foreign entities), see Form 8832 and its instructions.

If the answer to line 8a is "Yes," enter the number of LLC members. If the LLC is owned solely by an individual and his or her spouse in a community property state and they choose to treat the entity as a disregarded entity, enter "1" on line 8b.

 Don't file Form 8832 if the LLC accepts the default classifications above. If the LLC timely files Form 2553, it will be treated as a corporation as of the effective date of the S corporation election as long as it meets all other requirements to qualify as an S corporation. The LLC doesn't need to file Form 8832 in addition to Form 2553. See the Instructions for Form 2553.

Line 9a. Type of entity. Check the box that best describes the type of entity applying for the EIN. If you're an alien individual with an ITIN previously assigned to you, enter the ITIN in place of a requested SSN.

 This isn't an election for a tax classification of an entity. See Disregarded entities, *later.*

Sole proprietor. Check this box if you file Schedule C, or Schedule F (Form 1040) and have a qualified plan, or are required to file excise, employment, alcohol, tobacco, or firearms returns, or are a payer of gambling winnings. Enter your SSN or ITIN in the space provided. If you're a nonresident alien with no effectively connected income from sources within the United States, you don't need to enter an SSN or ITIN.

Corporation. This box is for any corporation other than a personal service corporation. If you check this box, enter the income tax form number to be filed by the entity in the space provided.

 If you entered "1120S" after the Corporation checkbox, the corporation must file Form 2553 no later than the 15th day of the 3rd month of the tax year the election to become an S corporation is to take effect. Until Form 2553 has been received and approved, you will be considered a Form 1120 filer. See the Instructions for Form 2553.

Personal service corporation. Check this box if the entity is a personal service corporation. An entity is a personal service corporation for a tax year only if:
• The principal activity of the entity during the testing period (generally the prior tax year) for the tax year is the performance of personal services substantially by employee-owners, and
• The employee-owners own at least 10% of the fair market value of the outstanding stock in the entity on the last day of the testing period.

Personal services include performance of services in such fields as accounting, actuarial science, architecture, consulting, engineering, health (including veterinary services), law, and the performing arts. For more information about personal service corporations, see the Instructions for Form 1120 and Pub. 542.

 If the corporation is recently formed, the testing period begins on the first day of its tax year and ends on the earlier of the last day of its tax year, or the last day of the calendar year in which its tax year begins.

Other nonprofit organization. Check the *Other nonprofit organization* box if the nonprofit organization is other than a church or church-controlled organization and specify the type of nonprofit organization (for example, an educational organization).

 If the organization also seeks tax-exempt status, you must file either Form 1023 (or Form 1023-EZ) or Form 1024. See Pub. 557 for more information.

Instr. for Form SS-4 (Rev. 2-2016) -3-

If the organization is covered by a group exemption letter, enter the four-digit group exemption number (GEN) in the last entry. (Don't confuse the GEN with the nine-digit EIN.) If you don't know the GEN, contact the parent organization. See Pub. 557 for more information about group exemption letters.

If the organization is a section 527 political organization, check the box for *Other nonprofit organization* and specify "Section 527 organization" in the space to the right. To be recognized as exempt from tax, a section 527 political organization must electronically file Form 8871, Political Organization Notice of Section 527 Status, within 24 hours of the date on which the organization was established. The organization may also have to file Form 8872, Political Organization Report of Contributions and Expenditures. Go to *www.irs.gov/polorgs* for more information.

Plan administrator. If the plan administrator is an individual, enter the plan administrator's taxpayer identification number (TIN) in the space provided.

REMIC. Check this box if the entity has elected to be treated as a real estate mortgage investment conduit (REMIC). See the Instructions for Form 1066 for more information.

State/local government. State and local governments generally have the characteristics of a government, such as powers of taxation, law enforcement, and civil authority. If you're unsure whether or not your organization is a government, search "Is My Entity a Government Entity?" at *www.irs.gov* for clarification.

Federal government/military. The federal government is made up of the Executive, Legislative, and Judicial branches, as well as independent federal agencies. Unions, VFW organizations, and political organizations aren't federal agencies.

Other. If not specifically listed, check the box for *Other*, enter the type of entity and the type of return, if any, that will be filed (for example, "Common trust fund, Form 1065" or "Created a pension plan"). Don't enter "N/A." If you're an alien individual applying for an EIN, see the instructions for *Lines 7a-b*.
• **Household employer.** If you're an individual that will employ someone to provide services in your household, check the box *Other* and enter "Household employer" and your SSN. If you're a trust that qualifies as a household employer, you don't need a separate EIN for reporting tax information relating to household employees; use the EIN of the trust.
• **Household employer agent.** If you're an agent of a household employer that is a disabled individual or other welfare recipient receiving home care services through a state or local program, check the box *Other* and enter "Household employer agent." For more information, see Rev. Proc. 84-33 and Rev. Proc. 2013-39. If you're a state or local government, also check the box for state/local government.
• **QSub.** For a qualified subchapter S subsidiary (QSub) check the box *Other* and specify "QSub."
• **Withholding agent.** If you're a withholding agent required to file Form 1042, check the box *Other* and enter "Withholding agent."

Disregarded entities. A disregarded entity is an eligible entity that is disregarded as separate from its owner for federal income tax purposes. Disregarded entities include single-member limited liability companies (LLCs) that are disregarded as separate from their owners, qualified subchapter S subsidiaries (qualified subsidiaries of an S corporation), and certain qualified foreign entities. See the Instructions for Form 8832 and Regulations section 301.7701-3 for more information on domestic and foreign disregarded entities.

The disregarded entity is required to use its name and EIN for reporting and payment of employment taxes. A disregarded entity is also required to use its name and EIN to register for excise tax activities on Form 637; pay and report excise taxes reported on Forms 720, 730, 2290, and 11-C; and claim any refunds, credits, and payments on Form 8849. See the instructions for the employment and excise tax returns for more information.

Complete Form SS-4 for disregarded entities as follows.
• If a disregarded entity is filing Form SS-4 to obtain an EIN because it is required to report and pay employment and excise taxes, or for non-federal purposes such as a state requirement, check the box *Other* for line 9a and write "Disregarded entity" (or "Disregarded entity-sole proprietorship" if the owner of the disregarded entity is an individual).
• If the disregarded entity is requesting an EIN for purposes of filing Form 8832 to elect classification as an association taxable as a corporation, or Form 2553 to elect S corporation status, check the box *Corporation* for line 9a and write "Single-member" and the form number of the return that will be filed (Form 1120 or 1120S).
• If the disregarded entity is requesting an EIN because it has acquired one or more additional owners and its classification has changed to partnership under the default rules of Regulations section 301.7701-3(f), check the box *Partnership* for line 9a.

Line 10. Reason for applying. Check only one box. Don't enter "N/A." A selection is required.

Started new business. Check this box if you're starting a new business that requires an EIN. If you check this box, enter the type of business being started. Don't apply if you already have an EIN and are only adding another place of business.

Hired employees. Check this box if the existing business is requesting an EIN because it has hired or is hiring employees and is therefore required to file employment tax returns. Don't apply if you already have an EIN and are only hiring employees. For information on employment taxes (for example, for family members), see Pub. 15, Pub. 51, or Pub. 80.

 You must make electronic deposits of all depository taxes (such as employment tax, excise tax, and corporate income tax) using EFTPS. See Pub. 15, Pub. 51, Pub. 80, and Pub. 966.

Banking purpose. Check this box if you're requesting an EIN for banking purposes only, and enter the banking purpose (for example, a bowling league for depositing dues or an investment club for dividend and interest reporting).

Changed type of organization. Check this box if the business is changing its type of organization. For example, the business was a sole proprietorship and has been incorporated or has become a partnership. If you check this box, specify in the space provided (including available space immediately below) the type of change made. For example, "From sole proprietorship to partnership."

Purchased going business. Check this box if you purchased an existing business. Don't use the former owner's EIN unless you became the "owner" of a corporation by acquiring its stock.

Created a trust. Check this box if you created a trust, and enter the type of trust created. For example, indicate if the trust is a nonexempt charitable trust or a split-interest trust.

Exception. Don't file this form for certain grantor-type trusts. The trustee doesn't need an EIN for the trust if the trustee furnishes the name and TIN of the grantor/owner and the address of the trust to all payers. However, grantor trusts that don't file using Optional Method 1 and IRA trusts that are required to file Form 990-T must have an EIN. For more information on grantor trusts, see the Instructions for Form 1041.

 Don't check this box if you're applying for a trust EIN when a new pension plan is established. Check the Created a pension plan box.

Created a pension plan. Check this box if you have created a pension plan and need an EIN for reporting purposes. Also, enter the type of plan in the space provided. For more information about pension plans, visit IRS.gov and enter "Types of retirement plans" in the search box.

Check this box if you're applying for a trust EIN when a new pension plan is established. In addition, check the Other box on line 9a and write "Created a pension plan" in the space provided.

Other. Check this box if you're requesting an EIN for any other reason; and enter the reason. For example, a newly-formed state government entity should enter "Newly-formed state government entity" in the space provided.

Line 11. Date business started or acquired. If you're starting a new business, enter the starting date of the business. If the business you acquired is already operating, enter the date you acquired the business. For foreign applicants, this is the date you began or acquired a business in the United States. If you're changing the form of ownership of your business, enter the date the new ownership entity began. Trusts should enter the date the trust was funded or the date that the trust was required to obtain an EIN under Regulations section 301.6109-1(a)(2). Estates should enter the date of death of the decedent whose name appears on line 1 or the date when the estate was legally funded.

Line 12. Closing month of accounting year. Enter the last month of your accounting year or tax year. An accounting or tax year is usually 12 consecutive months, either a calendar year or a fiscal year (including a period of 52 or 53 weeks). A calendar year is 12 consecutive months ending on December 31. A fiscal year is either 12 consecutive months ending on the last day of any month other than December or a 52-53 week year. For more information on accounting periods, see Pub. 538.

Individuals. Your tax year generally will be a calendar year.

Partnerships. Partnerships must adopt one of the following tax years.
- The tax year of the majority of its partners.
- The tax year common to all of its principal partners.
- The tax year that results in the least aggregate deferral of income.
- In certain cases, some other tax year.

See the Instructions for Form 1065 for more information.

REMICs. REMICs must have a calendar year as their tax year.

Personal service corporations. A personal service corporation generally must adopt a calendar year unless it meets one of the following requirements.
- It can establish a business purpose for having a different tax year.
- It elects under section 444 to have a tax year other than a calendar year.

Trusts. Generally, a trust must adopt a calendar year except for the following trusts.
- Tax-exempt trusts.
- Charitable trusts.
- Grantor-owned trusts.

Line 13. Highest number of employees expected in the next 12 months. Complete each box by entering the number (including zero (-0-)) of *Agricultural, Household,* or *Other* employees expected by the applicant in the next 12 months.

If no employees are expected, skip line 14.

Line 14. Do you want to file Form 944? If you expect your employment tax liability to be $1,000 or less in a full calendar year, you're eligible to file Form 944 annually (once each year) instead of filing Form 941 quarterly (every three months). Your employment tax liability generally will be $1,000 or less if you expect to pay $4,000 or less in total wages subject to social security and Medicare taxes and federal income tax withholding. If you qualify and want to file Form 944 instead of Forms 941, check the box on line 14. If you don't check the box, then you must file Form 941 for every quarter.

 For employers in the U.S. possessions, generally, if you pay $6,536 or less in wages subject to social security and Medicare taxes, you're likely to pay $1,000 or less in employment taxes.

For more information on employment taxes, see Pub. 15, Pub. 51, or Pub. 80.

Line 15. First date wages or annuities were paid. If the business has employees, enter the date on which the business began to pay wages or annuities. For foreign applicants, this is the date you began to pay wages in the United States. If the business doesn't plan to have employees, enter "N/A."

Withholding agent. Enter the date you began or will begin to pay income (including annuities) to a nonresident alien. This also applies to individuals who are required to file Form 1042 to report alimony paid to a nonresident alien. For foreign applicants, this is the date you began or will begin to pay income (including annuities) to a nonresident alien in the United States.

Line 16. Check the one box on line 16 that best describes the principal activity of the applicant's business. Check the box *Other* (and specify the applicant's principal activity) if none of the listed boxes applies. You must check a box.

Construction. Check this box if the applicant is engaged in erecting buildings or engineering projects (for example, streets, highways, bridges, and tunnels). The term "construction" also includes special trade contractors (for example, plumbing, HVAC, electrical, carpentry, concrete, excavation, etc. contractors).

Real estate. Check this box if the applicant is engaged in renting or leasing real estate to others; managing, selling, buying, or renting real estate for others; or providing related real estate services (for example, appraisal services). Also check this box for mortgage real estate investment trusts (REITs). Mortgage REITs are engaged in issuing shares of funds consisting primarily of portfolios of real estate mortgage assets with gross income of the trust solely derived from interest earned.

Rental & leasing. Check this box if the applicant is engaged in providing tangible goods such as autos, computers, consumer goods, or industrial machinery and equipment to customers in return for a periodic rental or lease payment. Also check this box for equity real estate investment trusts (REITs). Equity REITs are engaged in issuing shares of funds consisting primarily of portfolios of real estate assets with gross income of the trust derived from renting real property.

Manufacturing. Check this box if the applicant is engaged in the mechanical, physical, or chemical transformation of materials, substances, or components into new products. The assembling of component parts of manufactured products is also considered to be manufacturing.

Transportation & warehousing. Check this box if the applicant provides transportation of passengers or cargo, warehousing or storage of goods; scenic or sight-seeing transportation, or support activities related to transportation.

Finance & insurance. Check this box if the applicant is engaged in transactions involving the creation, liquidation, or change of ownership of financial assets and/or facilitating such financial transactions; underwriting annuities/insurance policies; facilitating such underwriting by selling insurance policies; or by providing other insurance or employee-benefit related services.

Health care & social assistance. Check this box if the applicant is engaged in providing physical, medical, or psychiatric care; or providing social assistance activities such as youth centers, adoption agencies, individual/family services, temporary shelters, daycare, etc.

Accommodation & food services. Check this box if the applicant is engaged in providing customers with lodging, meal preparation, snacks, or beverages for immediate consumption.

Wholesale-agent/broker. Check this box if the applicant is engaged in arranging for the purchase or sale of goods owned by others or purchasing goods on a commission basis for goods traded in the wholesale market, usually between businesses.

Wholesale-other. Check this box if the applicant is engaged in selling goods in the wholesale market generally to other businesses for resale on their own account, goods used in production, or capital or durable nonconsumer goods.

Retail. Check this box if the applicant is engaged in selling merchandise to the general public from a fixed store; by direct, mail-order, or electronic sales; or by using vending machines.

Other. Check this box if the applicant is engaged in an activity not described above. Describe the applicant's principal business activity in the space provided.

Line 17. Use line 17 to describe the applicant's principal line of business in more detail. For example, if you checked the *Construction* box on line 16, enter additional detail such as "General contractor for residential buildings" on line 17. An entry is required. For mortgage REITs, indicate mortgage REIT; and for equity REITs, indicate what type of real property is the principal type (residential REIT, nonresidential REIT, miniwarehouse REIT).

Line 18. Check the applicable box to indicate whether or not the applicant entity applying for an EIN was issued one previously.

Third Party Designee. Complete this section only if you want to authorize the named individual to receive the entity's EIN and answer questions about the completion of Form SS-4. The designee's authority terminates at the time the EIN is assigned and released to the designee. You must complete the signature area for the authorization to be valid.

Signature. When required, the application must be signed by (a) the individual, if the applicant is an individual; (b) the president, vice president, or other principal officer, if the applicant is a corporation; (c) a responsible and duly authorized member or officer having knowledge of its affairs, if the applicant is a partnership, government entity, or other unincorporated organization; or (d) the fiduciary, if the applicant is a trust or an estate. Foreign applicants may have any duly-authorized person (for example, division manager) sign Form SS-4.

Privacy Act and Paperwork Reduction Act Notice. We ask for the information on this form to carry out the Internal Revenue laws of the United States. We need it to comply with section 6109 and the regulations thereunder, which generally require the inclusion of an employer identification number (EIN) on certain returns, statements, or other documents filed with the Internal Revenue Service. If your entity is required to obtain an EIN, you're required to provide all of the information requested on this form. Information on this form may be used to determine which federal tax returns you're required to file and to provide you with related forms and publications.

We disclose this form to the Social Security Administration (SSA) for their use in determining compliance with applicable laws. We may give this information to the Department of Justice for use in civil and/or criminal litigation, and to cities, states, the District of Columbia, and U.S. commonwealths and possessions for use in administering their tax laws. We may also disclose this information to other countries under a tax treaty, to federal and state agencies to enforce federal nontax criminal laws, and to federal law enforcement and intelligence agencies to combat terrorism.

We will be unable to issue an EIN to you unless you provide all of the requested information that applies to your entity. Providing false information could subject you to penalties.

You're not required to provide the information requested on a form that is subject to the Paperwork Reduction Act unless the form displays a valid OMB control number. Books or records relating to a form or its instructions must be retained as long as their contents may become material in the administration of any Internal Revenue law. Generally, tax returns and return information are confidential, as required by section 6103.

The time needed to complete and file this form will vary depending on individual circumstances. The estimated average time is:

Recordkeeping	8 hr., 36 min.
Learning about the law or the form	42 min.
Preparing, copying, assembling, and sending the form to the IRS	52 min.

If you have comments concerning the accuracy of these time estimates or suggestions for making this form simpler, we would be happy to hear from you. You can send your comments from *www.irs.gov/formspubs*. Click on *More Information* and then click on *Give us feedback*. Or you can write to the Internal Revenue Service, Tax Forms and Publications Division, 1111 Constitution Ave. NW, IR-6526, Washington, DC 20224. Don't send Form SS-4 to this address. Instead, see *Where To File or Fax*, earlier.

Form **8832**
(Rev. December 2013)

Department of the Treasury
Internal Revenue Service

Entity Classification Election

OMB No. 1545-1516

▶ Information about Form 8832 and its instructions is at *www.irs.gov/form8832.*

Type or Print	Name of eligible entity making election	Employer identification number
	Number, street, and room or suite no. If a P.O. box, see instructions.	
	City or town, state, and ZIP code. If a foreign address, enter city, province or state, postal code and country. Follow the country's practice for entering the postal code.	

▶ Check if: ☐ Address change ☐ Late classification relief sought under Revenue Procedure 2009-41
☐ Relief for a late change of entity classification election sought under Revenue Procedure 2010-32

Part I   **Election Information**

1   **Type of election** (see instructions):

a   ☐ Initial classification by a newly-formed entity. Skip lines 2a and 2b and go to line 3.
b   ☐ Change in current classification. Go to line 2a.

2a   Has the eligible entity previously filed an entity election that had an effective date within the last 60 months?

☐ **Yes.** Go to line 2b.
☐ **No.** Skip line 2b and go to line 3.

2b   Was the eligible entity's prior election an initial classification election by a newly formed entity that was effective on the date of formation?

☐ **Yes.** Go to line 3.
☐ **No.** Stop here. You generally are not currently eligible to make the election (see instructions).

3   Does the eligible entity have more than one owner?

☐ **Yes.** You can elect to be classified as a partnership or an association taxable as a corporation. Skip line 4 and go to line 5.

☐ **No.** You can elect to be classified as an association taxable as a corporation or to be disregarded as a separate entity. Go to line 4.

4   If the eligible entity has only one owner, provide the following information:

a   Name of owner ▶ _____
b   Identifying number of owner ▶ _____

5   If the eligible entity is owned by one or more affiliated corporations that file a consolidated return, provide the name and employer identification number of the parent corporation:

a   Name of parent corporation ▶ _____
b   Employer identification number ▶ _____

For Paperwork Reduction Act Notice, see instructions.   Cat. No. 22598R   Form **8832** (Rev. 12-2013)

Form 8832 (Rev. 12-2013)   Page **2**

Part I	**Election Information** (Continued)

6   Type of entity (see instructions):

a ☐ A domestic eligible entity electing to be classified as an association taxable as a corporation.

b ☐ A domestic eligible entity electing to be classified as a partnership.

c ☐ A domestic eligible entity with a single owner electing to be disregarded as a separate entity.

d ☐ A foreign eligible entity electing to be classified as an association taxable as a corporation.

e ☐ A foreign eligible entity electing to be classified as a partnership.

f ☐ A foreign eligible entity with a single owner electing to be disregarded as a separate entity.

7   If the eligible entity is created or organized in a foreign jurisdiction, provide the foreign country of organization ▶ _____

8   Election is to be effective beginning (month, day, year) (see instructions) . . . . ▶ _____

9 Name and title of contact person whom the IRS may call for more information	**10** Contact person's telephone number

Consent Statement and Signature(s) (see instructions)

Under penalties of perjury, I (we) declare that I (we) consent to the election of the above-named entity to be classified as indicated above, and that I (we) have examined this election and consent statement, and to the best of my (our) knowledge and belief, this election and consent statement are true, correct, and complete. If I am an officer, manager, or member signing for the entity, I further declare under penalties of perjury that I am authorized to make the election on its behalf.

Signature(s)	**Date**	**Title**

Form **8832** (Rev. 12-2013)

Form 8832 (Rev. 12-2013)

Part II   **Late Election Relief**

11   Provide the explanation as to why the entity classification election was not filed on time (see instructions).

_____

_____

_____

_____

_____

_____

_____

_____

Under penalties of perjury, I (we) declare that I (we) have examined this election, including accompanying documents, and, to the best of my (our) knowledge and belief, the election contains all the relevant facts relating to the election, and such facts are true, correct, and complete. I (we) further declare that I (we) have personal knowledge of the facts and circumstances related to the election. I (we) further declare that the elements required for relief in Section 4.01 of Revenue Procedure 2009-41 have been satisfied.

Signature(s)	Date	Title

General Instructions

Section references are to the Internal Revenue Code unless otherwise noted.

Future Developments

For the latest information about developments related to Form 8832 and its instructions, such as legislation enacted after they were published, go to *www.irs.gov/form8832*.

What's New

For entities formed on or after July 1, 2013, the Croatian Dionicko Drustvo will always be treated as a corporation. See Notice 2013-44, 2013-29, I.R.B. 62 for more information.

Purpose of Form

An eligible entity uses Form 8832 to elect how it will be classified for federal tax purposes, as a corporation, a partnership, or an entity disregarded as separate from its owner. An eligible entity is classified for federal tax purposes under the default rules described below unless it files Form 8832 or Form 2553, Election by a Small Business Corporation. See *Who Must File* below.

The IRS will use the information entered on this form to establish the entity's filing and reporting requirements for federal tax purposes.

Note. An entity must file Form 2553 if making an election under section 1362(a) to be an S corporation

 A new eligible entity should not file Form 8832 if it will be using its default classification (see Default Rules *below).*

Eligible entity. An eligible entity is a business entity that is not included in items 1, or 3 through 9, under the definition of **corporation** provided under *Definitions*. Eligible entities include limited liability companies (LLCs) and partnerships.

Generally, corporations are not eligible entities. However, the following types of corporations are treated as eligible entities:

1. An eligible entity that previously elected to be an association taxable as a corporation by filing Form 8832. An entity that elects to be classified as a corporation by filing Form 8832 can make another election to change its classification (see the *60-month limitation rule* discussed below in the instructions for lines 2a and 2b).

2. A foreign eligible entity that became an association taxable as a corporation under the foreign default rule described below.

Default Rules

Existing entity default rule. Certain domestic and foreign entities that were in existence before January 1, 1997, and have an established federal tax classification generally do not need to make an election to continue that classification. If an existing entity decides to change its classification, it may do so subject to the 60-month limitation rule. See the instructions for lines 2a and 2b. See Regulations sections 301.7701-3(b)(3) and 301.7701-3(h)(2) for more details.

Domestic default rule. Unless an election is made on Form 8832, a domestic eligible entity is:

1. A partnership if it has two or more members.

2. Disregarded as an entity separate from its owner if it has a single owner.

A change in the number of members of an eligible entity classified as an **association** (defined below) does not affect the entity's classification. However, an eligible entity classified as a partnership will become a disregarded entity when the entity's membership is reduced to one member and a disregarded entity will be classified as a partnership when the entity has more than one member.

Foreign default rule. Unless an election is made on Form 8832, a foreign eligible entity is:

1. A partnership if it has two or more members and at least one member does not have limited liability.

2. An association taxable as a corporation if all members have limited liability.

3. Disregarded as an entity separate from its owner if it has a single owner that does not have limited liability.

However, if a qualified foreign entity (as defined in section 3.02 of Rev. Proc. 2010-32) files a valid election to be classified as a partnership based on the reasonable assumption that it had two or more owners as of the effective date of the election, and the qualified entity is later determined to have a single owner, the IRS will deem the election to be an election to be classified as a disregarded entity provided:

1. The qualified entity's owner and purported owners file amended returns that are consistent with the treatment of the entity as a disregarded entity;

2. The amended returns are filed before the close of the period of limitations on assessments under section 6501(a) for the relevant tax year; and

3. The corrected Form 8832, with the box checked entitled: Relief for a late change of entity classification election sought under Revenue Procedure 2010-32, is filed and attached to the amended tax return.

Also, if the qualified foreign entity (as defined in section 3.02 of Rev. Proc. 2010-32) files a valid election to be classified as a disregarded entity based on the reasonable assumption that it had a single owner as of the effective date of the election, and the qualified entity is later determined to have two or more owners, the IRS will deem the election to be an election to be classified as a partnership provided:

1. The qualified entity files information returns and the actual owners file original or amended returns consistent with the treatment of the entity as a partnership;

2. The amended returns are filed before the close of the period of limitations on assessments under section 6501(a) for the relevant tax year; and

3. The corrected Form 8832, with the box checked entitled: Relief for a late change of entity classification election sought under Revenue Procedure 2010-32, is filed and attached to the amended tax returns. See Rev. Proc. 2010-32, 2010-36 I.R.B. 320 for details.

Definitions

Association. For purposes of this form, an association is an eligible entity taxable as a corporation by election or, for foreign eligible entities, under the default rules (see Regulations section 301.7701-3).

Business entity. A business entity is any entity recognized for federal tax purposes that is not properly classified as a trust under Regulations section 301.7701-4 or otherwise subject to special treatment under the Code regarding the entity's classification. See Regulations section 301.7701-2(a).

Corporation. For federal tax purposes, a corporation is any of the following:

1. A business entity organized under a federal or state statute, or under a statute of a federally recognized Indian tribe, if the statute describes or refers to the entity as incorporated or as a corporation, body corporate, or body politic.

2. An association (as determined under Regulations section 301.7701-3).

3. A business entity organized under a state statute, if the statute describes or refers to the entity as a joint-stock company or joint-stock association.

4. An insurance company.

5. A state-chartered business entity conducting banking activities, if any of its deposits are insured under the Federal Deposit Insurance Act, as amended, 12 U.S. C. 1811 et seq., or a similar federal statute.

6. A business entity wholly owned by a state or any political subdivision thereof, or a business entity wholly owned by a foreign government or any other entity described in Regulations section 1.892-2T.

7. A business entity that is taxable as a corporation under a provision of the Code other than section 7701(a)(3).

8. A foreign business entity listed on page 7. See Regulations section 301.7701-2(b)(8) for any exceptions and inclusions to items on this list and for any revisions made to this list since these instructions were printed.

9. An entity created or organized under the laws of more than one jurisdiction (business entities with multiple charters) if the entity is treated as a corporation with respect to any one of the jurisdictions. See Regulations section 301.7701-2(b)(9) for examples.

Disregarded entity. A disregarded entity is an eligible entity that is treated as an entity not separate from its single owner for income tax purposes. A "disregarded entity" is treated as separate from its owner for:

• Employment tax purposes, effective for wages paid on or after January 1, 2009; and

• Excise taxes reported on Forms 720, 730, 2290, 11-C, or 8849, effective for excise taxes reported and paid after December 31, 2007.

See the employment tax and excise tax return instructions for more information.

Limited liability. A member of a foreign eligible entity has limited liability if the member has no personal liability for any debts of or claims against the entity by reason of being a member. This determination is based solely on the statute or law under which the entity is organized (and, if relevant, the entity's organizational documents). A member has personal liability if the creditors of the entity may seek satisfaction of all or any part of the debts or claims against the entity from the member as such. A member has personal liability even if the member makes an agreement under which another person (whether or not a member of the entity) assumes that liability or agrees to indemnify that member for that liability.

Partnership. A partnership is a business entity that has at least two members and is not a corporation as defined above under *Corporation.*

Who Must File

File this form for an eligible entity that is one of the following:

• A domestic entity electing to be classified as an association taxable as a corporation.

• A domestic entity electing to change its current classification (even if it is currently classified under the default rule).

• A foreign entity that has more than one owner, all owners having limited liability, electing to be classified as a partnership.

• A foreign entity that has at least one owner that does not have limited liability, electing to be classified as an association taxable as a corporation.

• A foreign entity with a single owner having limited liability, electing to be an entity disregarded as an entity separate from its owner.

• A foreign entity electing to change its current classification (even if it is currently classified under the default rule).

Do not file this form for an eligible entity that is:

• Tax-exempt under section 501(a);

• A real estate investment trust (REIT), as defined in section 856; or

• Electing to be classified as an S corporation. An eligible entity that timely files Form 2553 to elect classification as an S corporation and meets all other requirements to qualify as an S corporation is deemed to have made an election under Regulations section 301.7701-3(c)(v) to be classified as an association taxable as a corporation.

All three of these entities are deemed to have made an election to be classified as an association.

Effect of Election

The federal tax treatment of elective changes in classification as described in Regulations section 301.7701-3(g)(1) is summarized as follows:

• If an eligible entity classified as a partnership elects to be classified as an association, it is deemed that the partnership contributes all of its assets and liabilities to the association in exchange for stock in the association, and immediately thereafter, the partnership liquidates by distributing the stock of the association to its partners.

• If an eligible entity classified as an association elects to be classified as a partnership, it is deemed that the association distributes all of its assets and liabilities to its shareholders in liquidation of the association, and immediately thereafter, the shareholders contribute all of the distributed assets and liabilities to a newly formed partnership.

• If an eligible entity classified as an association elects to be disregarded as an entity separate from its owner, it is deemed that the association distributes all of its assets and liabilities to its single owner in liquidation of the association.

• If an eligible entity that is disregarded as an entity separate from its owner elects to be classified as an association, the owner of the eligible entity is deemed to have contributed all of the assets and liabilities of the entity to the association in exchange for the stock of the association.

Note. For information on the federal tax consequences of elective changes in classification, see Regulations section 301.7701-3(g).

When To File

Generally, an election specifying an eligible entity's classification cannot take effect more than 75 days prior to the date the election is filed, nor can it take effect later than 12 months after the date the election is filed. An eligible entity may be eligible for late election relief in certain circumstances. For more information, see *Late Election Relief,* later.

Where To File

File Form 8832 with the Internal Revenue Service Center for your state listed later.

In addition, attach a copy of Form 8832 to the entity's federal tax or information return for the tax year of the election. If the entity is not required to file a return for that year, a copy of its Form 8832 must be attached to the federal tax returns of all direct or indirect owners of the entity for the tax year of the owner that includes the date on which the election took effect. An indirect owner of the electing entity does not have to attach a copy of the Form 8832 to its tax return if an entity in which it has an interest is already filing a copy of the Form 8832 with its return. Failure to attach a copy of Form 8832 will not invalidate an otherwise valid election, but penalties may be assessed against persons who are required to, but do not, attach Form 8832.

Each member of the entity is required to file the member's return consistent with the entity election. Penalties apply to returns filed inconsistent with the entity's election.

If the entity's principal business, office, or agency is located in:	Use the following Internal Revenue Service Center address:
Connecticut, Delaware, District of Columbia, Florida, Illinois, Indiana, Kentucky, Maine, Maryland, Massachusetts, Michigan, New Hampshire, New Jersey, New York, North Carolina, Ohio, Pennsylvania, Rhode Island, South Carolina, Vermont, Virginia, West Virginia, Wisconsin	Cincinnati, OH 45999

If the entity's principal business, office, or agency is located in:	Use the following Internal Revenue Service Center address:
Alabama, Alaska, Arizona, Arkansas, California, Colorado, Georgia, Hawaii, Idaho, Iowa, Kansas, Louisiana, Minnesota, Mississippi, Missouri, Montana, Nebraska, Nevada, New Mexico, North Dakota, Oklahoma, Oregon, South Dakota, Tennessee, Texas, Utah, Washington, Wyoming	Ogden, UT 84201
A foreign country or U.S. possession	Ogden, UT 84201-0023

Note. Also attach a copy to the entity's federal income tax return for the tax year of the election.

Acceptance or Nonacceptance of Election

The service center will notify the eligible entity at the address listed on Form 8832 if its election is accepted or not accepted. The entity should generally receive a determination on its election within 60 days after it has filed Form 8832.

Care should be exercised to ensure that the IRS receives the election. If the entity is not notified of acceptance or nonacceptance of its election within 60 days of the date of filing, take follow-up action by calling 1-800-829-0115, or by sending a letter to the service center to inquire about its status. Send any such letter by certified or registered mail via the U.S. Postal Service, or equivalent type of delivery by a designated private delivery service (see Notice 2004-83, 2004-52 I.R.B. 1030 (or its successor)).

If the IRS questions whether Form 8832 was filed, an acceptable proof of filing is:

• A certified or registered mail receipt (timely postmarked) from the U.S. Postal Service, or its equivalent from a designated private delivery service;

• Form 8832 with an accepted stamp;

• Form 8832 with a stamped IRS received date; or

• An IRS letter stating that Form 8832 has been accepted.

Specific Instructions

Name. Enter the name of the eligible entity electing to be classified.

Employer identification number (EIN). Show the EIN of the eligible entity electing to be classified.

Do not put "Applied For" on this line.

Note. Any entity that has an EIN will retain that EIN even if its federal tax classification changes under Regulations section 301.7701-3.

If a disregarded entity's classification changes so that it becomes recognized as a partnership or association for federal tax purposes, and that entity had an EIN, then the entity must continue to use that EIN. If the entity did not already have its own EIN, then the entity must apply for an EIN and not use the identifying number of the single owner.

A foreign entity that makes an election under Regulations section 301.7701-3(c) and (d) must also use its own taxpayer identifying number. See sections 6721 through 6724 for penalties that may apply for failure to supply taxpayer identifying numbers.

If the entity electing to be classified using Form 8832 does not have an EIN, it must apply for one on Form SS-4, Application for Employer Identification Number. The entity must have received an EIN by the time Form 8832 is filed in order for the form to be processed. An election will not be accepted if the eligible entity does not provide an EIN.

Do not apply for a new EIN for an existing entity that is changing its classification if the entity already has an EIN.

Address. Enter the address of the entity electing a classification. All correspondence regarding the acceptance or nonacceptance of the election will be sent to this address. Include the suite, room, or other unit number after the street address. If the Post Office does not deliver mail to the street address and the entity has a P.O. box, show the box number instead of the street address. If the electing entity receives its mail in care of a third party (such as an accountant or an attorney), enter on the street address line "C/O" followed by the third party's name and street address or P.O. box.

Address change. If the eligible entity has changed its address since filing Form SS-4 or the entity's most recently-filed return (including a change to an "in care of" address), check the box for an address change.

Late-classification relief sought under Revenue Procedure 2009-41. Check the box if the entity is seeking relief under Rev. Proc. 2009-41, 2009-39 I.R.B. 439, for a late classification election. For more information, see *Late Election Relief*, later.

Relief for a late change of entity classification election sought under Revenue Procedure 2010-32. Check the box if the entity is seeking relief under Rev. Proc.

2010-32, 2010-36 I.R.B. 320. For more information, see *Foreign default rule*, earlier.

Part I. Election Information

Complete Part I whether or not the entity is seeking relief under Rev. Proc. 2009-41 or Rev. Proc. 2010-32.

Line 1. Check box 1a if the entity is choosing a classification for the first time (i.e., the entity does not want to be classified under the applicable default classification). Do not file this form if the entity wants to be classified under the default rules.

Check box 1b if the entity is changing its current classification.

Lines 2a and 2b. 60-month limitation rule. Once an eligible entity makes an election to *change* its classification, the entity generally cannot change its classification by election again during the 60 months after the effective date of the election. However, the IRS may (by private letter ruling) permit the entity to change its classification by election within the 60-month period if more than 50% of the ownership interests in the entity, as of the effective date of the election, are owned by persons that did not own any interests in the entity on the effective date or the filing date of the entity's prior election.

Note. The 60-month limitation does not apply if the previous election was made by a newly formed eligible entity and was effective on the date of formation.

Line 4. If an eligible entity has only one owner, provide the name of its owner on line 4a and the owner's identifying number (social security number, or individual taxpayer identification number, or EIN) on line 4b. If the electing eligible entity is owned by an entity that is a disregarded entity or by an entity that is a member of a series of tiered disregarded entities, identify the first entity (the entity closest to the electing eligible entity) that is not a disregarded entity. For example, if the electing eligible entity is owned by disregarded entity A, which is owned by another disregarded entity B, and disregarded entity B is owned by partnership C, provide the name and EIN of partnership C as the owner of the electing eligible entity. If the owner is a foreign person or entity and does not have a U.S. identifying number, enter "none" on line 4b.

Line 5. If the eligible entity is owned by one or more members of an affiliated group of corporations that file a consolidated return, provide the name and EIN of the parent corporation.

Line 6. Check the appropriate box if you are changing a current classification (no matter how achieved), or are electing out of a default classification. Do not file this form if you fall within a default classification that is the desired classification for the new entity.

Line 7. If the entity making the election is created or organized in a foreign jurisdiction, enter the name of the foreign country in which it is organized. This information must be provided even if the entity is also organized under domestic law.

Line 8. Generally, the election will take effect on the date you enter on line 8 of this form,

or on the date filed if no date is entered on line 8. An election specifying an entity's classification for federal tax purposes can take effect no more than 75 days prior to the date the election is filed, nor can it take effect later than 12 months after the date on which the election is filed. If line 8 shows a date more than 75 days prior to the date on which the election is filed, the election will default to 75 days before the date it is filed. If line 8 shows an effective date more than 12 months from the filing date, the election will take effect 12 months after the date the election is filed.

Consent statement and signature(s). Form 8832 must be signed by:

1. Each member of the electing entity who is an owner at the time the election is filed; or

2. Any officer, manager, or member of the electing entity who is authorized (under local law or the organizational documents) to make the election. The elector represents to having such authorization under penalties of perjury.

If an election is to be effective for any period prior to the time it is filed, each person who was an owner between the date the election is to be effective and the date the election is filed, and who is not an owner at the time the election is filed, must sign.

If you need a continuation sheet or use a separate consent statement, attach it to Form 8832. The separate consent statement must contain the same information as shown on Form 8832.

Note. Do not sign the copy that is attached to your tax return.

Part II. Late Election Relief

Complete Part II only if the entity is requesting late election relief under Rev. Proc. 2009-41.

An eligible entity may be eligible for late election relief under Rev. Proc. 2009-41, 2009-39 I.R.B. 439, if **each** of the following requirements is met.

1. The entity failed to obtain its requested classification as of the date of its formation (or upon the entity's classification becoming relevant) or failed to obtain its requested change in classification solely because Form 8832 was not filed timely.

2. Either:

a. The entity has not filed a federal tax or information return for the first year in which the election was intended because the due date has not passed for that year's federal tax or information return; or

b. The entity has timely filed all required federal tax returns and information returns (or if not timely, within 6 months after its due date, excluding extensions) consistent with its requested classification for all of the years the entity intended the requested election to be effective and no inconsistent tax or information returns have been filed by or with respect to the entity during any of the tax years. If the eligible entity is not required to file a federal tax return or information return, each affected person who is required to file a federal tax return or information return must have timely filed all such returns (or if not timely, within 6 months after its due date, excluding extensions) consistent with the entity's requested classification for all of the years the entity intended the requested election to be effective and no inconsistent tax or information returns have been filed during any of the tax years.

3. The entity has reasonable cause for its failure to timely make the entity classification election.

4. Three years and 75 days from the requested effective date of the eligible entity's classification election have not passed.

Affected person. An affected person is either:

• with respect to the effective date of the eligible entity's classification election, a person who would have been required to attach a copy of the Form 8832 for the eligible entity to its federal tax or information return for the tax year of the person which includes that date; or

• with respect to any subsequent date after the entity's requested effective date of the classification election, a person who would have been required to attach a copy of the Form 8832 for the eligible entity to its federal tax or information return for the person's tax year that includes that subsequent date had the election first become effective on that subsequent date.

For details on the requirement to attach a copy of Form 8832, see Rev. Proc. 2009-41 and the instructions under *Where To File.*

To obtain relief, file Form 8832 with the applicable IRS service center listed in *Where To File,* earlier, within 3 years and 75 days from the requested effective date of the eligible entity's classification election.

If Rev. Proc. 2009-41 does not apply, an entity may seek relief for a late entity election by requesting a private letter ruling and paying a user fee in accordance with Rev. Proc. 2013-1, 2013-1 I.R.B. 1 (or its successor).

Line 11. Explain the reason for the failure to file a timely entity classification election.

Signatures. Part II of Form 8832 must be signed by an authorized representative of the eligible entity and each affected person. See *Affected Persons,* earlier. The individual or individuals who sign the declaration must have personal knowledge of the facts and circumstances related to the election.

Foreign Entities Classified as Corporations for Federal Tax Purposes:

American Samoa—Corporation
Argentina—Sociedad Anonima
Australia—Public Limited Company
Austria—Aktiengesellschaft
Barbados—Limited Company
Belgium—Societe Anonyme
Belize—Public Limited Company
Bolivia—Sociedad Anonima
Brazil—Sociedade Anonima
Bulgaria—Aktsionerno Druzhestvo
Canada—Corporation and Company
Chile—Sociedad Anonima
People's Republic of China—Gufen Youxian Gongsi

Republic of China (Taiwan)
 —Ku-fen Yu-hsien Kung-szu
Colombia—Sociedad Anonima
Costa Rica—Sociedad Anonima
Croatia—Dionicko Drustvo
Cyprus—Public Limited Company
Czech Republic—Akciova Spolecnost
Denmark—Aktieselskab
Ecuador—Sociedad Anonima or Compania Anonima
Egypt—Sharikat Al-Mossahamah
El Salvador—Sociedad Anonima
Estonia—Aktsiaselts
European Economic Area/European Union
 —Societas Europaea
Finland—Julkinen Osakeyhtio/Publikt Aktiebolag
France—Societe Anonyme
Germany—Aktiengesellschaft
Greece—Anonymos Etairia
Guam—Corporation
Guatemala—Sociedad Anonima
Guyana—Public Limited Company
Honduras—Sociedad Anonima
Hong Kong—Public Limited Company
Hungary—Reszvenytarsasag
Iceland—Hlutafelag
India—Public Limited Company
Indonesia—Perseroan Terbuka
Ireland—Public Limited Company
Israel—Public Limited Company
Italy—Societa per Azioni
Jamaica—Public Limited Company
Japan—Kabushiki Kaisha
Kazakstan—Ashyk Aktsionerlik Kogham
Republic of Korea—Chusik Hoesa
Latvia—Akciju Sabiedriba
Liberia—Corporation
Liechtenstein—Aktiengesellschaft
Lithuania—Akcine Bendroves
Luxembourg—Societe Anonyme
Malaysia—Berhad
Malta—Public Limited Company
Mexico—Sociedad Anonima
Morocco—Societe Anonyme
Netherlands—Naamloze Vennootschap
New Zealand—Limited Company
Nicaragua—Compania Anonima
Nigeria—Public Limited Company
Northern Mariana Islands—Corporation
Norway—Allment Aksjeselskap
Pakistan—Public Limited Company
Panama—Sociedad Anonima
Paraguay—Sociedad Anonima
Peru—Sociedad Anonima
Philippines—Stock Corporation
Poland—Spolka Akcyjna
Portugal—Sociedade Anonima

Puerto Rico—Corporation
Romania—Societe pe Actiuni
Russia—Otkrytoye Aktsionernoy Obshchestvo
Saudi Arabia—Sharikat Al-Mossahamah
Singapore—Public Limited Company
Slovak Republic—Akciova Spolocnost
Slovenia—Delniska Druzba
South Africa—Public Limited Company
Spain—Sociedad Anonima
Surinam—Naamloze Vennootschap
Sweden—Publika Aktiebolag
Switzerland— Aktiengesellschaft
Thailand—Borisat Chamkad (Mahachon)
Trinidad and Tobago—Limited Company
Tunisia—Societe Anonyme
Turkey—Anonim Sirket
Ukraine—Aktsionerne Tovaristvo Vidkritogo Tipu
United Kingdom—Public Limited Company
United States Virgin Islands—Corporation
Uruguay—Sociedad Anonima
Venezuela—Sociedad Anonima or Compania Anonima

 See Regulations section 301.7701-2(b)(8) for any exceptions and inclusions to items on this list and for any revisions made to this list since these instructions were printed.

Paperwork Reduction Act Notice

We ask for the information on this form to carry out the Internal Revenue laws of the United States. You are required to give us the information. We need it to ensure that you are complying with these laws and to allow us to figure and collect the right amount of tax.

You are not required to provide the information requested on a form that is subject to the Paperwork Reduction Act unless the form displays a valid OMB control number. Books or records relating to a form or its instructions must be retained as long as their contents may become material in the administration of any Internal Revenue law. Generally, tax returns and return information are confidential, as required by section 6103.

The time needed to complete and file this form will vary depending on individual circumstances. The estimated average time is:

Recordkeeping . . . . 2 hr., 46 min.

Learning about the law or the form . . . . 3 hr., 48 min.

Preparing and sending the form to the IRS . . . . . 36 min.

If you have comments concerning the accuracy of these time estimates or suggestions for making this form simpler, we would be happy to hear from you. You can write to the Internal Revenue Service, Tax Forms and Publications, SE:W:CAR:MP:TFP, 1111 Constitution Ave. NW, IR-6526, Washington, DC 20224. Do not send the form to this address. Instead, see *Where To File* above.

MINUTES of a meeting of Members of
_____

A meeting of the members of the company was held on_____, at
_____.

The following were present, being all the members of the limited liability company:

_____   _____
_____   _____
_____   _____

The meeting was called to order and it was moved, seconded, and unanimously carried
that _____act as Chairman and that _____act as Secretary.

After discussion and upon motion duly made, seconded and carried the following
resolution(s) were adopted:

There being no further business to come before the meeting, upon motion duly made,
seconded, and unanimously carried, it was adjourned.

_____
Secretary

Members:

_____
_____
_____
_____

CHAPTER 6
STATE-BY-STATE RESOURCE GUIDE

"It's not about your resources, it's about your resourcefulness."
- Tony Robbins

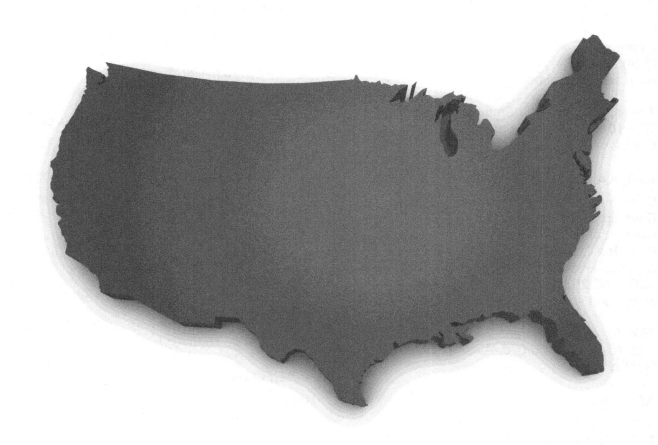

I've included the addresses for every state's office where you're supposed to file your Articles of Incorporation or LLC paperwork. I've also included the law codes (or statutes) of that state which deals with businesses. That way you can look it up at your facilities law library. Some states have books that cover just that state. The ones that are listed for you to possibly obtain and read? The one reason why you should consider setting up the business in your state is because you won't have to pay someone to be your registered agent. Remember, do your own research on your state's business law first. Write the state's corporation (or LLC) office, and ask them for the proper forms, if any? Not all states have forms, and you can use the ones in this book to do it. Every state has different fees. When I last checked, to incorporate in Wyoming it was $50.00, and Texas was the highest at $300. But the filing should not be what determines your decision. Your choice of state should be made after careful consideration and exhaustive research. Some of the things you should consider are the existing laws and statutes of your state, and your own personal preferences and situation. The resources in this section can help you get started. But it's up to you to begin.

"Do not spend any time in daydreaming or castle building; hold to the one vision of what you want, and act NOW."
- Wallace D. Wattles, *The Science of Getting Rich*

ALABAMA

Secretary of State
Corporation Section
P.O. Box 5616
Montgomery, AL 36103-5616
(334) 242-5324
www.sos.state.al.us

Title 10-2B, Alabama Statutes (Corporations)
Title 10, Chapter 12, Alabama Limited Liability Company Act (LLC.)

ALASKA

Department of Community and Economic Development
Division of B.S.C.
P.O. Box 110808
Juneau, AK 99811-0808
(907) 465-2530
www.dced.state.ak.us/bsc/corps.htm

Title 10, Alaska Statutes
Title 10, Section 50.010, Alaska Limited Liability Act

ARIZONA

Arizona Corporation Commission
1300 West Washington, 1st Floor
Phoenix, AZ 85007-3026
(602) 542-3026
www.cc.state.az.us/corp/index.ssi

Title 10, Arizona Statutes (Corporations)
Title 29, Chapter 4, Arizona Limited Liability Company Ad (UCs)

Recommended Reading
Doing Business in Arizona: A Legal Guide

ARKANSAS

Secretary of State
Corporation Division
State Capitol, Room 256
Little Rock, AR 72201
(501) 682-8032
www.sosweb.state.ar.us

Title 4, Chapter 27, Arkansas Statutes (Corporations)
Act 1003 of 1993, Arkansas Code Annotated, Section 4-32-101(UCs)

CALIFORNIA

Secretary of State
Corporate Division
1500 11th St.
Sacramento, CA 95814

(916) 657-5488
www.ss.ca.gov

Title 1, California Corporation Code
Title 1, Section 17000-17062

COLORADO

Secretary of State
Business Division
1700 Broadway, Suite 200
Denver, CO 80290
(303)894-2200
www.sos.state.co.us

Title 7, Colorado Revised Statutes
(Corporations)
Section 7080-107, Colorado Revised Statutes
(LLCs)

CONNECTICUT

Secretary of State
30 Trinity St.
Harford, CT 06106
(860) 509-6002
www.concord.sots.ct.gov

Chapter 601, Connecticut Business
Corporations Act
Public Act 93-267, Connecticut Statutes, Title
34 (LLCs)

DELAWARE

Secretary of State
Division of Corporations
P.O. Box 898
401 Federal St., Suite 4
Dover, DE 19901
(302)739-3073
www.state.de.us/corp.htm

Title B, Delaware Code (Corporations)
Title 6, Commerce and Trade, Chapter 18,
LLC Act

Recommended Reading
Incorporate in Delaware From Any State

DISTRICT OF COLUMBIA

Department of Commerce and Regulatory
Affairs
Corporate Division
941 North Capitol St., N.E.
Washington, DC 20002
(202) 442-4400
www.dcra.washingtondc.gov

Title 29, District of Columbia
Title 29, Chapter 10 (LLCs)

Recommended Reading
How to Start a Business in MD, VA or DC

FLORIDA

Secretary of State
Division of Corporations
P.O. Box 6327
Tallahassee, FL 32314
(800) 755-5111
www.sunbiz.org

Chapter 607 and 621, Florida Statutes
(Corporations)
Title 36, Chapter 608, Florida Statutes (LLCs)

Recommended Reading
How To Form a Corporation in Florida, Sixth
Edition
How to Form a Limited Liability Company in
Florida, Third Edition
How To Form a Partnership in Florida
How To Start a Business in Florida, Seventh
Edition

GEORGIA

Secretary of State
315 West Tower
#2 Martin Luther King, Jr. Drive
Atlanta, GA 30334-1530
(404) 656-2817
www.sos.state.ga.us/corporations

Title 14, Georgia Code (Corporations)
Title 14, Chapter 11, Georgia Code (LLCs)

Recommended Reading

How to Start a Business in Georgia, 4th Edition

HAWAII

Department of Commerce and Consumer Affairs
Business Registration Division
P.O. Box 40
Honolulu, HI 96810
(808) 586-2727
www.state.hi.us/dcca/brpg-sell/index.html

Title 32, Hawaii Revised Statutes (Corporations)
Title 23A, Chapter 428, Hawaii Revised Statutes (LLCs)

IDAHO

Secretary of State
700 West Jefferson
Basement West
Boise, ID 83720-0080
(208) 334-2301
www.idsos.state.id.us

Title 30, Idaho Code (Corporations)
Title 53, Chapter 6, Idaho Limited Liability Company Act

Recommended Reading
How To Start A Business In Idaho

ILLINOIS

Secretary of State
Business Services Department
328 Howlett Building
501 South 2nd St.
Springfield, IL 62756
(217) 782-6961
www.sos.state.il.us/departments/business_services/home.html

Business Corporation Act of Illinois
Illinois Limited Liability Company Act, 805 IL CS 180
Recommended Reading
How To Form Your Own Illinois Corporation Before the Ink Dries!

How To Start a Business in Illinois, Fourth Edition

INDIANA

Secretary of State
Business Services Division
302 West Washington St.
Room E018
Indianapolis, IN 46204
(317) 232-6576
www.in.gov/sos

Title 23, Indiana Statutes (Corporation)
Title 23, Chapter 18, Indiana Statutes (LLCs)

IOWA

Business Services
Lucas Building, First Floor
321 East 12th St.
State Capitol
Des Moines, IA 50319
(515) 281-5204
www.sos.state.ia.us

Chapter 490, Iowa Code (Cooperative)
Chapter 490A, Iowa Code, Limited Liability Company Act

KANSAS

Secretary of state
Memorial Hall
120 SW 10th St.
Topeka, KS 66612-1594
(785) 296-4564
www.ksos.org/business/business.html

Chapter 17, Kansas Statutes (Corporations)
Chapter 17, Section 7601, Kansas Statutes Annotated (LLCs)

KENTUCKY

Office of Secretary of State
P.O. Box 718
Frankfort, KY 40601
(502) 564-2848
www.sos.ky.gov/business

Chapter 271B, Kentucky Revised Statutes
Chapter 275, Kentucky Limited Liability
Company Act

LOUISIANA

Secretary of State
Corporations Division
P.O. Box 94125
Baton Rouge, LA 70804-9125
(225) 925-4704
www.sec.state.la.us

Title 12, Louisiana Revised Statutes
(Corporations)
Title 12, Section 1301, Louisiana Revised
Statutes (LLCs)

MAINE

Secretary of State
Bureau of Corporations, Elections and
Commissions
101 State House Station
Augusta, ME 04333
(207) 624-7736
www.state.me.us/sos/sos.htm

Title 13-A, Maine Revised Statutes
(Corporations)
Title 31, Chapter 13, Section 601-762, Maine
Revised Statutes (LLCs)

MARYLAND

State Department of Assessments and
Taxation
Charter Division
301 West Preston St.
Room 801
Baltimore, MD 21201
(410) 767-1340
www.sos.state.md.us

Corporations and Associations-Title 2, Code
of Maryland
Title 2, Section 4A-101, Code of Maryland
(LLCs)
Recommended Reading
How to Start a Business in MD, VA, or DC

MASSACHUSETTS

Secretary of the Commonwealth
Corporations Division
One Ashburton Place
17th Floor
Boston, MA 02108
(617) 727-9640
www.state.ma.us/sec/cor/corcon.htm

Chapter 156, Massachusetts General Laws
(Corporations)
Title 22, Chapter 156C, Massachusetts
Limited Liability Act

Recommended Reading
How To Form a Corporation in Massachusetts
How To Start a Business in Massachusetts,
Fourth Edition

MICHIGAN

Michigan Department of Commerce
Corporations and Securities Bureau
Corporation Divisional
P.O. Box 30054
Lansing, MI 48909
(517) 241-6470
www.michigan.gov/cis

Chapter 450, Michigan Compiled Laws
(Corporation)
Act 23, Public Arts of 1993, Michigan Limited
Liability Company Act

Recommended Reading
How To Form Your Own Michigan LLC Before
the Ink Dries!
How To Start a Business in Michigan, Fourth
Edition

MINNESOTA

Secretary of State
Division of Corporations
180 State Office Building
100 Rev. Martin Luther King Jr. Blvd.
St. Paul, MN 55155-1299
(651) 296-2803
www.sos.state.mn.us/bus.html

*Chapter 302A, Minnesota Statutes
(Corporations)*
Chapter 322B, Minnesota Statutes (LLCs)

Recommended Reading
How To Form A Corporation in Minnesota

MISSISSIPPI

Secretary of State
Business Services Division
P.O. Box 136
Jackson, MS 39205
(601) 359-1633
www.sos.state.ms.us
Title 79, Mississippi Code (Corporations)
*Section 79-29-101, Mississippi Code (Limited
Liability Company)*

MISSOURI

Secretary of State
Corporations Division
P.O. Box 778
600 W. Main, Room 322
Jefferson City, MO 65102
(573) 751-4153
www.sos.state.mo.us

Chapter 351, Missouri Statutes (Corporations)
Chapter 347, Missouri Statutes (LLCs)

MONTANA

Secretary of State
P.O. Box 202801
Helena, MT 59620-2801
(406) 444-2034
www.sos.state.mt.us/css

Title 35, Montana Code (Corporations)
Title 35, Chapter 8, Montana Code (LLCs)

Recommended Reading
How To Start A Business in Montana

NEBRASKA

Secretary of State
P.O. Box 94608
Suite 1301 State Capitol

Lincoln, NE 68509-4608
(402) 471-4079
www.sos.state.ne.us/business/corp_serv

*Chapter 21, Revised Nebraska Statutes
(Corporations)*
*Chapter 21, Section 2601, Revised Nebraska
Statutes (LLCs)*
Recommended Reading
How To Start a Business in Nebraska

NEVADA

Secretary of State
Capitol Complex
202 North Carson St.
Carson City, NV 89701
(775) 648-5708
www.sos.state./nv.us/comm_rec/index.htm

*Chapter 78, Nevada Revised Statutes
(Corporations)*
Chapter 86, Nevada Revised Statutes (LLCs)

Recommended Reading
Incorporate in Nevada from Any State

NEW HAMPSHIRE

Corporation Division
Department of State
107 North Main St.
Concord, NH 03301
www.sos.nh.gov/corporate/index.html

*Chapter 293-A, New Hampshire Business
Corporation Act*
*Section 304-C:1, New Hampshire Revised
Statutes Annotated (LLCs)*

NEW JERSEY

Department of Treasury
Division of Corporate Filing
P.O. Box 308
Trenton, NJ 08625-0308
(609) 292-1730
www.state.nj.us/treasury/revenue/index.html

Title 14A, New Jersey Revised Statutes

(Corporations)
*Title 42:2B, New Jersey Revised Statutes
(LLCs)*

Recommended Reading
How To Start A Business in New Jersey

NEW MEXICO

Public Regulation Commission
Corporation Department
P.O. Box 1269
Santa Fe, NM 87504-1269
(505) 827-4502
www.nmprc.state.nm.us/corporations/corpsho
me.html

*Chapter 53, New Mexico Statutes
(Corporations)*
*Title 53, Chapter 19, New Mexico Statutes
(LLCs)*

NEW YORK

Department of State
Division of Corporations and State Records
41 State St.
Albany, NY 12231
(518) 473-2492
www.dos.state.ny.us

*Chapter 4, Consolidation Laws of New York,
Corporation)*
*Chapter 34, Consolidation Laws of New York
(LLC Act)*

Recommended Reading
*How To Form A Corporation in New York,
Second Edition*
*How To Start A Business in New York,
Second Edition*
New York State Tax Law
New York Power of Attorney Handbook

NORTH CAROLINA

Department of Secretary of State
Corporations Division
P.O. Box 29622
Raleigh, NC 27626-0622

(919) 807-2225
www.secretary.state.nc.us/corporations

*Chapter 55, General Statutes of North
Carolina (Corporations)*
*Title 57C, General Statutes of North Carolina
(LLCs)*

Recommended Reading
*How To Start a Business in North Carolina or
South Carolina*

NORTH DAKOTA

Secretary of State
Capitol Building
600 East Boulevard Avenue
Department 108
Bismark, ND 58505
(701) 328-2910
www.state.nd.us/sec

*Title 10, North Dakota Century Code
(Corporations)*
*Chapter 10-32, North Dakota Century Code
(LLCs)*

OHIO

Secretary of State
Business Services Division
180 East Broad St., 16th Floor
Columbus, OH 43215
(614) 466-3910
www.state.oh.us/sos

Title 17, Ohio Revised Statutes
(Corporations)
Title 17, Chapter 1705, Ohio Revised Code
(LLC Act)
Recommended Reading
How To Form a Corporation in Ohio

OKLAHOMA

Secretary of State
Corporations Division
2300 North Lincoln Blvd, Room 101
Oklahoma City, OK 73105-4897

(405) 521-3912
www.sos.state.ok.us

Title 18, Oklahoma Statutes (Corporations)
Title 18, Chapter 32, Oklahoma LLC Act

OREGON

Corporations Division
Secretary of State
255 Capitol St., N.E.
Suite 151
Salem, OR 97310-1327
(503) 986-2200
www.filinginOregon.com

Title 7, Oregon Revised Statutes
(Corporations)
Title 7, Chapter 63, Oregon LLC Act

PENNSYLVANIA

Department of State
Corporation Bureau
P.O. Box 8722
Harrisburg, PA 17105-8722
(717) 787-1057
www.dos.state.pa.us/corps

Title 19, Pennsylvania Statutes (Corporations)
Title 15, Chapter 89, Pennsylvania
Consolidated Statutes (LLCs)

Recommended Reading
How To Form A Corporation in Pennsylvania
How To Start A Business in Pennsylvania,
Third Edition
The Pennsylvania Nonprofit Handbook

RHODE ISLAND

Secretary of State
Corporations Division
100 North Main St.
  1st Floor
Providence, RI 02903
(401) 222-3040
www.3.sec.state.ri.us/divs/corpos/index.html

Title 7, Chapter 7-1.2, General Laws of

Rhode Island (Corporations)
Title 7, Chapter 16, General Laws of Rhode
Island (LLCs)

SOUTH CAROLINA

Secretary of State
Division of Corporations
P.O. Box 11350
Columbia, SC 29211
(803) 734-2158
www.scsos.com/corporations.html

Title 33, Code of Laws of South Carolina
(Corporations)
Chapter 34-44, South Carolina Code of 1976
(LLCs)

Recommended Reading
How To Start a Business in North Carolina or
South Carolina

SOUTH DAKOTA

Secretary of State
State Capitol
500 East Capitol Avenue, Suite 204
Pierre, SD 57501
(605) 773-4845
www.sdsos.gov

Title 47, South Dakota Codified Laws
(Corporation)
Title 47, Chapters 34, 34A (LLCs)

TENNESSEE

Department of State
Division of Business Services
312 Eighth Avenue North, 6th Floor
Nashville, TN 37243
(615) 741-2286
www.tennessee.gov/sos/bus_svc/corporation
s.html

Title 48, Tennessee Code (Corporations)
Sections 48-201-101 through 48-248-606,
Tennessee Code (LLCs)

Recommended Reading
How To Form a Corporation, LLC or

Partnership in Tennessee

TEXAS

Secretary of State
Corporations Division
P.O. Box 1397
Austin, TX 78711
(512) 463-5555
www.sos.state.tx.us

*Business Corporations Act, Texas Civil
Statutes
Article 152BN, Texas Revised Civil Statutes
(LLC Act)*

Recommended Reading
*How To Form A Corporation in Texas, Third
Edition
How To Start A Business in Texas, Fourth
Edition
Texas Business and Commercial Code
Texas Corporation and Partnership Laws*

UTAH

Department of Commerce
Division of Corporation and Commercial Code
P.O. Box 146705
160 East 300 South
Salt Lake City, UT 84114-6705
(801) 530-4849
www.commerce.utah.gov/cor/index.htm

Title 16, Utah Code (Corporations)
Title 48-2B, Utah Code (LLCs)
Recommended Reading
Utah Corporation and Business Law Manual

VIRGINIA

State Corporation Commission
P.O. Box 1197
Richmond, VA 23218
(804) 371-9967
www.state.va.us/sec

*Title 13.1, Code of Virginia (Corporations &
LLCs)*

Recommended Reading
*How To Start a Business in Maryland,
Virginia, or DC*

VERMONT

Secretary of State
Division of Corporations
81 River St.
Montpelier, VT 05609-1104
(802) 828-2386
www.sec.state.vt.us/corps/corpindex.html

*Title 11A, Vermont Statutes (Corporations)
Title 11, Chapter 21, Section 3001, Vermont
Statues (LLCs)*

WASHINGTON

Secretary of State
Corporations Division
P.O. Box 40234
Olympia, WA 98504-0234
(360) 753-7115
www.secstate.wa.gov/corps

*Title 23B, Revised Code of Washington
(Corporations)
Chapter 25.15, Revised Code of Washington
(LLCs)*

WEST VIRGINIA

Secretary of State
Corporations Division
State Capitol, Building 1
Suite 157-K
1900 Kenawha Boulevard East
Charleston, WV 25305
(304) 558-8000
www.wvsos.com

*Chapter 31, West Virginia Code
(Corporations)
Chapter 31B, Section 1-101, Uniform LLC Act*

WISCONSIN

Department of Financial Institutions
Division of Corporate and Consumer Services

Corporate Section
P.O. Box 7846
Madison, WI 53707
(608) 26107577
www.wdfi.org/corporations

Chapter 108, Wisconsin Statutes
(Corporations)
Chapter 183, Wisconsin Statutes (LLCs)

Secretary of State
State Capitol Building
Room 110
200 West 24th St.
Cheyenne, WY 82002
(307) 777-7311
www.soswy.state.wy.us/corporat/corporat.htm

Title 17, Wyoming Statutes (Corporations)
Title 17, 15-101, Wyoming Statutes (LLCs)

WYOMING

RESOURCE BOX

All books listed above in the Recommended Reading listings in our state by state resource guide can ordered from our Bookstore on page 224 or online. Contact Freebird Publishers about ordering if you don't have anyone to help you.

ADDITIONAL RESEARCH RESOURCES

If your facility has a great law library, you may be able to find some of the below resource and law books? If not, you may order them from legal book publisher Thompson-West. They are the people behind WestLaw. Their contact information is included below. I suggest you try to find these books in your law library because otherwise, they are going to run you several hundred dollars, and up to over a thousand dollars. But knowing the current business law can save you a bunch of headaches down the road. Start your research at the law library!

Business and Commercial Litigation in Federal Courts, 2d, edited by Robert L Haig (8 hardback books, cost $1,100)
Modern Law of Contracts, 2016 ed. By Howard O. Hunter (2 softback books, costs $450)
Going Global: A Guide to Building an International Business by Alan S. Gutterman and Robert L. Brown (3 softback books, cost $357)
Cox and Hazen's Treatise on the Law of Corporations, 3d by James D. Cox and Thomas Lee Hazen (4 hardback books, cost $700)

CHAPTER 7
FINANCING YOUR CELLPRENEUR START-UP

"The idea that it takes money to make money has been contradicted countless times by modern business alchemists who've spun lead into gold."
- Jim Montavalli

TURNING IDEAS INTO MONEY

As a *Millionaire Prisoner,* your capital is your time, your ideas, your artwork, your manuscripts, and anything you produce. Turning these things into passive income is the way to prosperity. In *The Millionaire Prisoner* I share a bunch of prisoners who did just that. My first profitable venture was an

idea to sell a mailing list of 100 Wealthy Women. It cost me nothing but a few hours of my time to put the list together. I then tested it by placing an ad in *Prison Legal News*. Once I saw it worked we started selling it nationally. Your ideas can make you money if you act on them. For more information on turning ideas into money, you'll want to read How To Make Millions With Your Ideas: An Entrepreneurs Guide by Dan S. Kennedy.

One of my favorite ex-prisoners is Felix Dennis. He was sent to prison over censorship of one of his magazines in England. But he went from being "a hippie drops out on welfare, living in a room without money to pay rent, to being rich." Those are his own words from his must-read book, How to Get Rich. How Rich? Billionaire Rich, with a capital "B". He did it without a college degree or any capital. He vowed to never go back to prison and set out to get a piece of the wealth pie. His company, Dennis Publishing, owns magazines such as Stuff and Computer Shopper. He is also founder of Maxim Magazine. He did it, so can you.

OWNERSHIP IS EVERYTHING

One of the best principles that I learned from Felix Dennis is that the owner is the one that gets rich. Here's a prison example. Years ago, when I first came to prison I played football parlay tickets. I would put up a small sum of money, pick four teams and if they won, I could win 10 or 12 times my money. I was good at it and made some money. But I learned that the guy who ran the parlay makes the most money. So, I became a partner with the man, learned how he did it, then started my own parlay ticket business. I went from being a customer, to a partner, to an owner. And instead of making $50 or $60 every couple of weeks I started making hundreds of dollars every week! I learned a valuable lesson: *ownership determines who gets rich!* With that principle in mind, here are some tips to remember along your cellpreneur journey:

Try and keep ownership of anything you create, especially a business. Your goal is to cut out the middle men and become *the man*.

Never sell stock in something unless you absolutely have to. If you hold, you can get money for the rest of your life. If you sell, you get money once. With that being said, if you get offered something that will change your life, then maybe you should sell?

Even if you can't own it all, own a percentage of it. Remember my "Wealthy Women" list? I owned 50% of each sale. I have since made deals where I get 60% of net profits. My rule is this: *A percentage of something is better than nothing*. Have enough percentage deals and you can become a *Millionaire Prisoner* yourself.

*"To become rich, you must become an owner.
And you must try to own it all."*
– Felix Dennis

In this book, I've given you ways to keep ownership of your ideas and businesses. The rich use corporations and LLCs and you should also. I constantly hear prisoners say that they want to own a corporation, but you already own one – You Inc! That's what the Millionaire Prisoner lifestyle is all about: getting you to be the best you can be. If you can do that, then you can be successful in all you do.

"Never be a minion, always be an owner."
– Cornelius Vanderbilt

HOW TO GET START UP CAPITAL

Maybe you do have a business idea, but you don't have the funds to start it yet? So how do you get this money? It depends on how much you need? We started O'Barnett Publishing on the cheap. We registered it, opened a P.O. Box, and placed an advertisement for all under $400. Then we used money from the initial sales to build it up and spread out our marketing efforts. So, your first step is finding out how much you need to start.
Once you have that number then you can go after it.

Some of you may have personal savings in your prison trust fund account, and/or in a free-world bank account? I used $100 in my prison account to get 100 booklets printed of my *How to Get FREE Pen Pals* and $90 for an ad in *Prison Legal News.* George Kayer used money from a small inheritance to start *DiSSE* which became *Inmate Shopper*. It doesn't take much to start and if you got some cash stashed away you're one step ahead of everyone else. For those of you who have no savings, you have to beg, plead, and persuade others to give you capital. Because I'm against taking on a loan, I will not discuss that. Some people believe otherwise, but you're reading a *Millionaire Prisoner* book and not their books. I will show you some ways to get money, so you don't sell your soul in the process.

In his book, *How To Get Rich*, Felix Dennis has a chapter called "Obtaining Capital." He talks about people who you can borrow money from and calls these people one of three types: (1) Dolphins, (2) Sharks, or (3) Fishes. I'll talk about these three types, plus one more that I've added myself. A shark, or lean shark, is to be avoided at all costs. And there are different types of sharks. The prisoner who runs the "2 for 1" store is a shark. Stay away from him. There are places that will hold your paycheck and give you a loan off that check. You've seen these places in the hood with signs that say, "Cash Now" and "Payday Loans". But they charge crazy interest rates like 30-40%. In the same area are the "Title Loans" store. You take your car title or boat title in and they give you a loan on that for a small percentage of what it's actually worth. These places are sharks, stay away from them. You can, and should, study them and learn from them. But don't get money from them. A great TV show to watch by the way is ABC's *Shark Tank*. (FYI: I have a shark tattoo on my arm with the words: "A shark never sleeps." So maybe you should stay away from me?

Next, we have the venture capitalists or what Felix Dennis calls "dolphins". And I agree with him that you should stay away from these people in your start-up days. They only care about growing the business as fast as they can so they can get the most money back on investment. All the while taking a substantial piece of your business with them. I don't blame them either, because if I was a venture capitalist, I would do the same thing. But I'm not a dolphin, I'm your cellpreneur colleague and I'm advising you to stay away from them in your start-up days.

Before we discuss the "fishes", I want to discuss another creature of the wealth sea, I'm talking about the "whale" In the world of gambling, the whale is the player who isn't a professional, but is loaded from a business. But they like to gamble and because they're not a pro, they lose large sums of money. Yet their losses don't make a dent in their bankroll. If you can find a real-life whale and befriend them, by all means do so. You could be very close to your capital. There are whales in prison, especially in the federal system. Michael Santos tells how he made $100,000 using a Russian prisoner's money in *Earning Freedom*. So always be on the lookout for the whales around you. When you find one send them my way and I'll give you a finder's fee. Just kidding. Keep your eyes open because a whale can change your life.

If you don't know any whales, then you are left with the fishes. It has been through the fishes that I have started three different businesses. All of your pen pals, family members, acquaintances, friends, and everyone else you know are the fishes. Ask for their help. Beg them. Plead them. Persuade them. Do what you have to (as long as it's legal and ethical) and get your startup funds.

> *"Apply to all those whom you know will give something; next, to those whom you are uncertain whether they will give anything or not; And show them the list of those who have given; and lastly, do not neglect those you are sure will give nothing; for in some of them you will be mistaken."*
> – Benjamin Franklin

HOW TO ASK FAMILY & FRIENDS FOR MONEY

There are several steps that can make your request successful. They are as follows:

Step 1: Find out what their needs are for you and how much they could possibly contribute. You don't want to ask for $500 when they can only spare $50. Don't force them to say "no".

Step 2: Communicate your fears, needs and wants. You don't do this from a whiny perspective. But instead from the truth seat. My request went something like this: "I have to do this. For myself, for my lawyer money, for my daughters. But also, so I can take the burden off you and not be dependent on you."

Step 3: Focus your requests on compatible interests. Like them giving you money to start a business could save, and make, them money in the long run. And keep you out of prison!

Step 4: Deal with any conflicting interests. They may need a new muffler for their car? You need money to start an LLC or copyright your song? Those needs have to be worked out.

Step 5: Try and barter what you have or can do for the money. You don't want a loan, but a gift. (FYI: A family member can give you up to $11,000 a year as a gift and its tax deductible)

Step 6: If they don't want to send you the money, have them help with business supplies. Get them to order your business cards. Design your letterhead and have them order that. Have them get you a P.O. Box. You're going to get these things anyway, so why not have them do it.

That way they can see their money being put to use and not going to your honeybun and coffee habit.

Start small and work your way up. Grow your business slowly. You can start a business and claim tax deductions for up to two years so there's no rush. The money is out there, you just have to go and get it. President Obama did help us out in this aspect with the passage of the Second Chance Act. You can get free money from the government to start a business. There are also foundations that give out free money. Most of these places require you to fill out an application and write an essay on why you need the money. Troy Evans spent seven years locked up in a federal gulag. He used grants, foundation, and churches to finance his college education while inside. And he walked out with not one, but two degrees. He's also the author *of From Desperation to Dedication: An Ex-Con's Lessons on Turning Failure Into Success.* Check out his website at www.TroyEvans.com.

"The money is there, but the effort has to be there to make it happen.
It is only a matter of beating the bushes."
– Troy Evans

RESOURCE BOX

For more about getting a grant or free money, you'll want to grab a copy of one or more of the following:

- *Foundation Grants to Individuals* by The Foundation Center
- *Free Dollars From the Federal Government* by Laurie Blum
- *The Complete Guide to Getting a Grant: How To Turn Your Ideas Into Dollars* by Laurie Blum
- *Getting Funded: A Complete Guide to Proposal Writing* by Mary Hall
- *Investors In Your Backyard: How To Raise Business Capital From the People You Know* by Asheesh Advari

All books available on our Bookstore page 224 or online.
Contact Freebird Publishers about ordering if you don't have anyone to help you.

Or you can have someone check out www.fastweb.com. Fastweb is a database of more than 180,000 private sector grants and loans. It will let you match yourself to the grants that fit your project for free.

WHAT ABOUT CROWDFUNDING?

It seems every business magazine I read these days has a story about how a company got funded on a crowdsourcing website. What is crowdfunding? It's simply the process where a group of people connected through a website contribute small amounts of money to help someone (or some business) out with funding. Crowdfunding is such a big deal that the SEC passed rules that govern its uses. Here are some of those rules:

- You can only get up to $1 million a year through crowdfunding;
- Investors can't sell their shares for up to one year;
- You'll have to establish a company valuation;

- You have to disclose all information about the owners (if they own more than 20 percent) of your company;

- You have to deliver what you say you're going to do.

Before I tell you some tips on how to get funded you should be aware that it's going to be hard to get funded as a prisoner. My cellpreneur friend and colleague, George Kayer, said he tried to get it and was told no. But that doesn't mean it's impossible. In a *Prison Legal News* article ("*Crowdfunding Projects Present Opportunities For Prisoners*" July 2016, p. 54-44), Derek Gilna reported the following prison-based successful companies:

- $5,700 by New York women prisoners to produce "Amazing Grace";

- $582 to finance a creative writing class in a Connecticut prison;

- $5,000 to get a pizza oven for a Cook County Jail culinary arts program;

- $15,000 for the Prison Ecology Project;

- $2,600 to help a death row prisoner prove his innocence.

Keep those successes in mind as I write about the steps to getting money online.

> *"Don't delude yourself into believing that just because something is hard, it's impossible."*
> *– Robert Ringer*

SIX STEPS TO A SUCCESSFUL CROWDFUNDING CAMPAIGN

These tips have been gleaned from *Inc.*, *Money*, and *Entrepreneur* magazines.

Step 1: Define Your Project. Write out a few paragraphs that explain what you're trying to do and why people should support you.

Step 2: Decide How Much Money You Need. Then show possible donors how the money will be spent. For example, you could raise $10,000. And it could be broken down like this: $1,000 for website design, $3,000 for books printed; $2,000 for book cover design; $2,000 for editor, and $2,000 for interior designer/typesetter.

Step 3: Research which websites are best for your project or business. Not all of them cater to the same crowd. Ground floor is Real Estate. Indiegogo focuses on business start-ups. But Indigogo Life is for individual causes. So, make sure you're using the right one.

Step 4: Have a video of you, your sample product, or prototype, or something. You need to demonstrate, and your donors need to see the who or the what behind the campaign to be successful.

Step 5: Upload your campaign and begin tapping into your network. People can't contribute if they don't know about your campaign. So, have somebody spread the word using email, mail, phone, social media, free ads, and everything else under the sun.

Step 6: Keep asking until you reach your goal, or the time limit runs out. (Most sites set a time limit, like 90 days for you to run your campaign.)

Sound like a lot of work? It is. Success is not easy. But there's good news for those of you who don't want to do all this. There are consultants who can assist with your campaign for a percentage of the money you get. But before you hire help make sure you check out the consultant first. Ask for references. Never pay them up front, only pay them a fee based on your goal, like 10%.

33needs.com	FundMyWish.com	Peoplefund.it.com
AdoptAnything.com	Fund Razr.com	Petridish.org
Angelist.com	GiveForward.com	ProFounder.com
ArtistShare.com	GoFundMe.com	Quirky.com
Bolstr.com	GoGetFunding.com	Rockethub.com
Buzzbnk.org	Ignitiondeck.com	ScoutFunder.com
ChipIn.com	Indigogo.com	Seedrs.com
Circleup.com	Indigogolife.com	Seedups.com
Conzortia.com	Innovestment.com	Selfstarter.com
CrowdCube.com	Investedin.com	Somolend.com
Crowd Funder.com	Kickstarter.com	SponsorGoal.com
CrowdSupply.com	LendingClub.com	Sponsume.com
FansNextDoor.com	McKenson-Invest.com	Startupaddict.com
Fundable.com	MicroVentures.com	YouCaring.com
FundedByMe.com	MosaicInc.com	Zopa.com
FunderThunder.com	Mycofolio.com	
Fundly.com	Peerbackers.com	

FYI: I have never used a crowdfunding website. If you really want to know more about getting funded this way, I suggest you read Thomas Elliot Young's book, The Everything Guide To CrowdFunding: Learn How To Use Social Media for Small-Business Funding.

RESOURCE BOX

For more about financing your business here are some books that could help you learn more:

- *Starting On A Shoestring: Building A Business Without A Bankroll by* Arnold Goldstein

- *Guerrilla Financing: Alternative Techniques to Finance Any Small Business* by Bruce Blechman & Jay Conrad Levinson

- *Unlimited Business Financing* by Trent Lee & Chad Lee

- *The Six Secrets of Raising Capital* by Bill Fisher

Books can be ordered from our Bookstore on page 224 or online. Contact Freebir Publishers about ordering if you don't have anyone to help you.

FOR MORE INFORMATION

A lot of prisoners are looking for someone to help them with their legal appeals. But why wait for someone else? Take it upon yourself to find someone. That's what Anthony Faison did. In 1988, he and a codefendant were sent to prison for the murder and robbery of a cab driver. While inside, Faison wrote over 60,000 letters to attorneys, politicians, and anyone else who he thought might help prove his innocence. He found a taker in a Long Island, New York private detective. Faison and his rappy were released in 2001 after 13 years behind bars and awarded $1,650,000! Proof that you don't have to wait on someone else to take action when you can write letters yourself.

"Energy and persistence conquer all things."
– Ben Franklin

HOW TO START A LEGAL DEFENSE FUND

But when you do find someone willing to help you out with your criminal or civil cases you should set up a legal defense fund. My friend, Illinois prisoner Jamie Snow, and his wife, have set up a

website and she coordinate all his legal stuff through the site. Snow writes his URL (www.freejamiesnow.com) on the outside of all his outgoing envelopes and his family and friends write it on the money they spend. Guerrilla marketing at its best.

My info-cellpreneur comrade, Mike Enemigo, of *The Cell Block Publishing Group*, has an email address of freemikeenimigo@yahoo.com which helps get the word out.

Since Jody Cramer wrote about it already in the 2012 Edition #1 of *Inmate Shopper* I'll let her tell you how to do it the right way. She is an activist working to end the death penalty. In addition, she is the Executive Director of the Kevin Cooper Legal Defense Fund. See www.savekevincooper.org. She can be reached at Jody@activist-etc.org. I'll turn it over to her now.

Establishing a Legal Defense Fund

by Jody Cramer

LET'S START with the bad news. A legal defense fund is about raising money, and raising money is very hard work. Below is a discussion of the essential elements that will be required if the fundraising is going to be successful.

A Proactive Prisoner

The inmate for whom the fund is being established must be willing to work extensively on his or her own behalf. The work to be done includes identifying and writing to any and all family, friends, contacts, organizations, and acquaintances who might make a donation or help raise money. The prisoner must be active in developing a support system. In addition, when a person or an organization does respond, the prisoner must promptly write a personal thank you note. Finally, if the prisoner is able to write compellingly about his or her experiences in prison or with the criminal justice system, the writings can help "put a face" on the individual and can be used as part of brochures, a website, solicitation letters, media packets and group appeals.

A Support System Leader

Someone in the support system must be willing to act as the leader. The responsibilities of the leader include:
• working closely with the prisoner to ensure that he/she is fully informed and has as much control as possible;
• coordinating the efforts of the support group in order to ensure that there is ongoing communication among members, assignment of tasks and consensus on activities;
• actively seeking potential organizations and individuals who might donate, contacting them in writing, maintaining files, taking phone calls and providing accurate information;
• tracking donations and ensuring that donors are thanked;
• thanking and encouraging support members for their efforts;
• developing a mailing list, preparing and mailing a

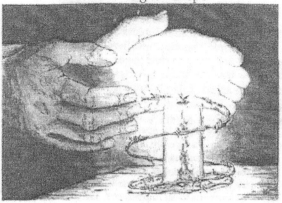

Warmth • Light • Hope

Dave Herman

periodic newsletter;
• demonstrating enthusiasm, providing a vision, being positive.

The Best Way to Raise Big Money

The single best way to raise big money is to get it directly from people who have it. In the nonprofit world this is called "development" because a nonprofit organization "develops" and nurtures relationships with people who have discretionary money and who have shown an interest in the cause. Sometimes someone with money will hear about a cause or a need and be instantly touched to write a check. Other times people show an initial interest and must be brought along to a large donation over time. Here are the steps to approaching people with money:
• Develop and print a professional-appearing business card like this:

> The XXXX Legal Defense Fund
> (Leader's Name), Executive Director
> Address
> phone, email, website, fax

(Having a logo will help)

Other team members can have a card which says "Associate Director" or "Support Team Member" or "Executive Committee Member."
• Get together with the support team for a brainstorming session in which you think of all the people you know who have money and all the people you know who know people with money. Write these names down. Go back through the list and put the names in priority order based on how easy it will be to gain access to them and how much money they might give. Talk about how to gain access. (Does your brother know them? Did you work for them in the past? Is there someone wealthy in your family?) Select five or six target people. Decide if

you will send a letter first or try to speak to them in person. Decide if two people from the support group should go together to ask. Set dates for accomplishing the goal.

•Develop professional materials to use when you approach people. Usually a brief flyer or brochure is best. People are not going to read pages and pages of material. Know the case, know the answers to the questions that will be asked. Role-play and practice with the support group what you will say when asking for financial support. Tell your potential donor why the money is needed and how it will be spent.

•Most people are really afraid of asking for money. Often people who have money are actually happy to find a cause they care about and to support it. Go ask them! The worse thing that can happen is that they will say "No." This happens to all fundraisers. There is a marvelous Chinese saying that I think applies perfectly to asking for money: "Do what you fear!"

Other Ways to Raise Money

Here are some ways to raise money without asking people face-to-face. Many of these ways are very time-consuming and energy draining. It's important for the support group to consider how to get the "biggest bang for the buck" and how to be successful so that the group doesn't burnout and feel discouraged.

•Collect items and hold a yard sale, or sell the "merchandise" at a flea market;

•Speak at service clubs and organizations, and ask the membership for a donation;

•Speak at your church, and ask the church membership for a donation;

•Prepare a brochure to use in a mail solicitation. Be sure there is a "coupon" the recipient can cut off and return. The coupon should suggest some "giving levels" such as ___$25 ___$50 ___$100. An addressed envelope should be included in the mailing to make it easier for the donor to respond. Send the mailing to everyone the prisoner knows, friends of the support group, and friends of the prisoner's family.

Activities That May Not Work

In my fundraising experience I haven't been successful in raising money by writing to celebrities, corporations, nonprofit organizations, or social organizations. It seems that in order to be successful, there must be some kind of personal connection.

When Donations Are Received

A separate account needs to be established for the donated funds and called something like "The XXXX Legal Defense Fund." A plan needs to be established to accurately track the donations, including collecting the addresses, phone numbers, dates of donations and donation amounts. The plan must include a sure way of promptly thanking all the donors. Addresses collected can be used in the future for a newsletter mailing, which can ask for additional financial help. Donations are *not tax deductible* unless the supporters are able to receive them under the umbrella of an existing nonprofit organization. Such an organization would have to be found and its cooperation would have to be gained. Supporters will not be able to acquire nonprofit status for a defense fund which helps only one person.

Keeping Your Donors Informed

As money is raised and progress is made on the prisoner's case, it is important to convey this information to your donors. They will know that their contribution helped, and they may be moved to give again. If you have a donor or donors who give a significant amount, it's a very good idea to invite them to a special meeting where the case is reviewed for them and they are able to ask individual questions. Also, if the donor and the prisoner are willing, a visit to meet the prisoner can be very helpful in soliciting future donations.

A Final Few Words

Raising money for a prisoner, especially for one on death row, is not like raising money for kids with cancer. If you undertake this project, you must be prepared for the probability that some people will be offended that you even asked them. Some people will wonder why you are "wasting your time and talent" on something like this. Many people who hear from you will simply ignore you because they don't know what to do and your request for help has put them in a difficult situation. Forge on! Persistence is the essence of success. If people question why you are doing this work, tell them that you are concerned about suffering and injustice *wherever* they exist. The positive part is that you will have an opportunity to educate people about a very dark side of American life. It takes guts and commitment to do this work, but the reward will go far beyond the effort.

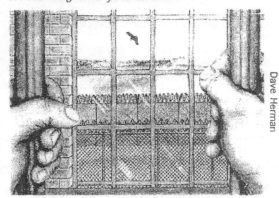

Dreams of Freedom

COSTS OF INCARCERATION

A lot of states are coming after prisoners for costs of incarceration charges. Some prisoners will use that as an excuse to not try and start a business. But you got to have money (or assets) before the state can seek reimbursement. I'll share some cases with you regarding costs of incarceration so that you can get a general understanding of these laws. Then it will be up to you to continue your research. Just remember that each state may have its own cost of incarceration laws and statutes.

In my state, the Illinois Department of Corrections has a rule codified in the Illinois Administrative Code and the Unified Code of Corrections which governs reimbursement for cost of incarceration. It states as follows:

> "The Director [of the Department], or the Director's designee, may, when he or she knows or reasonably believes that a committed person, or the estate of that person, has assets which may be used to satisfy all or part of a judgment rendered under this Act, or when he or she knows or reasonably believes that a committed person is engaged in gang-related activity and has a substantial sum of money or other assets,...authorize the Attorney General to institute actions on behalf of the Department and purse claims to require the persons, or estates of persons, to reimburse the Department for the expensed incurred by their incarceration."

See 730 ILCS S/3-7-6(d).

The key word thus being "assets". Here's how Illinois law defines prisoner's assets:

> "The assets of a committed person, for the purposes of this Section, shall include any property, tangible or intangible, real or personal, belonging to or due to a committed or formerly committed person including income or payments to the person from social security, worker's compensation, veteran's compensation, pension benefits, or from any other source whatsoever and any and all assets and property of whatever character held in the name of the person, held for the benefit of the person, or payable or otherwise deliverable to the person. Any trust, or portion of a trust, of which a convicted person is a beneficiary, shall be construed as an asset of the person, to the extent that benefits thereunder are required to be paid to the person, or shall in fact be paid to the person."

See 730 ILCS S/307-6(e)

There have been several challenges to this rule by Illinois prisoners which exempted certain assets.

Shortly after he went to prison, Lonnie Booth received a payment in settlement of $41,715.57 after attorney fees costs. This settlement stemmed from a lawsuit he brought against the Pace Suburban Bus Division of the Regional Transportation Authority (Chicagoland). When IDOC found out about the settlement they brought suit against him for costs of incarceration. The Court entered judgement against him but exempted $7,500 of the settlement because in Illinois, payments of $7,500 or less from personal injury suits are exempt. See *People ex rel. Director of Corrections v. Booth*, 215 Ill.2d 416 (2005).

Prisoner Leonce Ruckman got locked up in 1998. While inside, his mother died. Smarter than the average prisoner, Ruckman used proceeds from his mother's life insurance policy to purchase a MetLife Annuity of $32,178.22. When IDOC found out about this they came after Ruckman. The court entered judgement in the prison's favor and ordered MetLife to pay $29,156.60 to IDOC. The court exempted $2,000 for an Illinois personal property exemption. On appeal, Ruckman argued that everything was exempt because Illinois has an exemption for life insurance proceeds. But the Court stated that where life insurance proceeds have been converted to another form of property (like an annuity), that exemption does not apply. See *People Ex Rel. Director of Corrections v. Ruckman,* 363 Ill. App.3d 708 (2006).

The most interesting Illinois case is the Kensley Hawkins suit. Since 1983, Hawkins had been incarcerated at Stateville Correctional Center in Joliet, Illinois. He ended up getting a coveted job in the prison's industry program making furniture. Hawkins worked for IDOC and saved enough to stash away $11,000 in a freeworld bank account. In 2005, IDOC sought reimbursement for his 22 years of incarceration to the tune of $445,953.74. But part of Hawkins payment from his employment in the industry program had already been applied to his cost of incarceration. So, the court denied the state's lawsuit. The state appealed. After the Appellate Court reversed, the Illinois Supreme Court ruled in Hawkins favor and said it would be "unjust and inequitable" for IDOC to be able to seize wages a prisoner saved by working for the prison. See *People ex Rel. Illinois Dept. of Corrections v. Hawkins,* 2011 IL 110792, 952 N.E.2d 624 (2011).

According to existing IDOC rules, an Illinois prisoner must have assets worth $10,000 minimum before IDOC should refer the prisoner's case to the Illinois Attorney General. See the included IDOC Administrative Directive on the next few pages.

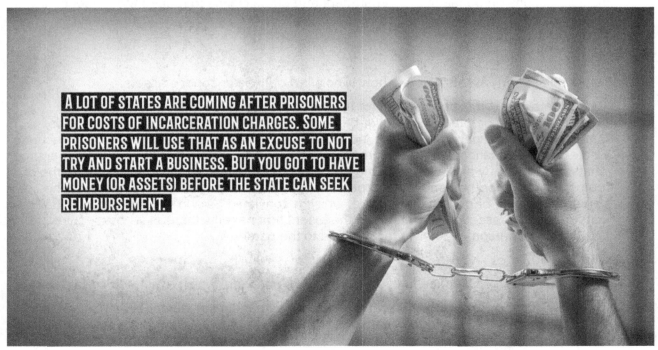

Illinois		Number	01.02.160
Department of	ADMINISTRATIVE	Page	1 of 4
Corrections	DIRECTIVE	Effective	12/1/2002 Amended 11/1/2005

Section	01	Administration and General Office
Subsection	02	Administration, Organization, and Management
Subject	160	Recovery of the Cost of Incarceration from Offenders

I. POLICY

A. Authority

730 ILCS 5/3-7-6, 3-12-1, 3-12-2 and 3-12-5

B. Policy Statement

The Department may recover the costs of incarceration from offenders committed to the Department to the extent of the offender's ability to pay.

II. PROCEDURE

A. Purpose

The purpose of this directive is to establish a procedure for recovering the costs of incarceration from offenders.

B. Applicability

This directive is applicable to all correctional facilities within the Department housing persons convicted as adults.

C. Internal Audits

An internal audit of this directive shall be conducted at least annually.

D. Designees

Individuals specified in this directive may delegate stated responsibilities to another person or persons unless otherwise directed.

E. Definitions

Asset – any property, tangible or intangible, real or personal, belonging to or due to an offender or former offender including income or payment to the offender from social security, worker's compensation, veteran's compensation, pension benefits, or from any other source whatsoever and any and all assets and property of whatever character held in the name of the offender, held for the benefit of the offender, or payable or otherwise deliverable to the offender.

Cost of incarceration - the cost to the Department for providing room, board, clothing, security, programs, health care, and other normal expenses of incarcerating offenders.

Offender - any person judicially committed to the Department who was convicted as an adult under both determinate and indeterminate sentences.

123

Illinois Department of **Corrections**

ADMINISTRATIVE DIRECTIVE	Effective DRAFT	Page 2 of 4	Number 01.02.160

F.   **General Provisions**

1. Effective January 1, 2003, all offenders shall be required to disclose their assets to the Department on the Offender Financial Status Report, DOC 0146.

2. The Director may require any offender to reimburse the State for his or her costs of incarceration to the extent of the offender's ability to pay said costs.

3. Factors to be considered in determining whether to require an offender to reimburse the State may include, among other matters:

   a. The offender's assets.

   b. The offender's Trust Fund account balance and account transactions;

   c. The amount needed by the offender to purchase essential personal hygiene items if such items are not provided by the facility where the offender is housed; and

   d. The offender's financial obligations, including support of legal dependents and payment of court ordered restitution.

4. The costs of incarceration shall be calculated on an average per capita/per day basis. The Deputy Director of Finance shall calculate this amount for each adult and juvenile correctional facility for each fiscal year commencing with fiscal year 1982.

   a. The average per capita cost of incarceration for a given Department correctional facility shall be computed by determining the total amount of expenditures made for a given fiscal year for a particular correctional facility, divided by the average daily offender population for that correctional facility during that fiscal year.

   b. The time period for determining the costs of incarcerating an offender shall be calculated from the date the offender was confined within the Department or from July 1, 1982, whichever date is later, until the date the offender is released.

   c. The offender shall be charged for the time he or she was housed at each correctional facility in accordance with the method of calculation described in Paragraphs II.F.4.a. and b.

5. Once the costs for incarcerating an offender have been determined, the Director may reduce the amount of those costs which an offender shall be required to pay if it is determined that the offender does not have the ability to pay the entire amount. The Director may consider, among other matters, an offender's:

   a. Obligation to pay taxes;

   b. Obligation to provide support for legal dependents;

   c. Obligation to provide court-ordered restitution;

   d. Outstanding debts; and

   e. Obligation to make mortgage payments.

6. When the Director requires an offender to reimburse the Department for the costs of his or her incarceration, the Director shall send a notice to the Attorney General authorizing

Illinois Department of **Corrections**

ADMINISTRATIVE DIRECTIVE	Effective **DRAFT**	Page **3 of 4**	Number **01.02.160**

him or her to institute an action pursuant to 730 ILCS 5/3-7-6 to recover the costs of incarcerating the offender. The Attorney General shall be informed of:

    a.   The offender's assets;

    b.   The amount of costs for incarcerating the offender that the Director has required the offender to pay at the time of the Director's authorization;

    c.   Any costs which the Director subsequently requires the offender to pay; and

    d.   Any offender compensation the Department has applied towards the offender's cost of incarceration.

G.   <u>**Requirements**</u>

    1.   The Chief Administrative Officer of each facility shall:

        a.   Notify offenders via methods such as Warden's Bulletins, posted notices, and orientation manuals of the statutory requirement to complete the Offender Financial Status Report and that failure to cooperate shall be considered for parole determination and shall subject the offender to disciplinary action including loss of good conduct credits of up to 180 days.

        b.   Provide each offender in custody on January 1, 2003 with an Offender Financial Status Report, DOC 0146, for completion.

        NOTE: At any time that it is suspected that the financial status of an offender has changed substantially since the latest Offender Financial Status Report, an updated report may be requested.

    2.   The Chief Administrative Officer of reception and classification centers shall ensure that each offender entering the Department after January 1, 2003 is provided with an Offender Financial Status Report for completion.

    3.   Copies of the completed Offender Financial Status Report shall be reviewed and placed in the offender's master file.

    4.   The Chief Administrative Officer shall be informed of known or suspected substantial sources of income and assets of offenders.

        a.   Upon notification of assets, a written report shall be submitted to the Deputy Director of Finance when it appears that an offender's known assets exceed or are expected to exceed $10,000.00.

        NOTE: The Office of the Illinois Attorney General set the minimum asset referral amount at $10,000.00. This amount is subject to change at the request of the Office of the Attorney General.

        b.   The report shall include:

            (1)   A copy of the Offender Financial Status Report;

            (2)   A summary of the offender's known assets including the specific sources;

            (3)   A summary of the offender's anticipated assets, including the specific sources; and

Illinois Department of **Corrections**

ADMINISTRATIVE DIRECTIVE	Effective DRAFT	Page 4 of 4	Number 01.02.160

  (4) A recommendation whether to require the offender to pay for all or some of the costs of the offender's incarceration.

 c. Updated reports shall be submitted upon request of the Deputy Director of Finance or when the offender's financial status is or is expected to be changed substantially.

5. The Deputy Director of Finance shall review all reports submitted and shall forward the reports with a recommendation to the Director.

6. The Director shall:

 a. Review the reports, requesting additional information when necessary;

 b. Make a determination whether to require the offender to pay all or part of the costs of incarceration; and

 c. Notify the Office of the Attorney General when costs are to be recovered.

7. The Director may authorize the Chief of Investigations and Intelligence to seek recovery of costs of incarceration when there is a reasonable belief that offender assets are proceeds from or facilitate the introduction or distribution of contraband within any departmental facility or are proceeds from organized criminal activity. Offender assets subject to recovery under this Paragraph may include State pay and the offender's principal residence unless occupied by the offender's legal dependents.

Authorized by:

Roger E. Walker Jr.
Director

Supersedes:
01.02.160 A-J   AD   2/1/1997

Illinois is not the only state coming after prisoners for money. In 1973, Lloyde Cowin was sentenced to three life sentences for murder in Missouri. The state filed suit to seek costs of incarceration after it learned that Mr. Cowin had assets of $16,025.68 through power of attorney with Jason Cowin. The court entered judgment for the state. But on appeal the court of appeals reversed because the trial court's order sought recovery from assets not identified. *See State ex rel. Koster v. Cowin*, 390 S. W. 3d 239 (2013); *also, Foster v. State*, 352 S.W. 3d 357, 361 (mo. banc.2011) ("prospect of a future gift does not constitute an asset because the offender is not entitled to it and it is not in the offender's account…").

PRISONER BANKRUPTCY

There's a bunch of literature out there that a bankruptcy proceeding is the answer to getting out from under that obligation. Even one judge has said as such: "…a convict who is subject to a money judgement does have the protection of any judgement debtor under state law and federal bankruptcy law." *Department of Corrections ex rel. People of the State of Illinois v. Adams*, 278 Ill.App.3d 803 (1996) (*Judge Green dissenting*).

But I'd advise you to use extreme caution before you decide to declare bankruptcy. You must examine your state's cost of incarceration and bankruptcy laws. You may be able to wipeout past debts, but not future obligations. If you structure your business entity properly then you may shield yourself from liability all together. A cellpreneur could set up a trust to control his business affairs, and as long as they aren't the beneficiary, they should be shielded from liability. Of course, you'd need someone you trust in the free world to be your trustee. This way may be better than bankruptcy.

> *"Bankruptcy is the answer only when you have too many debts*
> *to pay from your future income or from selling your assets."*
> *- Business attorney Hillel Presser, author of Asset Protection Secrets*
> *(www.AssetProtectionAttorneys.com)*

With that being said above, what do you do if you already owe hundreds of thousands of dollars in cost of incarceration fees? Maybe bankruptcy is the answer for you? If so, you should obtain a copy of cellpreneur Zachary Smith's book, Smith's Guide to Chapter 7 Bankruptcy for Prisoners. He has been through the process before and can help you. His book can be ordered for $31.90 ($34.08 in California) from Amazon.

If you form a LLC properly and that LLC files for bankruptcy it does not mess with your credit, unless you have personally guaranteed the debts. If you did guarantee them then you'll be liable or you'll have to file for bankruptcy yourself if you can't pay them. So, my advice on this subject is to never personally guarantee your LLC debts!

RESOURCE BOX

For more information on bankruptcy you may want to check out the following books:

- *The New Bankruptcy: Will It Work For You? By Stephen Elias & Leon Bayer*

- *Credit After Bankruptcy by Stephen Snyder*

Books can be ordered from our Bookstore on page 224 or online. Contact Freebird Publishers about ordering if you don't have anyone to help you..

MONEY MANAGEMENT FOR CELLPRENEURS

I love reading about my fellow lifers who are *Millionaire Prisoners* in their own right. Rahsaan Thomas wrote an article in the *San Quentin News* (January 2015) about lifer Curtis "Wall Street" Carroll. While in prison Carroll taught himself how to read, then advanced to picking stocks. Now he teaches a financial class at San Quentin with three modules: reentry, money management, and retirement. More proof that poor prisoners lay in bed all day watching tv while *Millionaire Prisoners* read *The Wall Street Journal*. But let's look at one of his modules: money management.

For me, you have one goal and one goal only: to extract the most profit from your info-cellpreneur system so you can invest in your future. I really like the money managing system that T.Harv Eker gives in his book *Secrets of the Millionaire Mind*. I like it so much that it's the one I now try to use to track and build my net worth. Here's how to do it:

1. Get a blank sheet of paper. Write "Net Worth" at the top. Then add up all your assets: bank accounts, home, cars, jewelry, TV, collectibles, etc. (But remember this: you use present value for cars, homes, jewelry, TVs, etc. If you had to sell those items – whatever you would get is what you use for this determination, not what you paid for the item.) The total is your net worth.

> *"An asset is worth only what it could be sold for, today."*
> *– Dan S. Kennedy, www.NoBSBooks.com*

2. Next, determine what you want your net worth to be, or the number you need to never have to work again. When I wrote my first book, The Millionaire Prisoner, I said my number was $6,000 a year for 40 years, or $240,000. But that number was reflective on what I wanted to live on in prison each year. I look at it different now. I've changed my number to 1 million! Why not be a net worth *Millionaire Prisoner* for real? (FYI: If I got out of prison it would change to 10 million!))

3. Write out a plan to get your number. Here's my simple version

Year One: Sell 2,000 copies of The Millionaire Prisoner
($16 profit per book sold = $32,000)

Year Two: Sell 2,000 copies of TMP + 2,000 copies of Pen Pal Success
($16 profit on TMP x 2,000 = $32,000 + $9 profit on Pen Pal Success = $18000) (32,000 + $18,000 = $50,000)

Year Three: Triple Net Worth through real estate, business and stock investments ($80,000 x 3 = $240,000)

Year Four: Put out 3rd book + continue to sell other books and triple net worth again ($240,000 +

$50,000 + $32,000 x 3 = $936,000)

Year Five: Sell all assets plus business to convert into net worth bank account of over 1 million cash after taxes!

Set up an investment / money managing program of profits as follows:
10% to a Long-Term Savings (SEP-IRA) Account
10% to an Education Account
10% to a Charity/Giving Account
20% to a Marketing Account
40% to a Necessities/Overhead Account
10% to a Play Account

This plan is simple, but it takes discipline to follow. Let's look at what the above accounts are for. Long-Term Savings Account is self-explanatory. This is money you put up and don't touch. So if you get $100, 10% is $10. That $10 goes into your savings account. Education Account is for books, study courses, college correspondence courses, or anything that helps you learn. Once again, if you get $100 - $10 goes to your education. Next is your charity/giving account. Practice good money karma by paying it forward. Another 10%. You may want to put more into the Marketing Account because that is what grows your customer base. I use 20% because that's what a lot of business books use, but it's not set-in-stone. Your necessities/overhead can consist of marketing, but since marketing is so important I think it should have its own account. 40% for a cellpreneur may be high or may be low? It depends on your business venture. You have to see how it goes, but you should keep costs as low as possible. 40% of $100 is $40. Lastly, you have your play account. 10% should be used to have fun or buy something you've always wanted. Reward yourself.

Most prisoners will not be able to follow this plan, but you're not in the most prisoners' category anymore. You have the *Millionaire Prisoner* mindset. You also have financial goals. The only way to reach them is to follow your money management plan. As you start growing your investment income you need to find a person to help manage your money and make it grow. You don't want a "broker." The reason they are called brokers is because without your money they will be broker than you! You want a fiduciary or an independent registered investment advisor. You can find them at:

      www.strongholdFinancial.com
      www.findanadvisor.napfa.or/home.aspx

The only credentials that you should be looking for is CFP or Certified Financial Planner. To get that certification the planner had to take a college-level course, pass a tough exam, and have at least three years as a full time personal financial planner. An accredited estate planner must be a lawyer or qualified professional, have taken two graduate-level courses, and have five years of estate planning experience. You can find background information and qualifications on brokers at www.brokercheck.finra.org. Be careful about who you hire to manage your money. If you need to understand all the different financial terms and make sense of money better, then read *How To Speak Money* by John Lanchester. I also really encourage you to read two other books:

    The Millionaire Fastlane by MJ DeMarco

    Money Master The Game by Tony Robbins

They will help demystify all the financial gobbledogook and show you how to make money fast and then invest it so you can achieve your dreams. Start your money management program today.

"I'd like to be rich enough, so I could throw
soap away after the letters are worn off."
– Andy Rooney

HOW TO SELL YOUR BUSINESS WITHOUT SELLING YOUR SOUL

In this great book, The Millionaire Fastlane, MJ Demarco says that the super-fast way to wealth is liquidation. Meaning to sell your business for a huge profit that makes you millions. An idea on paper is worthless but selling that idea outright; or through a license; is what makes you money. George Kayer built his book title, Inmate Shopper into a brand name then sold it to Freebird Publishers who revamped the title into what it is today. (FYI: He came to me also, but my offer was below his asking price.) If you build a brand and can show investors yearly  profit, then you can sell your business for a substantial sum. Here's how you do it without selling your soul.

- Pretend you don't need to sell. Trust me, if you're raking in money, buyers will come.

- Show the buyers the potential profit to come. Is your market share growing? Show them. Is your system producing more profit each month, quarter, or year? Show them.

- Be patient, let buyers come to you. Build something with quality and value and they will come.

- Don't pay attention to conventional business evaluations.
  You see it all the time on *Shark Tank* where one of the people pitching their businesses gets ripped by one of the sharks because they overvalued their business. Who cares about traditions, get what you want.

- Lastly, ask for a whole lot more than you really want. Never undervalue your business!

"Never be afraid to ask for too much when selling or offer too
little when buying. Once negotiations begin, you can come
down in your selling price or up in your buying price.
But it's impossible to do the opposite."
– Warren Buffett

You know how much money it will take to change your life. Keep that exit strategy in mind. A business that you have to work in everyday, 10-12 hours a day, is really just a job. And for any prisoner will just be another form of prison.

"Even if you trade golden handcuffs for
platinum handcuffs, you still are in prison."
– Robert G. Allen

CHAPTER 8
LICENSES, PARTNERSHIPS & TRUSTS

*"To become rich, you must be an owner,
and you must try to own it all."
- Felix Dennis*

LICENSES AND ASSIGNMENTS

Maybe you own a product, but because you're in prison you can't effectively market it? Or maybe you could, but instead want another company, a bigger one, to sell your product? You could license your product to them in return for a percentage of sales or even for a flat fee? You may even be approached by a company who wants to sell your product and pay you a licensing fee. That happened to me. Mike Enemigo of The Cell Block approached me about licensing my book, The Millionaire Prisoner. A copy of the original proposal agreement is included in this chapter. I didn't sign this one because I didn't want to give up all the rights to him for my book. We ended up

making a deal where The Cell Block would put out a "Special Edition" of The Millionaire Prisoner. He wrote a Forward for the special edition and changed the cover to give it a more "urban" feel. (see next page). We both win. I get a percentage of each book sold and he gets another book for his publishing empire. That's one way to do a licensing deal.

Another way is for you to purchase the "rights" to certain products and sell them. Ted Nicholas, author of Magic Words That Bring You Riches, said that he would do many of these types of deals and would pay a $250 advance on royalties. He said the advance was the key and he never paid more than $1,000. (FYI: An advance paid is taken out of the first sales. So, if my publisher gives me a $6,000 advance, they get to recoup that $6,000 up front from the initial sales. Sometimes publishers never recoup the advances paid if the book bombs. Authors normally do not have to pay advances back!) Most people would be happy to give you the rights to a product they couldn't sell. Especially if you pay them an advance and a royalty of each sale. You could find great products and make smart licensing deals. If I was in the free-world I would do this for a bunch of out-of-print books. But it can be used for any product type, not just books. Famous mail-order millionaire Joseph Sugarman built his business selling other people's products that he bought. He always tried to get an exclusive on the product. You could do the same.

If you want to approach another company or person about licensing your idea or product to that entity, I would suggest you first try and get them to sign a non-disclosure agreement. (I've included a sample one in this chapter.) I used an agreement like this before when I had an idea I wanted to pitch to my friend and fellow cellpreneur, George Kayer. We didn't use the idea, but I still might do it myself since I protected it with a non-disclosure agreement. Many people will not sign a non-disclosure agreement. In fact, one prison publisher sends a form wanting you to release all rights to your manuscript before they will even look at it. Thankfully I don't have to do that and neither should you. Elvis said it best: Don't Trust Anyone!

THE CELL BLOCK

PRESENTS

THE MILLIONAIRE PRISONER

SPECIAL TCB EDITION

JOSHUA KRUGER

FORWARD BY MIKE ENEMIGO

LICENSING AGREEMENT

This Agreement is entered into between The Cell Block, a California company with its principle address at PO BOX 212, Folsom, CA 95763 ("Licensee") and _____Josh Kruger_____, an individual with a principle address at _____ _____ ("Licensor"). The parties agree as follows effective this __8th__ day of _____February_____, __2015__ ("Effective Date").

(1) Distribution of Product: This agreement is for the distribution of new literary work written entirely by or containing contributions to collective work Licensor with a title of _____"THE MILLIONAIRE PRISONER"_____, manufactured and released by Licensee during the term of this agreement, all of which shall be referred to as "the Product". This agreement shall include the exclusive distribution through traditional retail and wholesale channels of literary works in book configuration, including all other forms of distribution, including but not limited to download and electronic transmission. The Product, including the cover artwork, shall, at all times, remain the property of Licensor, or any party responsible for its conceptualization and creation, financing and design.

(2) Exclusive Distribution: (a) Licensor hereby appoints Licensee as the exclusive distributor of the Product, with the right to manufacture, license, sublicense, publish, sell, promote and market the product, on a worldwide scale. Licensor shall neither allow nor permit any other person, company or entity to distribute the product without the express written consent of Licensee, and shall not assign any Product covered under the terms of this agreement to any entity, person, company or third party without written consent of Licensee.

(b) In the event that Licensee is unable to recoup all advances and expenses paid to or on behalf of Licensor, Licensee shall have the right to extend the terms of this agreement until such time as Licensee has recouped said advances and expenses, specific regard being given to any termination of this agreement, for any reason, as defined herein.

(3) Term: This agreement shall be binding and run in perpetuity for the life of the Product, unless and until such time as either party exercises its right to terminate said under the provisions set forth herein.

(4) Compensation: (a) Licensee shall pay Licensor an amount equal to __seventy__ (70%) of the net amount actually received by Licensee for the sale of the Product. For purposes of the foregoing sentence, the term "Net Amount Actually Received" shall mean the actual United States dollar amount received by Licensee less manufacturing, marketing, and promotional costs, which Licensee shall be entitled to recoup in its entirety from the Gross Sales of the Product. For purposes of the foregoing sentence, the term "Gross Sales" shall be defined as the amount paid to licensee by any party for sales of the product, prior to any and all deductions.

(b) Licensee shall make payment to Licensor on a quarterly basis based on total units shipped to and paid for by Licensee's customers less actual returns, customer inventory and return reserve, which shall not exceed 10%, and which shall be liquidated annually, beginning the first twelve months post publication of Product. The first payment to licensor shall be due approximately ninety (90) days from the commercial release date of the Product, at the first available calendar quarter. Thereafter, payments shall be made on a quarterly basis. All payments shall be accompanied by a Sales Report detailing all available information with regard to the computation of the royalty payment for which it represents.

(05) Termination: Licensee shall have the right to cancel this agreement at any time on thirty (30) days written notice to Licensor. Upon such termination, Licensee shall pay Licensor all royalties accrued as of such termination date. Licensee shall cease to publish, sell, distribute or market Licensor's Product, except as defined in Paragraph (02) (b) herein. In the event that Licensee fails to fulfill any provision set forth herein, Licensor may terminate the exclusivity of this Licensing Agreement effective thirty (30) days post receipt of written notice to Licensee, whereupon there is a failure to correct said grievance. In such instance, all other aspects of this agreement shall remain binding. Upon request for termination of this agreement by Licensor, Licensor shall make full remuneration to Licensee within thirty (30) days' time for any and all costs, materials, time and effort expended in good faith by Licensee for production, promotion, distribution, and any and all other services and costs related to the Product.

(06) Sales Reports: At Licensor's request, Licensee shall provide sales reports to Licensor detailing the sale of the Product. Each report shall include the number of units shipped and sold, as well as the format in which the Product was sold. Licensor may, within thirty (30) days written notice, audit all Licensee records pertaining to any product covered by this agreement at Licensor's own expense.

(07) Product Returnable: All product is 100% returnable to Licensee. Licensor recognizes that no sales are "final" and, although Licensee may report a "sale" of the Product and may have paid Licensor, such Product may be returned. In the event of a return for which Licensee has made payment to Licensor, such payment shall be deducted from the return reserve and/or Licensor's future royalty payments, whichever is great enough to cover the cost of said.

(08) Promotions: Promotional expenses shall be charged to Licensor's account and deducted from the quarterly statements provided to Licensor as well as the cost of any discounts necessary to issue to any of licensee's accounts.

(09) Representations: Both parties warrant and represent that they have the legal right to participate in this agreement and the ability to perform the terms hereof. Licensor further represents that all product which is the subject of this agreement is the legitimate Product of Licensor or that Licensor has acquired the lawful right to commercially exploit the same. Licensor warrants that the use and exploitation of the Product does and will not violate or infringe upon any copyright, trademark, or other intellectual property right claimed or owned by any other person, firm, or entity. Licensor warrants that it has the lawful right to publish and disseminate, for commercial purposes, the product to be distributed under the terms of this agreement including any and all copyrights, trademarks, service marks, names, likeness, images, and any other property right used in connection with the product.

(10) Hold Harmless and Indemnify: Both parties mutually agree to hold harmless and indemnify each other with respect to any claims, actions, suits, or the like, arising out of or connected with any claim by any third party which is inconsistent with the representations and warranties made by either party in connection with this agreement which have been reduced to final judgment or settled with Licensor's consent. Such indemnity and holding harmless shall include any and all losses and damages incurred by the affected party, including the party's reasonable costs and attorney fees in defending any legal action whether threatened or filed.

(11) Modification and Applicable Law: This agreement may only be modified in writing, mutually agreed upon and executed by the parties hereto. This agreement is made, and to be performed, in whole or in part, in the State of California and its law shall govern this agreement. This document contains the entire agreement between the parties.

(12) Mediation / Arbitration: In the event a dispute arises under the terms of this agreement the parties agree to attempt to resolve such dispute with the assistance of a mutually agreed upon mediator in the State of California. Any costs and fees, other than attorney's fees, shall be shared equally between the parties. In the event the parties do not resolve their differences by mediation the parties agree to submit the dispute to binding arbitration in the city of Sacramento, California.

(13) Notice / Breach: Notices to either party required under this agreement shall be made in writing and delivered by registered or certified mail, or private courier, to the address shown at the head of this agreement or such other addresses as may be designated in writing from time to time as well as legal counsel for both parties.

Either party claiming breach under the terms of this agreement shall provide notice of same in writing. Such notice must specifically set forth the facts constituting the breach. The party receiving such notice shall have thirty (30) days to cure the breach. Failure to cure a breach within thirty (30) days shall not be grounds for rescission of this agreement unless such breach is a material breach of this agreement. Acts of God and matters traditionally considered beyond the control of the party shall not be considered a breach of this agreement; provided, if Licensee cannot render services due to force majeure event for period in excess of sixty (60) days, Licensor may terminate contract via written notice and distribute the product through a third party.

WITNESS THE SIGNATURES OF THE UNDERSIGNED PARTIES:

Joshua Kruger

_____

By:

The Cell Block

By: _

R. Michael Werth, President

NON-DISCLOSURE AGREEMENT

WHEREAS, (Your name as inventor) has developed a (product type) and related technical and commercial information (collectively, Proprietary Information); and

WHEREAS, the undersigned and the firm of which he or she is an authorized representative (individually and collectively, the Undersigned) are interested in examining the Proprietary Information with a view to entering into a business arrangement in connection therewith; and

Whereas, (Your Name) considers the Proprietary Institution to be highly confidential; and

Whereas, (Your Name) is willing to allow the Undersigned to examine the Proprietary Information pursuant to the condition set forth herein;

Now therefore, in consideration of (Your Name) supplying the Undersigned with the aforesaid Proprietary Information, the Undersigned agree that for a period of two years from the date hereof such Proprietary Information shall be utilized only for the aforesaid purposes and that no other use or disclosure or copying thereof will be made without explicit prior written authorization from (Your Name).

Notwithstanding the above, the obligations of the Undersigned hereunder will be limited in regard to any specific portion of the Proprietary Information which (a) was in the public domain prior to the date of this agreement, or subsequently comes into the public domain other than as a result of actions of the Undersigned, or (b) is subsequently received by the Undersigned from a third party who did not acquire it directly or indirectly from (Your Name), or (c) the Undersigned can show as in their possession prior to the receipt thereof hereunder.

Date: _____

By: (Signature) _____

Printed Full Name: _____

Title: _____

Company: _____

WHAT IS AN AGREEMENT?

An agreement is simply a promise (or a set of promises) between two or more people to do something. It can also be used to prohibit someone from doing something. Like the previously mentioned non-disclosure agreement. Certain types of agreements must be in writing or they are invalid by law. Contracts for the sale of goods for more than $500 must be in writing. Agreements to purchase land and real estate must be in writing. Duties that can't be done in less than a year must be put into a written agreement. No matter what, I advise you to never rely on oral agreement. Always try to get a signed letter of agreement at least.

"An oral agreement isn't worth the paper it's written on."
– Samuel Goldwyn

TO LICENSE OR NOT?

Only you can answer that question. Do you want to spend your time filling orders or creating other products? Do you have the time, know-how, resources and zeal to do it all yourself? Or do you want to just sit back and relax while your mailbox fills up with royalty checks? It's a lot easier to license your product or idea to someone else. Robert Kiyosaki licenses his Rich Dad, Poor Dad series to another company who distributes them. I did it with my book, Pen Pal Success.

After putting out my first book, The Millionaire Prisoner, through my own publishing company, Carceral Wealth Services, I decided to try a different route. The reason why I did this was because I didn't want to keep going to segregation over my business or have to worry about stuff getting confiscated by Internal Affairs. So, I approached Freebird Publishers and told them what I wrote. They agreed to publish it and pay me a higher than usual royalty off each book sold. It was a hell of a lot easier I tell you. Most prisoners should do it that way. The downside? You lose a lot of profit. If you only sell a couple hundred products it doesn't really matter. But if you're selling thousands you could lose a nice chunk of change. So, make sure your decision to license or not is made with your eyes wide open. Here are some questions you ask yourself about the other company in the proposed deal:

- Can they reach new markets that I can't?

- Do they have great manufacturing, marketing and distribution capabilities that I don't have?

- Do they have an established customer base?

- Do they have brand name recognition?

If you answer yes to all of these questions, then you should probably license your product or idea to them. Still not sure? Contact a business law attorney for advice. You can also get a free evaluation and consultation with a patent attorney by contacting:

American Intellectual Property Law Association
2001 Jefferson Davis Highway, Suite 203
Arlington, VA 22202
www.aipla.org

Assignment Of Contract

You can also sell your intellectual property outright. This is called an "assignment." It's a simple transaction to do. I assigned all my rights to that book to my brother and his company, J&J Holdings. But be sure you want to do this because once it's done it's final. There are no refunds or do overs. You have to be sure you're getting a fair price. I hear a lot of prisoners say they would sell their books outright for $10,000. That is life changing money for a prisoner. But they should be careful about that. If the book is well written and properly promoted it could do well more than $10,000. But you may need money fast and this may be the way to go? Only you can make that decision. Just in case you decide to sell your intellectual property outright I've included a sample Assignment and the one I did for my book when I assigned it to J&J Holdings.

PRODUCT ASSIGNMENT

Date: _____, 20_____.

FOR GOOD AND VALUABLE CONSIDERATION, receipt of which is acknowledged, I/we hereby convey and assign to _____("Assignee") all my/our ownership rights and interest in the following product(s):

_____

_____

_____

The Assignee may use the product(s) as the owner of the same, as they see fit to do so.

s/ _____

_____

_____

_____

_____

LITERARY MATERIAL ASSIGNMENT

FOR GOOD AND VALUABLE CONSIDERATION, receipt of which is acknowledged, I hereby convey and assign to Joseph W. Kruger, J & J Holdings,   Danville, IL. 61834 ("Assignee") all my ownership rights and interest in the following literary material:

The Millionaire Prisoner: How To Turn Your Prison Into A Stepping-Stone To Succe$$(ISBN:978-0-9906154-4-5) by Josh Kruger

The Assignee may apply for copyrights on the material and utilize them as the owner of the same.

_____
Joshua Kruger

Date: March 14, 2016

]

_____
Notary Public

JENNIFER CLENDENIN
OFFICIAL SEAL
Notary Public, State of Illinois
My Commission Expires
May 29, 2018

FINDING BUSINESS AND SUCCESS MENTORS

Someone once said, "If the king likes you, it doesn't matter who dislikes you." It sounded cool, so I wrote it down. Later on, it dawned on me that they were talking about favor. I'm not talking about "favors" as in the exchange of gifts. With favor, there is no debt. To better illustrate what I'm talking about, let me give you a few examples. This will help you understand its power.

In 2007, I began a writing campaign in which I wrote to all the authors of books, which I read in research for my first book, *The Millionaire Prisoner*. I wrote them telling them how their book had helped me and that I was writing my own book for prisoners. Notice that I was telling the truth. It wasn't some form of jailhouse game. Their books had in fact changed my life and the way I thought. I wanted to share this with them. But did I really expect responses? No, but I hoped that someone I admired would validate my journey by giving me a reply. A few of them did write me back.

The famous motivational speaker and author, Zig Ziglar, sent me a copy of his autobiography: Zig. He's an inspiration to me and his books, *Top Performance* and *Secrets of Closing the Sale*, have helped me on my journey. His autobiography was a great read and showed me that by helping others get what they want out of life, my prosperity would be given to me. If I had questions, I'd write Zig and he'd give me an answer. He showed me favor and was my mentor. It's with deep sadness that I tell you that Zig passed away in 2012. But his son is carrying on the Ziglar tradition and you should read Zig's last book, *Born To Win*. Zig Ziglar didn't have to send me books or write me back. But he understood that helping someone else up the ladder of success is the right thing to do. You need to find your own Zig Ziglar's of the world.

"Favor must become your seed before it can become your harvest."
– Dr. Mike Murdock

The easiest way to find mentors is by reading books. The people who have gone through what you've gone through are who you need to be mentored by. Start by writing them. If you can't find their e-mail address or snail-mail address, then write them "in care of" the publisher. It works, I do it all the time. They'll get the letter. You should actively seek out other people. Whether you use email, phone, or regular old snail mail, you should be trying to contact everybody you admire. And anyone else that could help you reach your goals. Share with them and ask what they are doing.

"The more people you talk with, network with, develop a relationship with, the more opportunities and insights you will have. Opening one door leads to dozens of other doors. Opening dozens of doors leads to hundreds of others."
– Jay Abraham

RESOURCE BOX

For more about how to make money with licensing I suggest you grab copies of the following:

- *Franchising & Licensing: Two Ways to Build Your Business, 2nd Edition by Andrew J. Sherman*

- *How To License Technology*

- *How To License Your Million Dollar Idea* by Harvey Reese

- *The Licensing Business Handbook, 4th Edition* by Karen Raugust

- *The Complete Idiot's Guide to Cashing In on Your Inventions* by Richard C. Levy

Books can be ordered from our Bookstore on page 224 or online. Contact Freebird Publishers about ordering if you don't have anyone to help you.

SAMPLE LICENSE AGREEMENT

This _____ License Agreement ("Agreement") is made and entered into this _____,20_____("Effective Date"), by and between _____ _____, a _____ corporation with offices at _____ _____Street, _____("Licensee") and _____ _____, a _____ corporation with offices at _____ _____Street, _____("Licensor").

WHEREAS, Licensor has developed and owns all rights to a _____ known as the _____and more fully identified in Exhibit A;

WHEREAS, Licensee desires to use the _____for its own internal business purposes;

NOW, THEREFORE, in consideration of the mutual promises contained herein, the parties agree as follows:

1. Licensee Grant. Licensor grants to Licensee a nonexclusive license to use the _____ for its own internal business purposes, without the right of sublicense, subject to the terms and conditions of this Agreement. Licensee shall not copy or otherwise duplicate the _____, except for one copy for back up purposes, and shall not transfer, sell, or otherwise distribute the _____ to any third party. All rights not specifically granted to Licensee shall be reserved to Licensor.

2. Term. This agreement shall commence on the Effective Date and continue for a period of one (1) year, unless terminated according to this Agreement. This Agreement may be renewed for additional one (1) year periods, at the mutual consent of the parties.

3. Termination. Licensor may terminate this Agreement if Licensee material breaches any provision, subject to a thirty (30) day cure period. Upon termination, Licensee shall return all copies of the _____to Licensor.

4. Fees. During the term of this Agreement, Licensee shall pay Licensor a royalty of $_____per year. Payments shall be made every quarter for the duration of the term.

IN WITNESS WHEREOF, the parties have executed this Agreement as of the date first written above:

_____   _____
(Licensor)   (Licensee)

_____   _____
Name   Date   Name   Date

_____   _____
Title   Title

141

FORMING A PARTNERSHIP

Most advisors will tell you not to form a partnership. Why? Because it's rare for two people to complement each other well. You have to divide the work so that both will be happy. I did form a partnership with my friend John Halas of Superior Enterprises. We had a non-formal written agreement to share profits in a 50/50 split. It worked out well for several years. As John got older, and my twin brother got out of federal prison, I decided to transition all of my business interests into the control of my brother and his company, J&J Holdings. I'm still friends with John to this day. But this was a rare instance where I found a partner willing to work out there while I worked in here creating info-products. My mother did not make a good business partner. Some people just don't. Be careful when choosing your partners. If you do find someone reliable I suggest you draw up a formal partnership agreement like the sample one on the next page. Make two copies of your agreement, then sign both copies in front of a witness. Have your witness sign them. Then send both copies to your partner, they are to send a signed copy back to you after they sign it. And they should keep the other copy for their records. You never know, a partnership could be your step to getting started as a cellpreneur. Remember to be careful before you sign any agreement.

> *"If two or more people want to form a company,*
> *they should consider a corporation."*
> *–Dan Poynter*

PARTNERSHIP AGREEMENT

THIS AGREEMENT made this _____ day of _____, 20 _____, by and among _____ (hereinafter referred to as "Partner One") and _____ (hereinafter referred to as "Partner Two").

WHEREAS, Partner One and Partner Two desire to form a partnership in the state of _____.

NOW, THEREFORE, in consideration of the mutual covenants and agreements contained herein, the parties here to, intending to be legally bound hereby, agree as follows:

1. The parties hereby form a partnership that will engage in the business of _____ under the name of _____.

2. The partners ownership interest and capital account shall be as follows:
    _____
    _____
    _____

3. The principal office of the partnership is to be located at _____ _____, or in such other place as the parties may agree.

4. The partnership shall exist for a period of _____, commencing on _____, 20 _____ , and shall continue until _____, 20_____, unless terminated earlier as hereinafter provided.

5. Either party to this partnership agreement may withdraw from the partnership upon six (6) months notice to the remaining party to this partnership agreement.

6. The partners shall share the profits and losses of the partnership in relationship to their ownership interest.

7. This partnership agreement shall immediately terminate upon the death of either partner.

8. All controversies arising under or in connection with, or relating to any alleged breach of, this partnership agreement shall be settled by arbitration in accordance with the rules then obtaining of the American Arbitration Association, and judgement upon any award rendered may be entered in court having jurisdiction.

9. This partnership agreement shall be binding upon and inure to the benefit of the parties hereto and their respective heirs, executors, administrators, successors and assigns.

10. This partnership agreement constitutes the entire agreement between the parties hereto and supersedes all prior agreements, negotiations and understanding of any nature with respect to the subject matter hereto. No amendment, waiver or discharge of any of the provisions of this agreement shall be effective against any party unless that party shall have consented thereto in writing.

(continued on next page)

PARTNERSHIP AGREEMENT

11. This partnership agreement shall be construed, interpreted and enforced in accordance with the laws of the state of _____.

IN WITNESS WHEREOF, Partner One and Partner Two have caused this partnership agreement to be duly executed the day and year set out above.

IN WITNESS WHEREOF, the parties have executed this agreement the day and year frist above written.

s/ _____   s/ _____

_____   _____

"Partner One"   "Partner Two"

s/ _____   s/ _____

Witness   Witness

REVOCABLE LIVING TRUSTS

Some prisoners always say they want to set up a trust to protect their assets. The truth is that if the prisoner is the beneficiary of the trust the DOC could still try and seize the money they get from the trust. That prisoner would have to set up an "irrevocable" living trust and name someone else as the beneficiary. They may still be able to name themselves or a lawyer as the "trustee" that manages the trust. But that would still be a slippery slope when it comes to cost of incarceration charges. The thing about an irrevocable trust is that it couldn't be revoked or changed. Should you consider one of these types of trusts for an avenue of asset protection then I highly recommend you consult an attorney who specializes in trusts. That type of trust is beyond this guidebook area of discussion.

Another type of trust is a "special needs trust." For instance, I have a daughter who has cerebral palsy and is wheelchair bound. I would love to be able to set up a special needs trust so that she will have money to live on and that her many medical bills would be taken care of. That type of trust is not what I'm going to write about.

I'm talking about a "revocable living trust." This type of trust provides solutions to probate that a will cannot.

Some attorneys recommend these trusts, while others believe they are overvalued. A living trust is good in case you get disabled, sick or incapacitated. And they are written so you can alter or change them if you wish during your lifetime. A living trust is set up, so it has a trustee who manages the property that is transferred to the trust. Should you die, then the trustee will distribute the trusts property to the beneficiaries you've named or continue to manage the trust for the benefit of said beneficiaries. I think any prisoner that has children and decides to become a cellpreneur should set up a revocable living trust. Why? Because shit happens in prison. Prisons have the worst health care system in America. God, forbid you get sick without having taken this step beforehand. If anything, I hope that this section will get you thinking about your heirs and your legacy. As a cellpreneur your goal should not only be to eat commissary food when you want, but also to provide something for your loved ones. This is one to do it. I've included a sample trust on the next few pages. Just remember, I'm not an attorney and make no guarantee of the information contained therein.

"Put not your trust in money but put your money in trust."
– Oliver Wendell Holms

REVOCABLE LIVING TRUST AGREEMENT

THIS REVOCABLE LIVING TRUST AGREEMENT, (Hereinafter "Trust"), is being made this _____ day of _____, 20 _____, by and between _____, _____County _____, as the Trustor, and serving as Trustee. This Trust shall be known as THE _____ REVOCABLE TRUST, and shall be administered in accordance with the following terms:

ARTICLE I

INTRODUCTION

(A) TRUST PURPOSE

Any person shall deal with the Trustee without the approval of any court, the Trustor, or any beneficiary of any Trust created by this Trust and shall assume that the Trustee has the same power and authority to act as an individual does in the management of his or her own affairs. Father, any person presented with a copy of this page and any other page of the Trust shall accept same as conclusive proof of the terms and authority granted by this Trust and shall assume that no conflicting directions or terms are contained in the pages omitted.

(B) TRUST ASSETS

_____, as Trustor, does hereby assign, convey and deliver to the Trustee, all of the Trustor's right, title, and interest in and to all real and personal property, tangible or intangible, of any nature, in any location, which may be owned by the Trustor or later acquired by the Trustor, unless an exception to the conveyance of a particular property interest is made on Schedule A. Said property shall include,, but shall not be limited to, the assets listed on Schedule A, which may be attached to this Trust. However, this general assignment shall not alter any beneficiary designation unless specifically listed on Schedule A. A voluntary conveyance by the Trustor of a Trust asset which may remain registered to the Trustor individually shall convey any interest held by this Trust.

(C) ABSTRACT OF TRUST

In order to facilitate the convenient administration of the Trust, including the registration and transfer of assets to and from the Trust, the Trustee shall have the power to execute an Abstract of Trust describing any Trust matter, including but not limited to a description of the Trust terms, the administrative powers of the Trustee and the identity of any current Trustee. Any person who receives an original or photocopy of said Abstract of Trust shall be held harmless from relying on same, and shall not be obligated to inquire into the terms of the Trust or maintain a copy of the Trust.

(D) SUGGESTED TRUST REGISTRATION

During the life of the Trustor, assets may be registered to the Trust as follows: _____, Trustee, or his/her successors in trust, under THE _____ REVOCABLE TRUST date the _____ day of _____, 20 _____, and any amendments thereto.

Other forms of registration are permissible.

(E) TAX IDENTIFICATION

During the life of the Trustor, the Trust shall be identified by the Trustor's Social Security Number. Upon the death of the Trustor, the Trustee shall apply to the IRS for a tax identification number for the TRUST and any other TRUST created by this Trust Agreement

ARTICLE II

ADMINISTRATION DURING THE LIFE OF THE TRUSTOR

(A) The Trustee of this Trust shall be the Trustor. If the Trustee cannot continue to serve for any reason, the Successor Trustee shall be, and if he shall be not willing and/or able, then _____ shall serve as the Successor Trustee. The powers of the Trustee and the Successor Trustee are set forth in Article VI, below.

(B) DISPOSITION OF INCOME AND PRINCIPAL

1) AT THE DIRECTION OF THE TRUSTOR

The Trustee shall manage the property of the trust estate, collect the income, and shall pay from the income of the Trust such amounts and to such persons as the Trustor may from time to time direct. In the absence of direction, the Trustee may accumulate the net income or may disburse any portion of the net income to or for the benefit of the Trustor,

_____.

In addition, the Trustee shall pay from the principal of the Trust such amounts and to such persons as said Trustor may direct. In the absence of direction, the Trustee may pay from the principal of this Trust such amounts as may be necessary for the health or maintenance of the standard of living of _____.

2) DURING THE INCAPACITY OF THE TRUSTOR

In the event _____ is incapacitated as defined by this Trust Agreement, the Successor Trustee may apply or expend all or a part of the income and principle of this Trust, or both, for the health and maintenance of _____ in his/her accustomed manner of living.

During any period of incapacity of the Trustor, and provided sufficient resources exist for the care of the Trustor, the Successor Trustee is authorized to make distributions to or for the benefit of any issue of the Trustor who have no other financial resources and require said distribution for their health or support. In this regard the Successor Trustee shall consider all financial resources available to the beneficiary prior to making an invasion of this Trust, including, but not limited to, the ability of said beneficiary to earn a living and the ability of said beneficiary's spouse, if any, to earn a living. In no event may a Successor Trustee participate in the exercise of this power in favor of himself.

(C) RIGHT TO ADD TO PRINCIPAL

The Trustor, _____, or any other person may, at any time and from time to time add property acceptable to the Trustee to the Trust.

(D) RIGHT TO REVOKE AND AMEND

The Trustor, _____, reserves the right while alive, except any period when incapacitated, at any time and from time to time, by an instrument in writing, signed, acknowledged, and delivered to the Trustee:

1) To revoke this instrument entirely and to receive from the Trustee all property remaining after making payment or provision for payment of all expenses connected with the administration of this Trust,

2) From time to time to change the identity or number, or both, of the Trustee and, or Successor Trustee,

3) From time to time to alter or amend this instrument in any and every particular,

4) From time to time to withdraw from the operation of this Trust any or all of the Trust property.

ARTICLE III

ADMINISTRATION AFTER THE DEATH OF THE TRUSTOR

(A) TRUSTEE

The Trustee (meaning the Successor Trustee then acting as Trustee), shall continue to administer the assets of this Trust as well as any property received by this Trust under the terms of the Trustor's will or from any other source to the extent it is included in the Trustor's gross estate for Federal Estate Tax Purposes, and shall distribute said assets as provided below.

(B) COLLECTION OF PROCEEDS

The Trustee may take such action as is necessary to collect the proceeds of any life insurance policy, or provide for the payment of retirement plan, IRA, or other benefits payable to the Trust. If probate administration has not or will not be commenced, the Trustee shall have the power to collect tax refunds, health insurance proceeds, refunds under any contract, death benefits, or any other item which might otherwise be payable to the deceased Trustor's estate.

(C) DEBTS AND EXPENSES

The Trustee may, in the Trustee's sole and absolute discretion, pay to the estate of the Trustor from the principal or income of the Trust prior to distribution to any trusts created hereunder or any other distribute, such amounts as may be needed to pay all or any part of the deceased Trustor's just debts, funeral expense, and the administration expenses of the Trustor's estate. Alternatively, the Trustee may, but shall not be obligated to, pay such expenses directly.

(D) DEATH TAXES

The Trustee shall pay to the estate of the deceased Trustor or the appropriate tax authorities all estate and inheritance taxes that may become payable by reason of the Trustor's death in respect to all of the property comprising the Trustor's gross estate for death tax purposes, whether or not such property passes under this Trust, under the Trustor's will or otherwise.

Trust, under the Trustor's will or otherwise. However, the Trustee shall have the right of contribution as provided in Sections 2207 and 2207A IRC, if it is applicable.

(E) DISTRIBUTIONS TO THE TRUSTOR'S ESTATE

In addition to the distributions provided for in paragraphs C and D of this Article, the Trustee may pay to the Probate Estate of the deceased Trustor as much of the income and principle of this Trust as the Trustee deems necessary for any purpose.

(F) SPECIFIC GIFTS OF TANGIBLE PERSONAL PROPERTY

Upon the death of the Trustor, the Trustee shall make such gifts of the tangible personal property of the Trustor held or acquired by the Trust as may be directed by the Trustor's Will, or as may be directed by a list, letter, or other writing of the Trustor permitted by the Will, or as may be directed by a list, letter or other writing designated as Schedule B of this Trust. The cost of storing, packing, shipping and insuring any tangible personal property gift prior to delivery to its intended recipient shall be paid by the Trust.

ARTICLE IV

DEATH OF THE TRUSTOR

(A) DISTRIBUTIONS AND DISBURSEMENTS

Upon the death of the Trustor, and after the payment of the Trustor's just debts, funeral expenses and expenses of last illness, and the disbursements listed in Article III of this Trust, the following distributions shall be made:
_____ (state who is to receive property after termination of trust) I leave all the rest and remainder of the trust property to.

(B) DEATH OF BENEFICIARY BEFORE COMPLETE DISTRIBUTION OF TRUST ASSETS

1) In the event the Beneficiary dies before a complete distribution of his Trust is made, then their share shall go to: _____
_____

(C) PERPETUITIES CLAUSE

Notwithstanding any provision of this Trust to the contrary, all Trusts shall vest in their beneficiary twenty-one years after the death of the last of the issue of the Trustor who was alive when the Trustor died.

ARTICLE V
INCAPACITY, REHABILITATION, AND GUARDIANSHIP

Throughout this Trust Agreement, where there have been references to "incapacity" and "rehabilitation", these two terms shall have the following meanings:

(A) "INCAPACITATED"

If _____, as a Trustee or beneficiary, is under a legal disability or by reason of illness, or mental or physical disability is, in the written opinion of two doctors currently practicing medicine, unable to properly manage his/her affairs, they shall be deemed incapacitated for the purposes of this trust Agreement.

(B) "REHABILITATION"

_____, as a Trustee or beneficiary, once deemed incapacitated under Paragraph (A) of this Article, shall be deemed rehabilitated when she is no longer under a legal disability or when, in the written opinion of two doctors currently practicing medicine, he/she is able to properly manage their affairs. Upon rehabilitation, they shall resume the duties and powers they had prior to incapacity and his/her successors shall relinquish all powers and be relieved of all duties.

(C) "GUARDIANSHIP"

In the event the Trustor is adjudicated incompetent by any court having jurisdiction, pursuant to _____ statutes or similar provisions of the laws of any other state having jurisdiction, the Trustor does hereby nominate the same person(s) in name and order of succession who serve as Trustee as provided in Article II (A) as Guardian of the property of the incompetent Trustor, and the same person(s) in name and order of succession as provide in Article IX (B) as Guardian of the person of the incompetent Trustor. The Trustor further directs that the Court Honor Article 1(B) of the Trust by permitting the completion of the conveyance to the Trustee of any assets which remain registered to the Trustor.

ARTICLE VI

PROVISIONS REGARDING THE TRUSTEE

The following general provisions apply to the Trustee and any Successor Trustee of any Trust which is created by this Trust Agreement:

(A) GENERAL REVISIONS

1) TRUSTEE'S POWER: It is the intention of the Trustor to grant to the Trustee the power to deal with all the Trust property as freely as the Trustor could do individually, and the only requirement that the Trustor places upon the Trustee is that the Trustee act as a fiduciary in good faith. The trustee shall have all the powers and protection granted to Trustees by statute at the time of application, including all the powers enumerated below or contained in any Certificate of Trust signed by the Trustor; and the Trustor intends that such powers be construed in the broadest possible manner. Notwithstanding the foregoing, the Trustee shall not hold or exercise any power, or any discretion granted by Article VII which creates unexpected or adverse tax consequences to the Trustor's estate, any Trust created by this agreement, or any beneficiary, or which causes taxation to the Trustee or his/her estate by virtue of the existence of the power. The Trustee's powers are ministerial in nature and not intended to create or alter substantive rights. The limitations of this paragraph shall not affect the rights of any third person who deals with the Trustee.

(B) SPECIFIC POWERS OF THE TRUSTEE

1) RETAIN TRUST ESTATE: To retain, without liability for loss or depreciation resulting from such retention, the original assets and all other property later transferred, devised or bequeathed to the Trustee for such time as the Trustee shall deem advisable although it represents a large percentage of all of any

Trust; said original property may accordingly be held as permanent investment

2) HOLD UNINVESTED CASH AND UNDERPRODUCTIVE PROPERTY: For any periods deemed advisable, to hold cash, uninvested, even though the total amount so held is disproportionate under trust investment law or would not be permitted without this provision, and to retain or acquire and hold underproductive realty or personally.

3) INVEST AND ACQUIRE: To invest and reinvest Trust assets in any type of property or security or any interests in such property (including co-tenancies and remainders) without regard to the proportion that investments of the type selected may bear to the entire Trust Estate, without limitation to the classes of trust investments authorized by law, and without regard to the possibility that the investments may be in new issues or in new or foreign enterprises, and to write options against long positions. The property acquired may be realty or personally and may include life insurance, bonds, debentures, leaseholds, options, easements, mortgages, notes, mutual funds, investment trusts, common trust funds, voting trust certificates, limited partnership interest, U.S. Treasury obligations redeemable at par in payment of Federal Estate Tax, and any class of stock or rights to subscribe for stock, regardless of whether the yield rate is high or low or whether or not the new asset produces any income at all. It is intended that the Trustee shall have the authority to act in any manner deemed in the best interests of the Trust involved, regarding it as a whole, even though certain investments considered alone might not otherwise be proper.

4) OPTIONS, WARRANTS, PUTS, CALLS, COMMODITY AND MARGIN ACCOUNTS: The Trustee is specifically authorized, in her/his discretion, to buy, sell or transfer options, warrants, puts, calls, commodities, future contracts, repurchase contracts, and to maintain brokerage margin accounts.

5) EXERCISE OPTIONS AND CONVERSION PRIVILEGES: To exercise any options, rights, and conversion privileges pertaining to any securities held by the Trustee as Trust assets.

6) RECEIVE ADDITIONAL PROPERTY: To receive additional property from any source including the Personal Representative of a Trustor's estate and the Trustee or beneficiary of any other trust, by whomsoever created, and to hold and administer this property as part of the Trust Estate.

7) SELL AND LEASE: To sell, convey, grant options to purchase, lease, transfer, exchange or otherwise dispose of any Trust asset on any terms deemed advisable, to execute and deliver deeds, leases, bills of sale, and other instruments of whatever character, and to take or cause to be taken all action deemed necessary or proper.

8) INSURANCE: To carry any insurance deemed advisable with any insurer against any hazards, including public liability, and to use insurance proceeds to repair or replace the asset insured. In addition, the Trustee may carry or purchase life insurance on the life of any Trust beneficiary, and exercise or release any rights in such policy.

9) LEND: On any terms deemed advisable, to lend Trust funds to any borrower, including the personal representative of a Trustor's estate and the Trustee or beneficiary of any trust, by whomsoever created, and to change the terms of these loans. This authorization includes the power to extend them beyond maturity with or without renewal and without regard to the existence or value of any security, and to facilitate payment, to change the interest rate, and to consent to the modification of any guarantee.

10) BORROW: To borrow whatever money the Trustee deems desirable for any Trust on any terms from any lender, including the personal representative of a Trustor's estate, and the Trustee or beneficiary of any other trust, by whomsoever created, and to mortgage, pledge or otherwise encumber as security ay assets of the borrowing trust.

11) TERM OR DURATION OF OBLIGATION: Incident to the exercise of any power, to initiate or change the terms of collection or of payment of any debt, security, or other obligation of or due to any Trust, upon any terms and for any period, including a period beyond the duration or the termination of any or all trusts.

12) COMPROMISE OR ABANDONMENT OF CLAIMS: Upon whatever terms the Trustee deems advisable, to compromise, adjust, arbitrate, sue on, defend, or otherwise deal with any claims, including tax claims, against or in favor of any trust, to abandon any asset the Trustee deems of no value or of insufficient value to warrant keeping or protection: to refrain from paying taxes, assessments, or rents, and from repairing or maintaining any asset; and to permit any asset to be lost by tax sale or other proceeding.

13) DISTRIBUTION IN CASH OR IN PROPERTY: To distribute any share in cash or in property, or partly in each, and the Trustee's valuations of and selection of assets upon making distribution shall, if made in good faith, be final and binding on all beneficiaries.

14) USE OF NOMINEE: To hold any or all of the Trust assets, real or personal, in the Trustee's own name, or in the single name of any Co-Trustee, or in the name of any corporation, partnership, or other person as the Trustee's nominee for holding the assets, with or without disclosing the fiduciary relationship. A corporate Trustee shall have the power to appoint a Trustee to administer property in any jurisdiction in which it shall fail to qualify.

15) BID ON OR TAKE OVER WITHOUT FORECLOSURE: To foreclose any mortgage, to bid on the mortgaged property at the foreclosure sale or acquire it from the mortgagor without foreclosure, and to retain it or dispose of it upon any terms deemed advisable.

16) PAY OFF ENCUMBRANCES: To pay off any encumbrance on any Trust asset and to invest additional amounts to preserve it or to increase its productivity.

17) VOTE STOCK: To vote stock for any purpose in person or by proxy, to enter into a voting trust, and to participate in corporate activities related to a trust in any capacity permitted by law, including service as officer or director.

18) PARTICIPATE IN REORGANIZATION: To unite with other owners of property similar to any held in Trust in carrying out foreclosure, lease, sale, incorporation, dissolution, liquidation, re-incorporation, reorganization, or readjustment of the capital or financial structure of any association or corporation in which any Trust has a financial interest, to serve as a member of any protective committee, to deposit Trust securities in accordance with any plan agreed upon; to pay any assessments, expenses, or other sums deemed expedient for the protection or furtherance of the interests of the beneficiaries; and to receive and retain as Trust investments any new securities issued pursuant to the plan, even though these securities would not constitute authorized Trust investments without this provision.

19) PURCHASE PROPERTY FROM ESTATE OR TRUST: To purchase property, real or personal, from a Trustor's or beneficiary's estate or trust for their benefit upon such terms and conditions, price and terms of payment as the Trustee and the respective personal representative or Trustee shall agree upon, to hold the property so purchased in Trust although it may not qualify as an authorized Trust investment except for this provision, and to dispose of such property as and when the Trustee shall deem advisable.

20) EMPLOYMENT OF ASSISTANTS AND AGENTS: To any extent reasonably necessary, to employ attorneys-at-law, accountants, financial planners, brokers, investment advisors, realtors, managers for business or farms, technical consultants, attorneys-in-fact, agents and any other consultants and assistants the Trustee deems advisable for the proper administration of any Trust.

21) ESTABLISHMENT AND MAINTENANCE OF RESERVES: Out of the rents, profits, or other gross income received, to set aside and maintain reserves to the extent deemed advisable to meet present or future expenses, including taxes, assessments, insurance premiums, debt amortization, repairs, improvements, depreciation, obsolescence, general maintenance and reasonable compensation for services, including services of professional and other employees, as well as to provide for the effects of fluctuations in gross income and to equal or apportion payments for the benefit of beneficiaries entitle to receive income.

22) MANAGE REALTY: To deal with real and personally, including oil, gas, and mineral rights in any manner lawful to an owner. This authority includes the rights to manage, protect, and improve it, to raze, alter and repair improvements, to sell or contract to sell it in whole or in part, to partition it, to grant options to purchase it, to donate it, to convey it, to acquire it, release or grant easements or other rights relating to it, to dedicate parks and thoroughfares, to subdivide it, to vacate any subdivisions or any part thereof and resubdivide it from time to time, to lease it in whole or in part, and to renew, extend, contract for, and grant option in connection with contract entered into by the Trustee can be made on any terms and for any period, including a period beyond the duration or termination of any Trust.

23) CARRY ON BUSINESS: With respect to any business that may be or become a part of any Trust whether organized as a sole proprietorship, limited partnership, partnership or corporation, upon such terms, for such time, and in such manner as the Trustee deems advisable:

   a. To hold, retain and continue to operate such business solely at the risk of the Trust estate and without liability on the Trustee's part for any resulting losses;

   b. To incorporate, dissolve, liquidate, or sell such business at such times and upon such terms as the Trustee deems advisable. In this regard the Trustee's decision may be based upon qualified appraisal, and the Trustee shall not be obligated to seek other offers in contracting for sale to any person including another shareholder, trust, or beneficiary;

   c. To borrow money for business purposes and to mortgage, pledge or otherwise encumber the assets of any Trust to secure the loan;

   d. To engage in the redemption of stock and take such actions as are necessary to qualify the redemption under Sections 302 or 303 IRC and the applicable requirements of state law.

   e. To create a special lien for the payment of deferred death taxes under 6324 IRC, or similar provisions of state law.

   f. To create, continue, or terminate an S-Corporation election.

The following general provisions apply to the Trustee and any Successor Trustee of any Trust which is created by this Trust Agreement:

(C) DEALINGS WITH THE TRUSTEE

Any person who deals in good faith with the Trustee shall deal only with the Trustee and shall presume that the Trustee has full power and authority to act. No person shall require court confirmation or the approval of a beneficiary for any transaction with the Trustee. The signature of the Trustee shall bind the interest of any Trust beneficiary, including the Trustor, and no person need see the application of any property delivered to the Trustee.

(D) COMPENSATION OF TRUSTEE

Any Trustee who is also a beneficiary hereunder shall serve without compensation for his or her services except that the Trustee shall be reimbursed for reasonable expenses incurred in the administration of the Trust. Any Trustee not a beneficiary hereunder shall receive as compensation for its services, unless waived, such amount of compensation as is customarily being charge by commercial trust companies for services as a trustee of an inter vivos trust in the state of _____.

(E) BOND AND QUALIFICATIONS

No bond shall be required of the Trustee or any Successor Trustee. The Trustee and any successor Trustee shall not be required to qualify in any court and are relieved of the filing of any document and accounting in any court.

(F) SUCCESSOR TRUSTEE(S)

No Successor Trustee shall be responsible for acts of any prior Trustee. In the event a Trustee of any Trust is unable to serve or continued to serve as Trustee for any reason and no successor has been provided, the Successor Trustee shall be elected in writing by any of the person who have previously served as Trustee, with preference in the making of such appointment being determined in the same order of their succession as Trustee. If no appointment exists, the Successor Trustee shall be elected in writing by the majority in interest in the income of the Trust. No person shall be required to apply to any court in any jurisdiction for confirmation of said appointment. Any Successor Trustee so elected shall either be an issue of the Trustor or shall be a corporate Trustee qualified to exercise Trust powers.

(G) REMOVAL OF SUCCESSOR TRUSTEES

In the event a Successor Trustee is administering any Trust created hereunder, the Successor Trustee may be removed by the last individual to serve as Trustee; however, if that person is deceased or incapacitated, the Successor Trustee may be removed by a majority vote in interest in Trust income. Said removal must be in writing, stating the reasons for removal and indicate the successor trustee, which must be a corporate trustee. Removal of Successor Trustee shall be permitted for the purpose of influencing the exercise of discretion of a Successor Trustee which is granted by this instrument. For example, removal of a Successor Trustee that refuses to make a discretionary invasion of principal shall not be allowed. Removal of a successor Trustee shall be effective upon delivery of the notice of removal and the removed Trustee shall have a reasonable period of time to transfer assets to its successor. In the event the Successor Trustee believes that its removal is improper, it may, but shall not be required to, apply to a court of competent jurisdiction, at its expense, for a declaration of the propriety of the removal. In that event, the removal shall be effective only upon the order of said court and after any appeal. In the event the Successor Trustee prevails it shall be entitled to reimbursement from the Trust for its reasonable costs and attorney's fees.

(H) DELEGATION

Any Trustee may delegate any management function of any Trust to any other Successor Trustee (even though the Successor Trustee iss not then serving as Trustee) upon such terms as may be agreed by the Trustees. In the event more than one Trustee is serving, Trust assets may be held in the name of one Trustee.

(I) LIMITED POWER TO AMEND

The Trustee may amend this Trust to create or renounce management powers as may be required to facilitate the convenient administration of this Trust, deal with the unexpected or the unforeseen, or avoid unintended or adverse tax consequences. The amendment shall be in writing and shall be consented to by the Trustor, if not then deceased or incapacitated, or the beneficiaries of any Trust. The amendment may be retroactive. This limited power may only be exercised to provide for the convenient administration of any Trust; and shall not affect the rights of any beneficiary to enjoy Trust; and shall not affect the rights of any beneficiary to enjoy Trust income or principal without his consent, exercised to provide for the convenient administration of any Trust; and shall not affect the rights of any beneficiary to enjoy Trust; and shall not affect the rights of any beneficiary to enjoy Trust income or principal without his consent, shall not alter the dispositive provisions of any Trust, and shall not be exercisable in such a manner as to create gift, estate, or income taxation to the Trustee or any beneficiary. No amendment shall affect the rights of third persons who have dealt or may deal with the Trustee without their consent.

ARTICLE VII
ADMINISTRATIVE PROVISIONS

(A) CARRYING SEVERAL TRUSTS AS ONE ESTATE

To the extent that division of any Trust is directed, the Trustee may administer any Trust physically undivided until actual division becomes necessary. Further, the Trustee may add the assets of the Trust for any beneficiary to any other trust for such beneficiary having substantially the same provision for the disposition of trust income and principal, whether or not such trust is created by this agreement. The Trustee may commingle the assets of several trusts for the same beneficiary, whether or not created by this agreement, and account for whole or fractional trust shares as a single estate, making the division thereof by appropriate entries in the books of account only, and to allocate to each whole or fractional trust share its proportionate part of all receipts and expenses; provided, however, this carrying of several trusts as a single estate shall not defer the vesting of any whole or fractional share of a trust for its beneficiary at the times specified.

(B) ALLOCATION TO PRINCIPAL AND INCOME

All receipts of money or property paid or delivered to the Trustee and all expenses may be allocated to principal or income in accordance with the laws of the state of _____ or any other state in which a Trust is being administered.
However, the Trustee, in a reasonable and equitable manner, shall have the discretion to allocate, in whole or in part:

1. Administration expenses to income or principal.

2. Trustee's fees to income or principal.

3. To income, the gains or losses from option trading, and capital gains distributions from utility shares, or mutual funds, or tax managed funds; and

4. To income, any expense of the administrative of the Trust or its assets which is deductible for Federal Income Tax purposes; and

5. To income or principal, distributions from qualified or non-qualified pension plans, profit sharing plans, IRA accounts or deferred compensation arrangements.

(C) PROHIBITION OF ALIENATION

No income or principal beneficiary of any Trust (except the Trustor) shall have any right or power to anticipate, pledge, assign, sell, transfer, alienate or encumber his or her interest in the Trust, in any way. No interest in any Trust shall, in any manner, be liable for or subject to the debts, liabilities or obligations of such beneficiary or claims of any sort against such beneficiary.

(D) SMALL TRUST TERMINATION

If, at any time, any Trust shall be in the aggregate principal value of Ten Thousand Dollars ($10,000.00) or less, the Trustee may, in his/her sole discretion, terminate such Trust and distribute the assets to the beneficiary, or beneficiaries, the share of each being in the same proportion as he or she is a beneficiary under the terms of the Trust.

(E) DISCLAIMER

Any beneficiary of any Trust shall have the right to disclaim his or her interest in said Trust. Said disclaimer may be affected in compliance with the requirements of the laws of any jurisdiction in which any Trust may be administered. Alternatively, the Trustee may act upon any written disclaimer of any interest, in whole or in part, in any Trust. In the event any beneficiary is incapacitate, the Trustee may accept the disclaimer of a legal or natural guardian of said beneficiary; and if no such guardian exists, the Trustee of any Trust, acting on behalf of the beneficiary, shall have the power to disclaim all or a part of the property passing to said Trust.

(F) ELECTIONS

The Trustee and the Personal Representative of the Trustor's estate will have various options in the exercise of discretionary powers, some of which being limited only by the requirement that the Trustee and the Personal Representative act in good faith and within the bounds of their fiduciary duty. Specifically, the Trustee or Personal Representative may make certain elections for Federal Income Tax and Estate Tax purposes which may affect the administration of Trust income or principal. The Trustee or Personal Representative may exercise any such discretion without incurring liability to any beneficiary, nor shall any beneficiary have the right to demand a reallocation or redistribution of Trust income or principal as a result of the proper action of the Trustee or Personal Representative.

(G) CERTAIN DISTRIBUTIONS

The Trustee shall have the following options with regards to the distribution of principal or income to or for a beneficiary:

1. Directly to the beneficiary such amounts as the Trustee may deem advisable as an allowance;

2. To the Guardian of the person or of the property of the beneficiary.

3. To a relative of the beneficiary upon the agreement of such relative to expend such income or principal solely for the benefit of the beneficiary, which agreement may include a custodianship under the Uniform Transfers (or Gift) to Minors Act of any state.

4. By expending such income or principal directly for the beneficiary. After making a distribution as provided above, the Trustee shall have no further obligation regarding the distribution.

(H) Use of Residence

The Trustee may purchase or hold a residence to be occupied by the income beneficiary of any Trust (and/or their family) without rent, and the expense of maintaining the residence may be borne by the Trust, the beneficiary, or partly by each, as the Trustee may deem proper.

(I) DESIGNATION OF BENEFICIARY

The Trustee shall act upon any written designation of a beneficiary by a Trustor for qualified plan or IRA benefits made payable to this Trust by distributing the right to receive such benefits to the designated beneficiary. If no such designation exists the Trustor gives the Trustee the power, on behalf of the Trustor, to distribute the right to receive such benefits as a part of the share otherwise to be distributed to any beneficiary, and such person shall be the Trustor's designated beneficiary. It is intended that the operation of this paragraph qualify under the requirements of 401(a)(9) and 408(a)(6) IRC and it shall be interpreted in all regards in accordance with this intent.

(J) INVESTMENT ADVISOR

The Trustor or any person then having the power to remove and replace a corporate Trustee shall have the right to appoint an investment advisor who is duly registered with the Securities Exchange Commission. Such appointment shall be in writing effective upon delivery to the corporate Trustee. Upon receiving such appointment, the corporate Trustee shall follow such investment directions regarding such Trust assets the investment discretion as to which has been delegated to the investment advisor. During such time as an investment advisor is acting, the Corporate Trustee shall have absolutely no liability for investment decisions which have been delegated to the investment advisor. Such appointment shall not cause the reduction of the fees charged by the corporate Trustee, nor shall it create any new liabilities of the Corporate Trustee without its consent. The Corporate Trustee may enter into such written agreements with the investment advisor or the person appointing the investment advisor as may be appropriate to carry out the intent of this paragraph.

ARTICLE VIII

MISCELLANEOUS PROVISIONS

(A) SURVIVORSHIP

This agreement shall be binding upon the heirs, personal representatives, successors, and assigns of the parties hereto.

(B) _____LAW

This Agreement shall be construed and regulated in all respects by the laws of the State of _____. In the event any Trust or asset is being administered in another state, this Trust may be regulated by the laws of such state if required to avoid excessive administrative expense, or to uphold the validity of any of the terms of this Trust

(C) TRUSTEE AND TRUST

The term "TRUSTEE" refers to the single, multiple and Successor Trustee, who at any time may be appointed and acting in a fiduciary capacity under the terms of this agreement. Where appropriate, the term "TRUST" refers to any trust created by this agreement.

(D) GENDER-SINGULAR AND PLURAL

Where appropriate, words of the masculine gender include the feminine and neuter; words of the feminine gender include the masculine and neuter; and words of the neuter gender include the masculine and feminine. Where appropriate, words used in the plural or collective sense include the singular and vice-versa.

(E) IRC

The term "IRC" refers to the Internal Revenue Code and its valid regulations

(F) SERVE OR CONTINUE TO SERVE

A person cannot "serve or continue to serve" in a particular capacity if they are incapacitated, deceased, have resigned, or are removed by a court of competent jurisdiction.

(G) ISSUE

The term "issue", unless otherwise designated herein, shall include adopted "issue" of descendants and lineal descendants, both natural and legally adopted indefinitely. Such term shall specifically exclude individuals adopted out of the family of the Trustor or out of the family of a descendant of the Trustor. The word "living" shall include unborn persons in the period of gestation.

(H) NOTICE

No person shall have notice of any event or document until receipt of written notice. Absent written notice to the contrary, all persons shall rely upon the information in their possession, no matter how old, without recertification, verification, or further inquiry.

(I) MERGER

The doctrine of merger shall not apply to any interests under any Trust.

(J) REPRESENTATION

In any Trust matter a beneficiary whose interest is subject to a condition (such as survivorship) shall represent the interests in the Trust of those who would take in default of said condition. The members of a class shall represent the interests of those who may join the class in the future (e.g. living issue representing unborn issue). The legal natural guardian of a person under a legal disability shall represent the interests of the disabled person.

ARTICLE IX

POWER OF ATTORNEY

By virtue of the signing of this Trust below, the Trustor makes the following appointments of Attorneys-in-Fact:

(A) FOR FINANCIAL MATTERS

The Trustor appoints _____, as Attorney-in-Fact for the Trustor for the

(A) purpose of signing any state or federal income or gift tax return on behalf of the Trustor, collecting and endorsing to the Trust any tax refund, making claims against any insurance policy, providing for the collection and payment to the Trust of any amount due on account of Social Security, Medicare, Salary or other compensation, disability payments, contract, employee benefit program, IRA Account or any other benefits payable to the Trustor. In the event that _____._____, is unable or unwilling to so serve, then _____ shall serve in such capacity.

(B) FOR CARE OF THE TRUSTOR
The Trustor first appoints _____, and _____; jointly if then alive and competent, and then either of them individually, if then alive and competent if the other of them has predeceased Trustor or is incompetent, as Attorney-in-Fact to make any and all decisions regarding the personal care of the Trustor during any period when the Trustor may be incapacitated.

(C) DURABILITY
In the hands of a qualified holder, the appointments above, shall create a durable family power of attorney. This durable family power of attorney shall not be affected by the disability of the Trustor except as provided by statute; and the powers in the hands of a qualified holder may not be delegated.

IN WITNESS WHEREOF, on this the _____ day of _____, 20_____, has signed this instrument as Trustor, and has signed this Instrument as Trustee, to evidence acceptance of the Trust Agreement.

_____
TRUSTOR

_____
TRUSTEE

STATE OF _____

COUNTY OF _____

_____, Trustor and Trustee, being first duly sworn, does hereby declare to the undersigned officer / notary public that the Trustor signed the instrument as the Trustor's Revocable Trust Agreement, that the Trustee accepted this instrument as such, that the Trustor and Trustee signed the Trust Agreement as their voluntary act and deed on the date and year shown therein.

_____
TRUSTOR

_____
TRUSTEE

SUBSCRIBED and sworn before me by _____, the Trustor and Trustee, on this _____ day of _____, 20 _____.

_____
NOTARY PUBLIC

SOFT COVER BOOK, 70 PAGES, B&W, SIZE 6 X 9"

S.T.O.P : Start Thinking Outside Prison

Inspiring Motivating Self-Help

by Jermaine Ali Williams

Regain Your Power Beyond Prison Walls

Greatness lies within many of my brothers and sisters. The problem is we tend to find ourselves incarcerated before we discover this greatness. Our thought patterns and consistent inability to think on a positive level leads us straight to prison.

Thinking is very critical to one's success, failure, and survival. Every decision requires thinking. If not, many actions will be done on impulse. And impulsive behavior tends to bring about situations from which one needs to be rescued. Think of a preteen, teenager, or young adult, all of whom can possess the impulsive behaviors of children. If the impulses aren't tamed or controlled, the behavior patterns will be present in each stage of life. Maybe this is the reason I see so many 40-year-olds that lack self-control or the ability to deal with some of life's simplest problems. They can't attack the situations from a professional, calm, and diplomatic standpoint.

S.T.O.P. was written as a movement to help promote a greater thinking process - a thinking process I believe will slow down the recidivism rate within our communities. This will mean that more fathers will be available in the household, more parents around to pass down the guidance that will enable our young boys to become men. Men who will stand accountable for the direction of their community.

As a man, I ask all men to join together and help rebuild what many of us helped destroy. It starts with you. It starts with me. No outside force can aid this cause until the aid is given from within. A better future is literally in our hands. It is my intent that the following ten chapters will provide enlightenment and force all of us to S.T.O.P. - Start Thinking Outside Prison!

Regain Your Power
Beyond Prison Walls

Only... $13.99 plus $5 s/h with tracking

In 10 Chapters Learn How-to:

- ◊ The Foundation: Focus
- ◊ Life Skills
- ◊ Your Moral Compass
- ◊ Practice Your Principles
- ◊ Assert Your Values
- ◊ Teach the Youth
- ◊ Make Money Make Money

NO ORDER FORM NEEDED

On paper clearly write your full contact information and what you are ordering.

S.T.O.P: Start Thinking Outside Prison

Send $18.99 or TO: FREEBIRD PUBLISHERS

MAIL TO: POST OFFICE BOX 541, NORTH DIGHTON, MA 02764

ORDER ONLINE AT: WWW.FREEBIRDPUBLISHERS.COM OR AMAZON

EMAIL: DIANE@FREEBIRDPUBLISHERS.COM

We accept all forms of payments.

MoneyGram.

CHAPTER 9
GETTING THE HELP YOU NEED

"People are bridges you must cross to get where you want to go."
– Bob Beaudine

You cannot run a business from inside prison without some outside help. All you need is one good reliable personal assistant or family member. I understand that a lot of you don't have that person in your network. This chapter is designed to help you. From my personal experience I can tell you that a paid personal assistant is better than a family member, or even a trusted friend. Why? Because family and friends tend to procrastinate on doing tasks. It's better if you can walk them through it step-by-step on the phone. Also, try to keep your requests to only one task for each phone call or letter. If you start asking them to do multiple things you can overwhelm them and nothing will get done.

But there's another reason for employing a qualified personal assistant. You'll save money. And a good assistant will make you money. Here's how. If it costs you $20 an hour for your personal assistant, yet they get things done faster than your family member, you save time and make money. Why? Because it frees you from having to go round and round with a family member. If your assistant processes orders faster, you make money. A good, reliable personal assistant is the key to success from prison.

Here are my suggestions on how a prisoner could find and hire a good administrative assistant and never have to leave the prison.

NEWSPAPER CLASSIFIED ADS

Start with the local newspaper closet to your prison. Or the biggest town closet to your prison. Try to get a copy of the latest issue of that newspaper. Your prison's library may have a copy of it? You can also have someone get a copy of the FREE trader newspapers or magazine weekly that are found in gas stations and convenience stores. Once you get a copy of the latest issue, you need to look in the classified ad section. You'll want to place ads in the "Help Wanted" or "Job Opportunities" sections. Placing an ad in the help wanted section is a lot less costly than hiring an employment agency to find

someone for you. Of course, you could use a free online classified website like *Criagslist*® if you have someone outside in the free-world to help you. Since I'm writing this section for the prisoner who has no one to help and is trying to find that person, you probably can't use online classified websites. After you get the newspaper classified section you must write an ad for it.

But you can't just write any ad asking for help. You should use the classified ad to test your prospective assistant. You need to see if they can follow instructions and communicate through mail. That's mainly how you'll dictate your business affairs. Here's a sample ad that you could use to do this.

Administrative Assistant Needed

Prison-based writer seeks best secretary in St. Louis. Top office skills including editing, computer and bookkeeping are required. Media or publishing background helpful. Work from home. References Required. Do not email your resume to joshkrugerauthor@gmail.com. Do not call 1-800-BUY-JOSH. Instead, please send your two-page letter by mail to: Josh Kruger, Street Address, City, State and Zip Code

---

FYI: The ad is a combination of tactics I learned from two books. They are: *How To Publish A Book and Sell A Million Copies* by Ted Nicholas and *No B.S. Ruthless Management of People and Profits* by Dan S. Kennedy. Both are must-reads for into-cellpreneurs.

Notice that my ad on the previous page tells the prospect what not to do and what to do. This is how you weed out those who can't comprehend and follow instructions. Once you get responses from those who mailed you their two-page letter you must take another step. Background checks! Google® them. Use your state's DOC database. Check their social media pages. You're looking for red-flags like drug use, theft convictions, or a history of mental illness. According to business advisor Scott Tucker, your best employee would be a person who had a business in the family or was honorably discharged from the military.

After you find a qualified prospect, put them on probation. Test them. Are they completing tasks on time? Are they done in a quality manner? Can they visit your prison? Do they have a phone you could call and pay the collect call bill? Those are some questions you should ask. Always keep control of everything. Whatever you do, don't rush into hiring someone. But be quick to fire someone who doesn't measure up. I fired my mom once, then rehired her. She quit on me before I could fire her a second time. Remember, it's your business and your life. So be ruthless. There's no room to be nice if someone is screwing up and costing you money. Get rid of them.

> *"I believe in benevolent dictatorships,*
> *provided I am the dictator."*
> *– Richard Branson*

USING VOLUNTEERS AND INTERNS

You can sometimes find volunteers to help you. All you have to do is post notices on church bulletin boards detailing what you need. Or you could offer people a percentage of sales or profits. In *Magic Words That Bring You Riches*, Ted Nicholas said he ran a bookstore this way. He said instead of giving them a salary you could place your help wanted ads and give them several options:

- Percentage of sales
- Percentage of profits
- Royalty on sales
- Fixed payment for units produced.
- Percentage of savings

The key to the above type of help is that they are only an "independent contractor." This helps with taxes because they are not considered employees on your payroll. My assistant is an independent contractor who gets a fee for each book order processed. It depends on what type of business you've built and what products or services you're selling. Keep this idea in mind when looking for help.

Another way to get help is to use college students who act as interns. Someone going to school for small business would be a good fit. Maybe a criminology student as well? Some interns work for free just to get the experience, but most are paid minimum wages. To find interns you can post ads at your local university or college. You want to post them in your field's academic department. For instance, my fields are publishing, business and prison. I would do well to place my ads in the publishing school's hallways. Same for the business' and penology departments. You can also check out the following websites for interns:

www.internweb.com   www.ucanintern.com   www.internjobs.com

PRISONER ASSISTANT COMPANIES

I have used Prisoner Assistant, Inc. and Help From Outside for certain tasks and book fulfillment. But Prisoner Assistant and Lifetime Liberty Group are out of business. There are others that can be used for simple tasks. My cellmate uses EPS and doesn't have problems, but he's doing small stuff. If you're looking for a legit personal assistant company, then I recommend Help From Outside (HFO). The owner of HFO is Julia Capel and she provides good, timely services. But they do charge $30 an hour for most services. So be sure to have sufficient income before you set up an account. You can start the process by contacting HFO at:

> Help From Outside
> 2620 Bellevue Way NE #200
> Bellevue, WA 98004
> (206) 486-6042
> www.helpfromoutside.com

One caution. If you require someone to do something in your name like open a bank account or start a business, you'll need to sign power of attorney over to them. I've included two different power of attorney forms at the end of this chapter. One is "limited". The other is "full". Do not sign full power of attorney over to anyone unless you absolutely trust them. If you want to learn more about the use of power of attorney, then order *The Power of Attorney Handbook, Fourth Edition*.

WHAT ABOUT SOCIAL MEDIA NETWORKING?

A lot of prisoners think they can find new friends on Facebook, Instagram and other social media websites. But I ask you what kind of friends would these people be and what kind of help could they do for you? My thoughts are that people who spend their time on social media would not make good helpers. Unless you need help doing something on a social media site. Then it might be worth engaging them in a social media blast or shout-out. LinkedIn may be the one exception because people go there looking for business connections and help. Once you've started your business or corporation, you should set up a LinkedIn profile for yourself. Just remember that you'll need someone to monitor your pages for you. Now a few words about Facebook.

Facebook and other social networking sites do offer a prisoner an avenue to expand their network. But you must use caution because numerous prisons have enacted rules that ban prisoners from using these sites. South Carolina is the most drastic. The Electronic Frontier Foundation (www.eff.org) reported that some South Carolina prisoners are getting years in segregation for "Creating and/or assisting with a social networking site." (See October 2015 *Prison Legal News*, p. 24-26). Facebook was shutting down prisoner pages at the whim of prison administrators and even had a special page called: "Inmate Account Takedown Request." How did they justify this? By saying that it violated Facebook's Terms of Service (TOS) when prisoners use aliases or give their passwords to third parties to access their pages. But it has got a little better.

With the help of the EFF and other free speech lobbyists, Facebook has changed how it deals with prisoner pages. It now has a "Report An Inmate's Account" page. That page asks for information regarding the prisoner's offense, the date he or she was incarcerated, and their release date. Most of us are used to providing that type of information on pen pal sites anyway. It also requires prison officials to include links to the "law or legal authority regarding inmate social media access." If there is no law prohibiting a prisoners' access to social media, officials must provide specific reasons why granting Facebook access to the prisoner "poses a serious safety risk."

With all of the above in mind, here are some rules to remember when using Facebook:

- Do not use an alias when setting up your profile.

- Do not gang bang on your profile pages or posts.

- Do not do anything illegal or advocate criminal acts or scams on your pages.

- Learn your prison's rules and regulations first.

- Have your free-world assistant setup a support page or business page instead of a personal one that they control.

- Use your page to network and build your brand.

There will always be prisoners who mess things up. But for cellpreneurs who truly want to build something legit, we have to follow the rules. Doing it the right way can help the multitude. And build your bankroll at the same time.
What about prison pen pal websites?

A lot of prisoners think they are going to go online and find someone to help them make moves out there in the free-world. It's not impossible to find someone like that, but it's not probable using a prison pen pal website. I've been on about 10 different prison pen pal websites. I've included one of my current profiles. I got a few hits off of this site, but only one of the women is business minded. Yet it will take six months to a year to get to know her and by then I will have missed out on getting things done. (FYI: Freebird Publishers now owns Penacon.com. And even though they are my publisher I still paid to post my profile!)

Some website like writeaprisoner.com will not even let you talk about business stuff in your profile. Over the years, I've tried to get pen pals to help out with some of my business stuff. But that didn't turn out well. One gal told me "You just want a secretary." She was right! ☺ I have been more successful when I just asked for some needed internet research. It's better for me, and a lot less stressful, to just open an account with a prisoner assistance company and pay them to do what I need done. Maybe that's what you should do also? Or maybe you can find someone off a website to help you? If that is what you want to try and do, then I suggest you get a copy of my second book, Pen Pal Success. (See ad on next page.) It will show you everything you need to know.

Wish You Could Get Mail From Interesting People Each and Every Day?

Tired of Wasting Money On Pen Pal Lists & Services With Too Few Results?

Then this book was written especially for you!

PEN PAL SUCCESS: The Ultimate Proven Guide to Getting & Keeping Pen Pals

You've heard it said "The game is to be sold not told." Well, now a new book is doing all the telling about the game.

In 20 information-dense chapters you'll DISCOVER the following secrets:

▶ How to find FREE pen pals that are willing to write prisoners.

▶ Make money legally in the pen pal game without running any bogus prison scams!

▶ *Effectively use online pen pal websites, including which ones actually work and real profiles the author used to get HITS!*

▶ What to do once you get your pen pal so you keep them on your team for years!

▶ How to write letters to pen pals that get you responses!

▶ One successful letter can get you multiple responses from different pen pals;

▶ Learn the website that the author used to get 20+ hits in the first week his profile was up!

▶ Find out some of the biggest myths in the prison pen pal game and how not to fall victim to them or waste your money!

▶ How to rekindle a lost pen pal correspondence and keep pen pals coming back for more;

"I'm pleased to say that your system does work, one gal has fallen madly in love with me."

– John H. , Akron OH

▶ Get your pen pal to write you hot, freaky letters and send you sexy photos without paying!

▶ The act of giving gifts so you don't look like a trick-off artist;

▶ *What's more, this book is jam-packed with the full contact information of the people and companies that can help you succeed today!*

And There's Much, Much More!!

You have never seen a pen pal resource this detail on what it takes to succeed in the pen pal game today! Written by lifer, Josh Kruger author of *The Millionaire Prisoner.*

Pen Pal Success contains "insider's" wisdom especially for prisoners. You owe it to yourself to invest in this book!

CAUTION: This book is only of those prisoners who want to achieve their pen pal dreams and get lots of mail! ...Every word is designed so that prisoners can succeed now!

It's All Included Here In This Book!!

NO ORDER FORM NEEDED
On paper clearly write your full contact information and product info.

PEN PAL SUCCESS
Only $22.99
plus $7 s/h (priority with tracking)
Softcover, 8" x 10" over 225 pages

FREEBIRD PUBLISHERS

Box 541,
North Dighton, MA 02764
www.FreebirdPublishers.com
or Amazon.com
Diane@FreebirdPublishers.com
We accept all forms of payment

MoneyGram

We accept all major credit cards
VISA   DISCOVER AMERICAN EXPRESS PayPal

© COPYRIGHT 2015 BY FREEBIRD PUBLISHERS

Get to know an Inmate

38 year old male in Menard, IL

| Josh Kruger's Profile | SEND MESSAGE |

Hi there, hope you are having a great day? I'll be honest, prison can be lonely at times. So I'm trying to meet someone new. Are you tired of the same old lies? Or people who are lacking honesty, sincerity and respect? Well, I promise to shower you with attention, affection and appreciation. To always lend a helping hand... deliver a prompt reply to all your letters... and time devoted to you and you alone!

I'm a tall, slim, witty, confident, athletic, spontaneous and open-minded guy. I spend my time reading and writing and have published two books: The Millionaire Prisoner and Pen Pal Success. In my spare time, I like to watch baseball, but would so much rather turn off the TV and write you.

I'm searching for a meaningful and lasting friendship, maybe more? I'll be honest, plus-size women turn me on! But inner warmth is more important than anything else because I want to get to know you from the inside out. If this sounds like something you're interested in, don't hesitate to send me an email so we can get acquainted. Talk to you soon.

** Some information (such as contact info) has been removed to comply with facility mailroom rules and regulations.

About Me

NEW MEMBER

Name: Josh Kruger
Sex: Male
DOB: 1978-06-13
Ethnicity: Caucasian/White
Height: 6 ft 4 in.
Weight: 190
Hair Color: Brown
Eye Color: Blue
Sexual Orientation: Straight
People I'm Willing to Write: Anyone
On Death Row: No
Crime for which incarcerated:

| Click to View |

There are non-prisoner websites that cater to business people. One is elitesingles.com, a dating website for professional people. But that's not what you need. You need to network with other like-minded business people. One of the best things you can do is create a LinkedIn profile and start building your contacts.

RESOURCE BOX

For more information about building your business and network by using LinkedIn you should grab a copy of:

- *The Power Formula for LinkedIn Success: Kick-Start Your Business Brand and Job Search by* Wayne Breithbarth

- *The Power in a Link: Open Doors, Close Deals, and Change the Way You Do Business Using LinkedIn by* Dave Gowel

Books can be ordered from our Bookstore on page 224 or online. Contact Freebird Publishers about ordering if you don't have anyone to help you.

Here are some tips to remember when seeking mentors:

- Choose the right mentor. If you want to be a writer, you don't seek out someone who builds motorcycles for a living. You want someone that's successful in your chosen vocation.

- Be honest with yourself and your mentor about what is happening. Seek to understand what your mentor has to offer, and what you hope to gain. Discuss this with your mentor, if possible.

- Be open-minded and humble. Don't allow what you think you know to stop you from learning what you need to know. Don't brag about who's mentoring you to other prisoners either.

- Have a hunger for learning. Always ask questions. Your mentor will not get mad or upset if they see that you're honestly trying to learn. Become a protégé, not a parasite. You want what's in their head, not anything they could hand out. If you ask the right questions, you'll get the right answers.

- Find a business or success author that you like? Collect all their books. Reread them over and over again. It's just like having them in your cell talking to you!

Attn: Prisoners. I know some of you will want to write me and have me mentor you. But I cannot write prisoners directly. You must use a third party. Please don't write me from your prison or you'll get me in trouble.

A good example of a prisoner taking advantage of a mentorship is that of former prisoner Lawrence Carpenter. He did time for dealing drugs and armed robbery. He used mentors to help with his business ideas. Now he runs his own janitor service company that has 53 employees and provides services for businesses in several states. Carpenter even helps out other prisoners now. In 2010, he went back inside at the Eastern Correctional Institution in North Carolina as a part of the Inmates to Entrepreneurs program. Maybe one day they will come to your prison? If they do, sign up immediately. But don't wait till they do, seek out your mentors by writing them.

"Successful people rely heavily on their mentors.
Ordinary people don't."
– Robert G. Allen

RESOURCE BOX

For more on getting a mentor, you should get a copy of:

- *Who's In Your Top Five? Your Guide to Finding Your Success Mentors* by Bertrand Gervais

Books can be ordered from our Bookstore on page 224 or online. Contact Freebird Publishers about ordering if you don't have anyone to help you.

LETTER REQUESTING A MENTORSHIP

Dear _____:

I hope this letter finds you in the best of health and spirits. I just finished reading your book, _____, and I can honestly say that it has truly changed my life. I am trying to learn more about becoming successful at _____, and would like for you to mentor me if possible?

In making this request I would like to know what you've learned over the years, and I'm not out to get what you've earned. I would like to be a protégé and not a parasite. I don't want you to tell me, but to show me. I do understand that your time is valuable, so what I propose is sending you a letter here and there with any questions that I may have. Then you can answer them whenever you get some free time. If it's more convenient you can respond by emailing me at _____@gmail.com.

Once again, thank you for writing _____. I really like the part about _____. It was a great read. You can quote me on that in any promotions that you do. Thank you for taking the time to consider my letter and request. I look forward to hearing from you soon.

Respectfully Requested,

_____

_____

_____

_____

HOW TO SET UP A SYSTEM SO ANYONE CAN RUN YOUR BUSINESS

If you find someone that is willing to help out then you need to make it as easy on them as you can. Don't assume they know what you know. Or think like you think. People in the free-world are easily distracted. Too much pressure by you may cause them to quit. But there is a way to make it less stressful for everyone. All you have to do is create a business manual. If you do this, it also helps out when it's time to sell the business. Here's how you create your manual:

Step 1: List all jobs that need to be done and define each one. These descriptions should be explicit.

Step 2: For each job description, you must write out the specifics of that job and the tasks they'll need to complete daily.

Step 3: Next, write the skill needed for each job description.

Step 4: Write a summary of how the business should operate on a day-to-day basis.

When you write these lists, descriptions and manuals be sure to be as explicit and detailed as possible. Try to write them so that any high school graduate could read them and then run the business. Have blank pages in the back of each job manual so the people running things can write

notes, tips, or changes that need to be made. You should review these manuals periodically and make any amendments as needed. Even if you're only planning to hire one administrative assistant you should still create a manual for them, so they know what is expected.

The reason why this is so important is because your business should work without you needing to be there all the time. You need to create, innovate, and meditate on building your business. If you have the right person helping out combined with the right process, you can do pretty good. Having a business manual is a step in the process. A word of caution: these manuals are not "proposals" or "business plans." These manuals are for your in-house staff to read and study. Say you had to fire someone. If you have a manual, then the person who substitutes for the employee that got fired can step right in and follow the steps in the manual. Running a business from inside prison is hard. It's not impossible, but it takes a lot of patience. It takes understanding and empathy. You have to listen to the person out there managing your affairs. But that doesn't mean you lose your authority as the owner. You should always retain final decision-making authority when it comes to the big stuff. Don't sweat the small stuff. Unless it's costly, you profit. Just remember to go slow and have patience. Being a cellpreneur requires a lot of patience.

A FEW FINAL WORDS ABOUT FINDING (AND HIRING) HELP

There's only two reasons to hire someone to help you out:

- You can't do from inside prison what they can;

- They help make you money.

Try to do everything that you can from your cell at first. This will help keep costs down. When Hugh Hefner started Playboy®, his office was his bedroom. The desk was his bed. He'd use his typewriter and type up his own letterheads. If he was writing about marketing he'd put "marketing department". If he was writing about circulation he'd put "circulation department." You can do the same. Got access to a typewriter? Do your own letterheads just like Hugh Hefner did. Prison-based CEO Mike Enemigo does his work from his cell on his typewriter. So, does D. Razor Babb. I started my info-cellpreneur empire with a typewriter and $200. You can do it also.

After you've grown your business or sales you can outsource everything you can't do or don't want to do. Use independent contractors, interns and volunteers. Once you have a proven profitable venture, then you can hire an administrative assistant. But always remember to take your time when hiring someone and be quick to fire them if needed.

RESOURCE BOX

For more about hiring help and managing businesses I recommend you order two books:

- *The Complete Hiring and Firing Handbook*

- *No B.S. Ruthless Management of People and Profits* by Dan S. Kennedy

Books can be ordered from our Bookstore on page 224 or online. Contact Freebird Publishers about ordering if you don't have anyone to help you.

173

LIMITED POWER OF ATTORNEY

KNOW ALL PERSONS BY THESE PRESENTS, that I, _____
residing at _____, do hereby make, constitute and
appoint _____, residing at _____,
as the true and lawful attorney-in-fact for me and in my name, place and stead, and on my
behalf, and for my use and benefit with respect to the following matter(s):_____
_____
_____
_____

This instrument shall be construed and interpreted as a limited power of attorney.

The enumeration of specific items, rights or powers herein shall not limit or restrict, and is
not to be construed or interpreted as limiting or restricting, the limited powers herein
granted to said attorney-in-fact.

The rights, powers and authority of said attorney-in-fact granted in this instrument shall
commence and be in full force and effect on _____, 20 _____,
and such rights, powers and authority shall remain in full force and effect thereafter until I,
_____, give notice in writing that such power is terminated.

It is my desire, and I so freely state, that this power of attorney shall not be affected by my
subsequent disability or incapacity. Furthermore, upon a finding of incompetence by a
court of appropriate jurisdiction, this power of attorney shall be irrevocable until such time
as said court determines that I am no longer incompetent.

s/ _____

I, _____, whose name is signed to the foregoing instrument,
having been duly qualified according to the law, do hereby acknowledge that I signed and
executed this power of attorney; that I am of sound mind; that I am eighteen (18) years of
age or older; that I signed it willingly and am under no constraint or undue influence; and
that I signed it as my free and voluntary act for the purpose therein expressed.

s/ _____

s/ _____
(Notary Public)

FULL POWER OF ATTORNEY
DATE:

KNOW ALL PERSONS BY THESE PRESENTS, that I, _____
residing at _____, do hereby make, constitute and
appoint _____, residing at _____,
as the true and lawful attorney-in-fact for me and in my name, place and stead, and on my
behalf, and for my use and benefit, in the following matters:

1. To ask, demand, sue for, recover and receive all manner of goods, chattels, debts,
    rents, interest, sums of money and demands whatsoever, due or hereafter to
    become due and owing, or belonging to me, and to make, give and execute
    acquaintances, receipts, satisfactions or other discharges for the same, whether
    under seal or otherwise;

2. To make, execute, endorse, accept and deliver in my name or in the name of my
    aforesaid attorney all checks, notes, drafts, warrants, acknowledgements,
    agreements and all other instruments in writing, of whatever nature, as to my said
    attorney-in-fact may seem necessary to conserve my interests;

3. To execute, acknowledge and deliver any and all contracts, debts, leases,
    assignments of mortgage, extensions of mortgage, satisfactions of mortgage,
    releases of mortgage, subordination agreements and any other instrument or
    agreement of any kind or nature whatsoever, in connection therewith, and affecting
    any and all property presently mine or hereafter acquired, located anywhere, which
    to my said attorney-in-fact may seem necessary or advantageous for my interests;

4. To enter into and take possession of any lands, real estate, tenements, houses,
    stores or buildings, or parts thereof, belonging to me that may become vacant or
    unoccupied, or to the possession of which I may be or may become entitled, and to
    receive and take for me and in my name and to my use all or any rents, profits or
    issues of any real estate to me belonging, and to let the same in such manner as to
    my attorney shall seem necessary and proper, and from time to time to renew
    leases;

5. To commence, and prosecute in my behalf, any suits or actions or other legal or
    equitable proceedings for the recovery of any of my lands or for any goods,
    chattels, debts, duties, demand, cause or thing whatsoever, due or to become due
    or belonging to me, and to prosecute, maintain and discontinue the same, if he or
    she shall deem proper;

6. To take all steps and remedies necessary and proper for the conduct and
    management of my business affairs, and for the recovery, receiving, obtaining and
    holding possession of any lands, tenements, rents or real estate, goods and
    chattels, debts, interest, demands, duties, sum or sums of money or any other
    thing whatsoever, located anywhere, that is, or shall be, by my said attorney-in-
    fact, thought to be due, owning, belonging to or payable to me in my own right or
    otherwise;

7. To appear, answer and defend in all actions and suits whatsoever that shall be commenced against me and also for me and in my name to compromise, settle and adjust, with each and every person or persons, all actions, accounts, dues and demands, subsisting or to subsist between me and them or any of them, and in such manner as my said attorney-in-fact shall thing proper; hereby giving to my said attorney power and authority to do, execute and perform and finish for me and in my name all those things that shall be expedient and necessary, or which my said attorney shall judge expedient and necessary in and about or concerning the premises, or any of them, as fully as I could do if personally present, hereby ratifying and confirming whatever my said attorney shall do or cause to be done in, about or concerning the premises and any part thereof.

This instrument shall be construed and interpreted as a general power of attorney.

The enumeration of specific items, rights or powers herein shall not limit or restrict, and is not to be construed or interpreted as limited or restricting, the general powers herein granted to said attorney-in-fact.

The rights, powers and authority of said attorney-in-fact granted in this instrument shall commence and be in full force and effect on _____ 20_____, and such rights, powers and authority shall remain in full force and effect thereafter until I give notice in wiring that such power is terminated.

It is my desire, and I so freely state, that this power of attorney shall not be affected by my subsequent disability or incapacity. Furthermore, upon a finding of incompetence by a court of appropriate jurisdiction, this power of attorney shall be irrevocable until such time as said court determines that I am no longer incompetent.

s/ _____

I, _____, whose name is signed to the foregoing instrument, having been duly qualified according to the law, do hereby acknowledge that I signed and executed this power of attorney; that I am of sound mind; that I am eighteen (18) years of age or older; that I signed it willingly and am under no constraint or undue influence; and that I signed it as my free and voluntary act for the purpose therein expressed.

s/ _____

s/_____
(Notary Public)

NEW 2018-19

MADE IN THE USA

Freebird Publishers

NEW-All In ONE Book

GIFT LOOK BOOK

We carry hundreds of high quality gifts for every occasion to fit every budget. <u>Our gifts are made in America!</u>
Gift Baskets, Flowers, Chocolates & Candies, Personalized Gifts and more...

WANT TO SEE MORE OF OUR GIFT COLLECTIONS...

◇ Baby	◇ Holiday
◇ Birthday	◇ Meat & Cheeses
◇ Care Packages	◇ Mini Baskets
◇ Children's Gifts	◇ Mother's Day
◇ Easter	◇ New Home
◇ Fall Gifts	◇ Pet Gifts
◇ Father's Day	◇ Plush
◇ Gardening Gifts	◇ Snack Baskets
◇ Get Well	◇ Special Diets
◇ Gifts for Men	◇ Specialty Foods
◇ Gifts for Women	◇ Sports
◇ Gourmet	◇ St. Patrick's
◇ Halloween	◇ Sympathy Gifts
	◇ Thank You
	◇ Valentine's
	◇ Wedding & Romance
	◇ And more

Order our full size, color GIFT LOOK BOOK with hundreds of our high quality, beautifully handcrafted gifts to choose from, all made in U.S.A. We offer a complete line of gift baskets that have been custom designed. We have flowers that get delivered fresh in bud-form so they open up to full bloom in front of your loved ones. Our chocolates are of the finest quality, all made fresh. All of our gifts are skillfully featured in detailed full color photographs on 8.5 X 11" size, 110+ pages, softcover with full descriptions, prices, order forms with instructions. Over hundred of high quality gifts.

<u>**HOW TO ORDER**</u>: on blank paper, write GIFT LOOK BOOK, and include your complete contact info with payment of $15.00 to Freebird Publishers. All catalogs are mailed USPS tracking with packing slip/invoice.

<u>**WITH EVERY BOOK RECEIVE A $15.00 VOUCHER**</u>, good towards a purchase of any gift order from our GIFT LOOK BOOK for $75.00 or more. (not including shipping & handling)

PayPal.me/FreebirdPublishers
WE ACCEPT ALL FORMS OF PAYMENT

Only... $15.00 FREE S/H
With Each Book <u>GET</u>
$15 Credit Voucher
good on order from book

Box 541 North Dighton, MA 02764
www.FreebirdPublishers.com
Diane@FreebirdPublishers.com
Phone/Text 774-406-8682

PENACON

 Penacon is owned and operated by Freebird Publishers, your trusted inmate service provider.

Penacon.com dedicated to assisting the imprisoned community find connections of friendship and romance around the world. Your profile will be listed on our user-friendly website. We make sure your profile is seen at the highest visibility rate available by driving traffic to our site by consistent advertising and networking. We know how important it is to have your ad seen by as many people as possible in order to bring you the best service possible. Pen pals can now email their first message through penacon.com! We print and send these messages with return addresses if you get one. We value your business and process profiles promptly.

To receive your informational package and application send two stamps to:

PENACON

Box 533
North Dighton, MA 02764

Penacon@freebirdpublishers.com
Corrlinks: diane@freebirdpublishers.com
JPay: diane@freebirdpublishers.com

NEW... PEN PAL BOOK
A PERSONAL GUIDE FOR PRISONERS
Resources, Tips, Creative Inspiration and more

Pen Pals: A Personal Guide for Prisoners

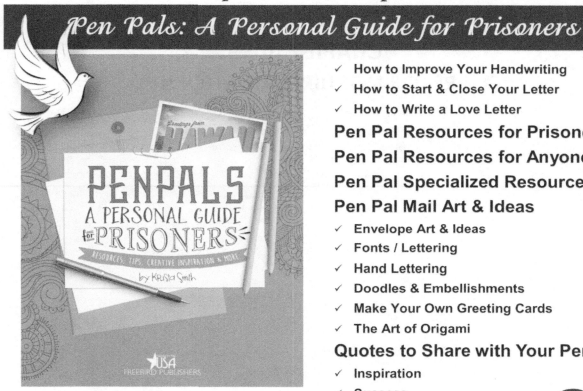

✓ How to Improve Your Handwriting
✓ How to Start & Close Your Letter
✓ How to Write a Love Letter

Pen Pal Resources for Prisoners

Pen Pal Resources for Anyone

Pen Pal Specialized Resources

Pen Pal Mail Art & Ideas

✓ Envelope Art & Ideas
✓ Fonts / Lettering
✓ Hand Lettering
✓ Doodles & Embellishments
✓ Make Your Own Greeting Cards
✓ The Art of Origami

Quotes to Share with Your Pen Pal

✓ Inspiration
✓ Success
✓ Friendship
✓ Love

Pen Pal Stationary

My Pen Pal Notes & Address Book Section

Pen Pal Profiles & Writing Tips

✓ **Creating Your Profile**
✓ **Writing Your First Letter**
✓ **Pen Pal Etiquette**
✓ **100 Things to Tell Your Pen Pal**
✓ **100 Getting to Know You Questions**
✓ **How to Keep It Interesting**

Softcover, 8x10", 200 Pages, B&W Interior

PEN PALS: A PERSONAL GUIDE FOR PRISONERS **$22.99** PLUS $7. S/H WITH TRACKING
<u>NO ORDER FORM NEEDED</u> clearly write on paper & send payment to:

Freebird Publishers Box 541, North Dighton, MA 02764

Diane@FreebirdPublishers.com www.FreebirdPublishers.com

We take all forms of payments. All credits cards, MoneyGram and PayPal.me/FreebirdPublishers

CHAPTER 10
TO HIRE (OR NOT HIRE) AN ATTORNEY

*"A lawyer can generally do a better job than a prisoner... by virtue
of experience and of not being locked up..."*
– John Boston & Daniel E. Manville

GETTING THE ASSISTANCE OF AN ATTORNEY

Most of us prisoners have had bad experiences with ineffective public defenders appointed to us by the state in criminal proceedings. So, we may automatically distrust lawyers. But not all attorneys are bad, lazy or unresponsive. I have participated in 17 years of criminal court proceedings as a defendant. I have also represented myself in six different lawsuits as a plaintiff and numerous small court claims. I've had eight different attorneys represent me in numerous matters. With all of this experience I've learned that going to court should be avoided if possible. This chapter should help you avoid costly legal warfare. But should you find yourself in need of a good litigator I'll share what I've learned over the years so you get the best representation possible.

If you decide to go the Millionaire Prisoner route and follow the strategies in this book you may need an attorney sooner or later. God forbid someone sues you. But if you can afford it, I suggest you hire an attorney for the following purposes:

- Setting up your LLC or Corporation properly.

- Obtaining Employer Identification Numbers (EINs) and Resale Certificates, if they are needed?

- Review your licenses, contracts and agreements.

- Advising you on your business regulation if applicable?

Having an attorney assist you with these initial matters can save you time and hassle in the long run.

HOW TO FIND THE RIGHT ATTORNEY?

Your criminal attorney can't help you with business law. You don't want a general practitioner either. You need to find an attorney who specializes in business law and formation. If you're a prison author like me, then you need to find an attorney who specializes in the intellectual property areas of copyrights, permissions, trademarks and licensing agreements. You need an attorney who specializes in only those matters!

Here's something I learned from Harvey Mackay, author of *Swim With the Sharks Without Being Eaten Alive*. You should ask an attorney that you trust and know to be ethical who they would hire if they had the problem you have. Good advice. Attorney Lee Wilson says you should ask for three or four names. He says when they come back with the names you can ask them the following three questions:

- How do you know these lawyers?

- What do you know about them?

- Why do you think one of them could help me?

Be careful if the lawyer you ask refers you to another attorney in the same firm. That lawyer could possibly be the best lawyer for your situation? Or it could be because they're trying to pad the firm's coffers. Further research is needed.

If you don't know any attorneys that you trust you have other options available. You can begin your search in your prison's law library. You are looking for your state's law directory. In Illinois it's called the Sullivan's Law Directory. You may also be able to use the Martindale-Hubbell Legal Directory. In my prison law library, they have an older set of the comprehensive Martindale-Hubbell Legal Directory. You can also find it online at www.martindale.com. A lot of the attorney addresses in this chapter came from that directory.

If you have someone in the free world who can search online, you may check the below websites for attorneys:

- American Intellectual Property Law Association
  www.aipla.org

- American Bar Association
  www.abanet.org

- Attorney Find
  www.attorneyfind.com

Sometimes you can get an attorney to help you pro bono or on a volunteer basis. A good place to find this kind of help will be the national directory of Volunteer Lawyers for the Arts at: www.vlany.org/legalservices/vladirectory.php.

Once you get a list of possible attorneys you should look for the following qualifications:

- Experience of 10 years or more;

- Specialist in business law; and

- No disciplinary actions on their record.

Most law directories list how long an attorney has been practicing and what they specialize in. To find out if an attorney has had any disciplinary action taken against them you should contact your state's lawyer-licensing board. In Illinois, it's called the Attorney Registration & Disciplinary Committee. Once they pass those initial tests you're ready to begin your hiring priceless. A few words about this are needed before we proceed.

The bigger the legal problem you have the longer you should take to hire an attorney. Your business life may depend on you making the right choice! And the same attorney who forms your business may not be the same one who can litigate in court. Be sure you know what you actually need before you venture down the road of hiring an attorney.

> *"Talk is cheap...until you hire a lawyer."*
> *– Dan S. Kennedy, www.NoBSBooks.com*

You should prepare an initial letter to each attorney on your list. It should briefly describe your problem and or need. Next it should ask if they would be willing to represent a prisoner in this kind of matter? (Some attorneys do not like doing work for prisoners.) Lastly, and this is key, request that they set up a legal call with you that you pay for as an initial consultation.

Most lawyers waive their fees for the initial consultation, but since you're in prison you can't travel to the lawyer's office. You must do it by phone and letter only. Unless the attorney is nearby and chooses to come to the prison for a visit? From my experience, you'll get a better response if you have someone in the free world contact the lawyer's office first. They should pay the collect call fees and lawyer's time to set up the legal call. I've found that $75.00 normally covers that initial phone consultation. At the end of your phone consultation you should say this:

"I must be honest with you at this time. You are not the only attorney I'm contacting in regard to this matter. But I promise to let you know within two weeks if I'm going to hire you or going to go a different route."

Don't allow the attorney to pressure you into agreeing to hiring them until you find out if you can work together. You must understand this: Your lawyer works for you! That doesn't mean they should blindly follow your instructions. It does mean they should counsel you on all the available options and educate you about the risks behind each option. You have to figure out if the attorney will do that in your initial talks.

The last thing you need to inquire about is their fees for handling the matter. Ask for an estimate? Some attorneys will quote an hourly fee ($150-500 an hour), others may quote a flat fee. Should you be the plaintiff in a lawsuit the attorney may represent you on a contingency fee? You should be aware that the more experienced attorney will probably charge you more. In one of my hiring experiences, one attorney quoted me a $10,000 fee. But he was honest that he had never filed the particular petition I needed. I ended up going with a more experienced attorney, albeit for $15,000. You get what you pay for.

After you've contacted the attorneys on your list you need to decide which attorney you will hire. You can base this on a few factors that you should have gleaned from your phone conversations. These factors are:

- Response Time. Did the attorney get back to you promptly? If you contacted them by phone, they should have returned your call within 24 hours; or their secretary should have contacted you to set up a time and date to call. If you contacted them by mail, they should have written back within seven business days.

- Chemistry. Did you and the attorney have a good rapport? Did they try and talk down to you? Or did they explain things to you honestly? This matters a lot because this is someone that you're going to have numerous conversations with. You need to be able to communicate.

- Style. Business attorney, and author, Helen Sedwick says you shouldn't hire a bully because they'll waste time and money. I tend to agree. But you don't want to hire a timid or polite lawyer if you're suing someone either. There is a difference from being polite, but aggressive and a bully.

- Command. This comes from experience and being up-to-date with the latest law and tactics. Some attorneys love the law and what they do. Others don't. Hopefully you'll hire one that is experienced and loves the law.

Just remember that there are numerous attorneys that you could hire. So be careful when choosing your attorney.

WHAT TO DO AFTER YOU HIRE AN ATTORNEY

Your legal obligations do not stop just because you've hired an attorney. You need to do the following to ensure that your case proceeds in a timely and effective manner.

1. Follow up every meeting or phone call with a written letter, and start your letter by saying, "Just to make sure I understand our meeting (phone conversation) today, we're agreed to..." Then you list any deadlines, etc. Make a copy of this letter for your files.

2. Monitor any detailed billing statement your attorney sends. If you're paying by the hour you are entitled to this statement. If something is questionable, bring it to your attorney's

attention politely. They should explain it to you. On a side note: "fees" are what attorneys charge you for their time and experience; "costs" are what they charge you for things they must pay for. There can be copy fees, gas mileage, collect calls, etc.

3. Be polite and considerate with your attorney. But you don't have to be a pushover. Remember that when you hire an attorney they work for you. A good lawyer will help you make the right decisions instead of making them for you.

4. Provide your lawyer with all the information and paperwork you have. Let them decide what is relevant and what isn't.

5. Allow your attorney to do their work. That means after your initial consultations you don't need to sweat them or bug them every day with calls and letters. As a prisoner this can be hard, but your attorney isn't just working for you, they have other clients. Give them time to get the work done.

Those are some of the things you should do once you hire an attorney. But your attorney has certain legal obligations to you as a client as well. A good one will do the following:

- Keep you informed of all court filings, meetings, phone calls or investigations on your behalf. This is probably the biggest sign of a good attorney. You should get a copy of everything, or a letter/memo explaining it.

- Meets all deadlines and keeps commitments. Everyone in the world should do this, but especially attorneys. If you're attorney misses a deadline, bring it up to them immediately. If they fail to respond or give an inadequate response, consult another attorney and consider filing a legal malpractice claim.

- Tells you the truth and doesn't guarantee success. No attorney can guarantee how a jury or judge will decide a case or an issue. If they do you should hire another attorney fast.

If a lawyer lies to you or steals from you – fire them immediately! Write them a letter and demand delivery of your file and return any fees/retainer not yet billed and deducted. And file a complaint with your state's attorney disciplinary committee. Hopefully it never comes to that.

RESOURCE BOX

For more information about issues concerning dealing with your attorneys you should consider reading the following books which may be in your prison's law library:

- *How To Help Your Lawyer Win Your Case, Second Edition*
- *Finding the Right Lawyer*
- *Attorney Responsibilities and Client Rights*
- *How & When To Sue Your Lawyer: What You Need To Know*
- *What Your Lawyer Doesn't Want You To Know*
- *Legal Street Smarts: How To Survive in a World of Lawyers.*

If not? Contact Freebird Publishers about them.

BUSINESS LAW ATTORNEYS

Ralph R. Storto
Storto, Finn & Rosinksi
100 West Green St.
Bensenville, IL 60106

Jo Anna E. Rentschler
999 Old Decatur Rd.
Dawson, IL 62520-3000

Gregory W. Coffey
Mathis, Marifian & Richtee, Ltd.
125 N. Buchanan St.
Edwardsville, IL 62025

Beers, Maller, Backs & Salin, LLP.
110 West Berry St. Suite 1100
Fort Wayne, IN 46802
(219) 426-9706

Andrew K. Carruthers
Hepler Brown, LLC.

130 N. Main St.
P.O. Box 510
Edwardsville, IL 62025-05510

David L. Antognoli
Goldenberg, Heller, Antognoli P.C.
2227 S. State Route 157
P.O. Box 959
Edwardsville, IL 62025

Bay Venture Counsel, LLP.
Suite 1300
Lake Merrit Plaza
1999 Harrison St.
Oakland, CA 94612
(510) 273-8750
www.vclaw.com

Howard W. Fisher
The Fisher Company
7618 N. La Cholla Blvd.
Tucson, AZ 85741
www.thefishercompany.com
(520) 547-2460

COPYRIGHT & TRADEMARK ATTORNEYS

Phillip R. Van Ness
Webber & Thies, PC
202 Lincoln Square
P.O. Box 189
Urbana, IL. 61803

Bradley & Riley, P.C.
Attorneys & Counselors
2007 First Avenue SE
Cedar Rapids, IA 52402
www.bradleyrileypc.com
(319) 363-0101

Hall, Render, Killian, Heath & Lyman
Suite 2000
One American Square, Box 82064
Indianapolis, IN 46282

www.hrkhl.com
(317) 633-4884

Ashen & Lippman
1737 Franklin Canyon Drive
Beverly Hills, CA 90067
(310) 274-8060

Gretta Bieber
Alschuler, Simantz & Hem, LLC.
1961 West Downer Place
Aurora, IL 60506-4384

Wenzel & Harms, P.C.
2750 1st Avenue, NE, Suite 420
Cedar Rapids, IA 52402-4831

www.lawyers.com/wenzel-harms
(319) 363-8905

Lawrence A. Steward
Brinks, Hofer, Gilson & Lione
Suite 2425
One Indiana Square
Indianapolis, IN 46204-2001
www.brinkshofer.com
(317) 636-0886

Evans & Walsh
Suite 206
119 North San Vincente Blvd.
Beverly Hills, CA 90211
(310) 273-0938

Bose, McKinney & Evans, LLP
2700 First Indiana Plaza
135 North Pennsylvania St.
Indianapolis, IN 46204
www.boselaw.com
(317) 684-5000

Donald E. Knebel
Barnes & Thornburg
11 South Meridian St.
Indianapolis, IN 46204
www.btlaw.com
(317) 236-1313

Arnold, White & Durkee
155 Linfield Drive
Menlo Park, CA 94025-3741
www.awd.com
(650) 614-4500

Weil, Gotshal & Manges, LLP.
2882 Sand Hill Road, Suite 280
Menlo Park, CA 94025-7022
www.weil.com
(650)926-6200

Baker & Daniels
300 North Meridian St.
Indianapolis, IN 46204
www.bakerdaniels.com
(317) 236-0300

Lyon & Lyon, LLP
Suite 800
4225 Executive Square
La Jolla, CA 92037
(619) 552-8400
www.lyonlyon.com

Fish & Richardson, P.C.
2200 Sand Hill Road, Suite 100
Menlo Park, CA 94025
www.fr.com
(650) 322-5070

Cooley Godward, LLP.
Five Palo Alto Square
3000 El Camino Real
Palo Alto, CA 94306-2155
www.cooley.com
(650) 843-5000

Fish & Neave
525 University Avenue, Suite 300
Palo Alto, CA 94301
www.fishneave.com
(650) 617-4000

Hoffman & Baron, LLP
6900 Jericho Turnpike
Syosset, NY 11791
(516) 822-3550

Dillworth & Barrese
333 Earl Ovington Blvd.
Uniondale, NY 11553

Bazerman & Drangel, P.C.
60 East 42nd St., Suite 1158

New York, NY 10165
www.ipcounselors.com
(212) 292-5390

Cobrin & Gittes
750 Lexington Avenue
New York, NY 10022
(212) 486-4000

Colucci & Umans
670 White Plains Road
Scarsdale, NY 10583
(914) 472-1500

Trapani & Molldrem
333 East Onondaga St.
Syracuse, NY 13202
(315) 422-4323

Baker Botts, LLP.
599 Lexington Avenue
New York, NY 10022-6030
www.bakerbotts.com
(212) 705-5000

Coleman Sudol, LLP.
708 Third Avenue, 14th Floor
New York, NY 10017
(212) 679-0090

Cooper & Dunham, LLP.
1185 Avenue of the Americas
New York, NY 10036
www.cooperdunham.com
(212) 278-0400

Darby & Darby
805 Third Avenue
New York, NY 10022-7513
www.darbylaw.com
(212) 527-7700

Helfgott & Karas, P.C.
Suite 6024
350 Fifth Avenue
New York, NY 10118-6098
(212) 643-5000

KaLow, Springut & Bressler, LLP.
488 Madison Avenue
New York, NY 10022-5702
www.creativity-law.com
(212) 813-1600

Lieberman & Nowak, LLP.
805 Third Avenue, 21st Floor
New York, NY 10022
www.lieberman-nowak.com
(212) 532-4447

Frommer, Lawrence & Haug, LLP.
754 Fifth Avenue
New York, NY 10151
www.FLHLaw.com
(212) 588-0800

Kenyon & Kenyon
One Broadway
New York, NY 10004
(212) 425-7200

Ladas & Parry
26 West 61st St.
New York, NY 10023
www.ladas.com
(212) 708-1800

Malina & Wilson
Lincoln Building
60 East 42nd St.
New York, NY 10165
(212) 986-7410

Pennie & Edmonds, LLP.
1155 Avenue of the Americas
New York, NY 10036
www.pennie.com
(212) 790-9090

Shenier & O'Connor
380 Lexington Avenue
Suite 2518
New York, NY 10168
(212) 682-1986

White & Case, LLP.
1155 Avenue of the Americas
New York, NY 10036-2787
www.whitecase.com
(212) 819-8200

Gonzales & Oberlander, LLP.
Carol Desmond
www.golawny.com
(914) 220-5474

Robin, Blecker & Daley
330 Madison Avenue
New York, NY 10017
www.robinblecker.com
(212) 682-9640

Steinberg & Raskin, P.C.
1140 Avenue, NY 10036
(212) 768-3800

Wood, Herron & Evans, LLP.
2700 Carew Tower
441 Vine St.
Cincinnati, OH 45202
www.whepatent.com
(513) 241-2324

Law Clerk
Aaron Aguirre

Office Manager
Debi Jonigian-Schmidt

377 W. Fallbrook #205
P.O. Box 25001
Fresno, CA, 93729

559.261.2222
Fax: 559.436.8163
legal.schmidt@gmail.com

March 11, 2015

Joshua Kruger

Re: *Money Management*

Dear Mr. Kruger:

Thank you for your recent letter. Over the years, we have obtained millions for our clients in civil suits. We have earned the trust of those clients and when the money was distributed they asked us to hold the funds. Through word of mouth, the quality of our services to those clients spread. We now hold a significant amount of money for our incarcerated clients.

It is not clear whether the $10,000 limit is "income" or the amount in your prison trust account. If it's in the account, we could simply hold the money for you and pay it to whomever you designate. If it's income, we need to do research. Of course we can set up a trust, or complete other legal work. My rate is $350/hour, and we would need a $2,500 retainer.

Half my practice continues to be focused on "Prison Law", while the other is general practice- divorce, civil litigation, injury, business management, etc. I have many clients with substantial assets who require complete confidentiality. An attorney is uniquely situated by law to provide this protection through the attorney-client privilege.

We can hold money indefinitely in our Attorney-Client Trust Account. However, be advised, the interest generated goes to the California State Bar by statute, not to the law firm or the client. From that account we can write checks or distribute the money as instructed by the client. Money can be invested for the client in any number for investment vehicles including stocks, bonds, mutual funds, savings accounts and real estate. We do not give investment advice, all investments are client selected. We have relationships with several stock brokers and we can open an account for you, but cannot determine what or when to buy. We frequently are retained to serve as a liaison between clients and their businesses.

Our fees are as follows:

One time account setup fee:	1.5% ($500.00 minimum)
Check writing fee:	$25.00 (1 free per month)
Cashier's check fee:	$10.00 each (plus check writing fee)
Yearly maintenance fee:	1.5% of annual deposits ($500.00 minimum)
Quarterly package fee:	$35.00 each
Internet Orders:	$37.50 each
Std Mail included, Priority mail:	$20.00 each
Hourly fee for other services:	$95.00
Third Party Deposit fee:	$35.00
Wire Transfer fee:	$40.00 (plus costs)
Stop Payment fee:	$40.00
Attorney hourly fee:	$350.00
Collect call fee:	$5.00 (plus time)

All instructions regarding any account we establish for you, including requests for checks to be issued, must be submitted in writing. No requests made by phone or through a third party will be accepted. All fees will be withdrawn directly from your account by us.

To move forward, or if you would like us to draft a contract for your signature, please contact my assistant, Debi, at the address above.

Regards,

William L. Schmidt

WLS:djs

190

Freebird Publishers

Presents A New Cookbook

You will find these scrumptious recipes and more...

Refried Beanie Chicken Winnies

Slightly Sweet Nuttier Chicken

Chipotle Chicken-n-Ranch Burritos

Ted's Po`boy BBQ Crunch

Caffeine-Cino Rush

Sweet Vanilla Sin Coffee

Margaret's Non-Alcoholic Strawberry Margaritas

Charlie's Butterscotch Brownies

Dream Bar Cake

Are you eating the same thing day in and day out? Tired of the same boring, bland tasting food? Are your meals lacking flavor and originality? Then our Cell Chef Cookbook will hit the spot!

The Cell Chef Cookbook is filled with hundreds of fantastic recipes, that can be simply made with everyday, commonly sold commissary/store foods. Every recipe has been tried and thoroughly tested. Loved by everyone.

In the Cell Chef Cookbook the recipes are divided into four sections:

√ **Meals and Snacks**

√ **Sauces, Sandwich Spreads, Salsa and Dips**

√ **Drinks**

√ **Sweet Desserts**

The Cell Chef Cookbook, has an extensive Glossary and Index, created to assist you in the process of your preparations and leading to the pleasure of enjoying these wonderful, tasty dishes.

The Cell Chef Cookbook's recipes have each been organized with a list of all the needed ingredients, and easy-to-follow directions on how to make them to perfection.

Food is essential to life; therefore, make it great.

The CELL CHEF Cookbook

Only $13.99

Plus $5 S/H with tracking

Softcover, Square 8.25" x 8.25", B&W, 183 pages

NO ORDER FORM NEEDED CLEARLY WRITE ON PAPER & SEND PAYMENT TO:

Freebird Publishers Box 541, North Dighton, MA 02764

Diane@FreebirdPublishers.com   www.FreebirdPublishers.com

amazon.com

CHAPTER 11
THE BETTER BUSINESS BUREAU

"To help establish your credibility with your customers,
join the Better Business Bureau (BBB)."
– Ted Nicholas

JOIN THE BETTER BUSINESS BUREAU

When you first start out it will be hard to build credibility and establish trust in your customer's eye. To help with this you should join the Better Business Bureau (BBB). Better Business Bureaus are non-profit organizations that encourage honest advertising and selling practices. They are supported mostly by local businesses. BBBs offer numerous consumer services, including business reports, mediation and arbitration services, information about charities and other organizations that seek public donations. They also provide ratings of local companies to express the BBB's confidence that the company operates in a trustworthy manner and demonstrates a willingness to resolve customer concerns and complaints. To join the BBB you can contact the council of Better Bureaus at:

Council of Better Business Bureaus, Inc.
4200 Wilson Blvd., 84th Floor
Arlington, VA 22203-1838
www.bbb.org/online
(703) 276-0100

You can also contact your local chapter of the BBB with any complaints regarding local businesses, or about how you can join the local chapter. Here are the many different local chapters and their contact information

ALABAMA

BBB-Birmingham
1210 S. 20th St.
Birmingham, AL 35205
1-800-824-5274 (AL)
(205) 558-2222

BBB-Decatur
254 Moulton St., E, 3rd Floor
Decatur, AL 35601
(256) 35502226

BBB-Huntsville
107 Lincoln St., SE
Huntsville, AL 35801
(256) 533-1640

BBB-Montgomery
4750 Woodmere Blvd., Suite D
Montgomery, AL 36107
(334) 273-5530

ALASKA

BBB-Anchorage
341 W. Tudor Rd., Suite 209
Anchorage, AK 99503
(907) 562-0704

BBB-Cullman
202 1st Ave., SE, Suite 1
Cullman, AL 35055
(256) 775-2917

BBB-Dothan
1971 S. Brannon Stand Rd.
Suite 1
Dothan, AL 36305
(334) 794-0492

BBB-Mobile
960 S. Schillinger Rd., Suite 1
Mobile, AL 36695
(251) 433-5494

ARIZONA

BBB-Phoenix
4428 N. 12th St.
Phoenix, AZ 85014-4585
(620) 624-1721

BBB-Tucson
434 S. Williams Blvd., Suite 102
Tucson, AZ 85711
(520) 888-5353

ARKANSAS

BBB-Little Rock
1251 Kanis Rd.
Little Rock, AR 72211
(501) 664-4888

BBB-Siera Vista
2160 E. Fry Blvd.
Suite C5 PMB 172
Sierra Vista, AZ 85635
(520) 888-5353

CALIFORNIA

BBB-Bakersfield
1601 H. St, Suite 101
Bakersfield, CA 93301
(661) 322-2074

BBB- Culver City
6125 Washington Blvd., 3rd Floor
Culver City, CA 90232
(310) 945-3166

BBB-Fresno
4201 W. Shaw Ave., Suite 107
Fresno, CA 93722
(559) 222-8111

BBB-Long Beach
3363 Linden Ave., Suite A
Long Beach, CA 90807
(562) 216-9242

BBB-Los Angeles
315 N. La Cadena Dr.
Cotton, CA 92324
(909) 825-7280

BBB-Oakland
1000 Broadway, Suite 625

Oakland, CA 94607
(510) 844-2000

BBB-Placentia
550 W. Orangethorpe Ave.
Placentia, CA 92870
(714) 985-8922

BBB-Sacramento
3075 Beacon Blvd.
west Sacramento, CA 95691
(916) 443-6843

BBB-San Diego
5050 Murphy Canyon Rd., Suite 110
San Diego, CA 92123
(858) 496-2131

BBB-San Jose
1112 S. Bascom Ave.
San Jose, CA 92128
(408) 278-7400

BBB-Santa Barbara
P.O. Box 129
Santa Barbara, CA 93101
(805) 963-8657

BBB-Stockton
11 S. San Joaquin St., 8th Floor
Stockton, CA 95202
(209) 948-4880

COLORADO

BBB-Colorado Springs
25 N. Wahsatch Ave.
Colorado Springs, CO 80903
(719) 636-1155

BBB-Denver
1020 Cherokee St.
Denver, CO 80204-4039
(303) 758-2100

BBB-Fort Collins
8020 S. County Rd., 5, Suite 100
Fort Collins, CO 80528
(800) 564-0371

CONNECTICUT

BBB-Wallingford
94 S. Turnpike Rd.
Wallingford, CT 06492-43322
(203) 269-2700

DELAWARE

BBB-Wilmington
60 Reads Way
New Castle, DE 19720
(302) 221-5255

DISTRICT OF COLUMBIA

BBB-Washington
1411 K. St., NW, Suite 1000
Washington, DC 20005-3404
(202) 393-8000

FLORIDA

BBB-Clearwater
2655 McCormick Dr.
Clearwater, FL 33759
(727) 535-5522

BBB-Jacksonville
4417 Beach Blvd., Suite 202
Jacksonville, FL 32207
(904) 721-2288

BBB-Longwood
1600 S. Grant St.
Longwood, FL 32750
(407) 621-3300

BBB-Miami Lakes
14750 N.W. 77 ct., #317
Miami Lakes, FL 33016
(561) 842-1918

BBB-Pensacola
912 E. Gadsen St.
Pensacola, FL 32501
(850) 429-0002

BBB-Stuart
101 S.E. Ocean Blvd., Suite 202
Stuart, FL 34994
(772) 223-1492

BBB-West Palm Beach
4411 Beacon Circle, Suite 4
West Palm Beach, FL 33407
(561) 842-1918

GEORGIA

BBB-Atlanta
503 Oak Place, Suite 590
Atlanta, GA 30349
(404) 766-0875

BBB-Augusta
1227 Augusta West Parkway
Suite 15
Augusta, GA 30909
(706) 210-7676

BBB-Columbus
P.O. Box 2587
Columbus, GA 31902
(706) 324-0712

BBB-Macon
277 Martin Luther King Jr. Blvd.
Suite 102
Macon, GA 31201-3495
(478) 742-7999

BBB-Savannah
6555 Abercorn St., Suite 120
Savannah, GA 31405-5817
(912) 354-7521

HAWAII

BBB-Honolulu
1132 Bishop St., Suite 615
Honolulu, HI 96813
(808) 536-6956

IDAHO

BBB-Boise
1200 N. Curtis Rd.
Boise, ID 83706
(208) 342-4649

BBB-Idaho Falls
453 River Parkway
Idaho Falls, ID 83402
(208) 523-9754

ILLINOIS

BBB-Chicago
330 N. Wabash Ave., Suite 2006
Chicago, IL 60611-7621
(312) 832-0500

BBB-Peoria
112 Harrison St.
Peoria, IL 61602
(309) 688-3741

BBB-Rockford
810 E. State St., 3rd Floor
Rockford, IL 61104-1001

INDIANA

BBB-Evansville
3101 N. Green River Rd., Suite 410
Evansville, IN 47715
(812) 473-0202

BBB-Fort Wayne
4011 Parnell Ave.
Fort Wayne, IN 46805
(260) 423-4433

BBB-Indianapolis
151 N. Delaware St., Suite 2020
Indianapolis, IN 46204-2599
(317) 488-2222

BBB-Merriville
7863 Broadway, Suite 124
Merriville, IN 46410
(219) 791-9550

BBB-Osceola
10775 McKinley Highway, Suite B
Osceola, IN 46561
(574) 675-9315

IOWA

BBB-Bettendorf
2435 Kimberly Rd., Ste 260 N.
Bettendorf, IA 52722-4100
(563) 355-6344

BBB-Des Moines
505 5th Ave., Suite 950
Des Moines, IA 50309
(515) 243-9137

KANSAS

BBB-Wichita
345 N. Riverview St., Suite 720
Wichita, KS 67203
1-800-856-2417

KENTUCKY

BBB-Lexington
1460 Newton Pike
Lexington, KY 40511
(859) 259-1008

BBB-Louisville
844 S. Fourth St.
Louisville, KY 40203
(502) 583-6546

LOUISIANA

BBB-Alexandria
5220-C Rue Verdun
Alexandria, LA 71303
(318) 473-4494

BBB-Baton Rouge
748 Main St.
Baton Rouge, LA 70802
(225) 346-5222

BBB-Houma
801 Barrow St., Suite 400
Houma, LA 70360
(985) 868-3456

BBB-Lafayette
4007 W. Congress St., Suite B
Lafayette, LA 70506
(337) 981-3497

BBB-Lake Charles
2309 E. Prien Lake Rd.
Lake Charles, LA 70601
(337) 478-6253

BBB-Monroe
212 Walnut St., #210
Monroe, LA 71201
1-800-960-7756

BBB-New Orleans
710 Baronne St., Suite C
New Orleans, LA 70113
(504) 581-6222

BBB-Shreveport
401 Edwards St., Suite 135
Shreveport, LA 71101
(318) 222-7575

MARYLAND

BBB-Baltimore
502 S. Sharp St., Suite 1200
Baltimore, MD 21201
(410) 347-3990

MASSACHUSETTS

BBB-Marlborough
290 Donald Lynch Blvd., Suite 102
Marlborough, MA 01752
(508) 652-4800

BBB-Worcester
340 Main St., Suite 802
Worcester, MA 01608
(508) 755-2548

MINNESOTA

BBB-St. Paul
2706 Gannon Rd.
St. Paul, MN 5516—2600
(651) 699-1111

MISSISSIPPI

BBB-Ridgeland
601 Renaissance Way, Suite A
Ridgeland, MS 39157
(601) 707-0960

MICHIGAN

BBB-Grand Rapids
40 Pearl St., NW, Suite 354
Grand Rapids, MI 49503
(616) 774-8236

BBB-Detroit
26777 Central Park Blvd., Ste 100
Southfield, MI 48076-4163
(248) 223-9400

MISSOURI

BBB-Kansas City
8080 Ward Parkway, Suite 401
Kansas City, MO 64114
(816) 421-7800

BBB-Springfield
430 S. Glenstone Ave., Suite A
Springfield, MO 65802
(417) 862-4222

BBB-St. Louis
211 N. Broadway, Suite 2060
St. Louis, MO 63102
(314) 645-3300

NEBRASKA

BBB-Lincoln
3633 O St., Suite 1

Lincoln, NE 68510
(402) 436-2345

BBB-Omaha
11811 P. St.
Omaha, NE 68137
(402) 391-7612

NEVADA

BBB-Las Vegas
6040 S. Jones Blvd.
Las Vegas, NV 89118
(702) 320-4500

BBB-Sparks
4834 Sparks Blvd., Suite 102
Sparks, NV 89436
(775) 322-0657

NEW HAMPSHIRE

BBB-Concord
48 Pleasant St.
Concord, NH 03301
(603) 224-1991

NEW JERSEY

BBB-Trenton
1700 Whitehorse-Hamilton Square Rd.
Suite D-5
Trenton, NJ 08690-3596
(609) 588-0808

NEW MEXICO

BBB-Albuquerque
2625 Pennsylvania St., NE, Suite 2050
Albuquerque, NM 87110-3658
(505) 346-0110

BBB-Farmington
308 N. Locke Ave.
Farmington, NM 87401-5855
(505) 326-6501

NEW YORK

BBB-Amherst
100 Bryant Woods South
Amherst, NY 14228
(716) 881-5222

BBB-Farmingdale
399 Conklin St., Suite 300
Farmingdale, NY 11735
(516) 420-0500

BBB-NYC
257 Park Ave S, 4th Floor
New York, NY 10016
(212) 533-6200

BBB-Rochester
55 St. Paul St.
Rochester, NY 14604
(716) 881-5222

BBB-Tarrytown
150 White Plains Rd, Ste. 107
Tarrytown, NY 10591-5521
(914) 333-0550

NORTH CAROLINA

BBB-Asheville
112 Executive Park
Asheville, NC 28801
(828) 253-2392

BBB-Charlotte
12860 Ballatyne Corporate Place, Ste. 225
Charlotte, NC 28277
(704) 927-8611

BBB-Greensboro
3608 W. Friendly Ave.
Greensboro, NC 27410-4895
(336) 852-4240

BBB-Raleigh
5540 Munford Rd., Suite 130
Raleigh, NC 27612-2655
(919) 277-4222

BBB-Winston-Salem
500 W. 5th St., Ste 202
Winston-Salem, NC 27101-2728
(336) 725-8348

OHIO

BBB-Akron
222 W. Market St.
Akron, OH 44303
(330) 253-4590

BBB-Canton
1434 Cleveland Ave., NW
Canton, OH 44703
(330) 454-9401

BBB-Cincinnati
Seven W 7th St., Suite 1600
Cincinnati, OH 45202
(513) 421-3015

BBB-Cleveland
2800 Euclid Ave., 4th Floor
Cleveland, OH 44115
(216) 241-7678

BBB-Columbus
1169 Dublin Rd.
Columbus, OH 43215-1005
(614) 486-6336

BBB-Dayton
15 W. Fourth St., Suite 300
Dayton, OH 45402-1830
1-800-776-5301

BBB-Lima
219 N. McDonel St.
Lima, OH 45801
(419) 223-7010

BBB-Toledo
Integrity Place
7668 King's Pointe Rd.
Toledo, OH 43617
(419) 531-3116

OKLAHOMA

BBB-Oklahoma City
17 S. Dewey St.
Oklahoma City, OK 73102-2400
(405) 239-6081

BBB-Tulsa
1722 S. Carson Ave., Suite 3200
Tulsa, OK 74119
(918) 492-1266

OREGON

BBB-Lake Aswego
4004 S.W. Kruse Way PL., Ste. 375
Lake Oswego, OR 97035
(503) 212-3022

PENNSYLVANIA

BBB-Bethlehem
50 W. North St.
Bethlehem, PA 18018-3907
(610) 866-8780

BBB-Harrisburg
1337 N. Front St.
Harrisburg, PA 17102
(717) 364-3250

BBB-Scranton/Wilkes-Barre
4099 Birney Ave.
Moosic, PA 18507
(570) 342-5100

BBB-Philadelphia
1880 John F. Kennedy Blvd., Ste. 1330
Philadelphia, PA 19103
(215) 985-9313

BBB-Pittsburgh
400 Holiday Dr., Ste 220
Pittsburgh, PA 15220
(412) 456-2700

PUERTO RICO

BBB-San Juan
530 Avenida De La Constitución #206
San Juan, PR 00901
(787) 289-8710

SOUTH CAROLINA

BBB-Columbia
1515 Burnette Dr.
Columbia, SC 29210
(803) 254-2525

BBB-Conway
1121 3rd Ave
Conway, SC 29526
(843) 488-2227

BBB-Greenville
408 N. Church St., Suite C
Greenville, SC 29601-2164
(864) 242-5052

SOUTH DAKOTA

BBB-Sioux Falls
300 N. Phillips Ave., #202
Sioux Falls, SD 57104
(605) 271-2066

TENNESSEE

BBB-Chattanooga
1010 Market St., Suite 200
Chattanooga, TN 37402
(423) 266-6144

BBB-Clarksville
214 Main St.
Clarksville, TN 37040
(931) 503-2222

BBB-Columbia
502 N. Garden St., Suite 201
Columbia, TN 38401
(931) 388-9222

BBB-Cookeville
18 N. Jefferson St.
Cookville, TN 38501
(931) 520-0008

BBB-Franklin
367 Riverside Dr., Suite 110
Franklin, TN 37064
(615) 250-7431

BBB-Knoxville
255 N Peters Rd, Suite A
Knoxville, TN 37923
(865) 692-1600

BBB-Memphis
3693 Tyndale Dr.
Memphis, TN 38125
(901) 759-1300

BBB-Murfreesboro
530 Uptown Square
Murfreesboro, TN 37129
(615) 242-4222

BBB-Nashville
201 4th Ave. N., Suite 100
Nashville, TN 37219
(615) 242-4222

TEXAS

BBB-Abilene
3300 S. 14th St., Suite 307
Abilene, TX 79605-5052
(325) 691-1533

BBB-Amarillo
720 S. Tyler St., Suite B112
Amarillo, TX 79101

BBB-Austin
1005 La Posada Dr.
Austin, TX 78752
(512) 445-2911

BBB-Beaumont
550 Fannin St., Suite 100
Beaumont, TX 77701-2011

(409) 835-5348

BBB-College Station
418 Tarrow St.
College Station, TX 77840-1822
(979) 260-2222

BBB-Corpus Christi
719 S. Shoreline, Suite 304
Corpus Christi, TX 78401
(361) 852-4949

BBB-Dallas
1601 Elm St., Suite 3838
Dallas, TX 75201-3093
(214) 220-2000

BBB-El Paso
720 Arizona Ave.
El Paso, TX 79902
(915) 577-0191

BBB-Fort Worth
101 Summit Ave., Suite 707
Fort Worth, TX 76102-5978
(817) 332-7585

BBB-Harker Heights
445 E. Central Texas Expressway, Suite 1
Harker Heights, TX 76548
(254) 699-0694

BBB-Houston
1333 W. Loop South, Suite 1200
Houston, TX 77027
(713) 868-9500

BBB-Longview
2401 Judson Rd., #102
Longview, TX 75605
(903) 758-3222

BBB-Lubbock
3333 66th St.
Lubbock, TX 79413-5711
(806) 763-0459

BBB-Midland

10100 Liberator Ln.
Midland, TX 79711
(432) 563-1880

BBB-San Angelo
3134 Executive Dr., Suite A
San Angelo, TX 76904
(325) 949-2989

BBB-San Antonio
1800 Northeast Loop 410, Suite 400
San Antonio, TX 78217-5296
(210) 828-9441

BBB-Tyler
3600 Old Bullard Rd.
Building 1, Suite 101
Tyler, TX 75701
(903) 581-5704

BBB-Weslaco
502 E. Expressway 83, Suite C
Weslaco, TX 78596
(956) 968-3678

BBB-Wichita Falls
4245 Kemp Blvd., Suite 900
Wichita Falls, TX 76308-2830
(940) 691-1172

UTAH

BBB-Salt Lake City
5673 S. Redwood Rd., Suite 22
Salt Lake City, UT 84123-5322
(801) 892-6009

VIRGINIA

BBB-Norfolk
586 Virginia Dr.
Norfolk, VA 23505
(757) 531-1300

BBB-Richmond
720 Moorefield Park Dr., Suite 300
Richmond, VA 23236

(804) 648-0016

BBB-Roanoke
31 W. Campbell Ave.
Roanoke, VA 24011
(540) 342-3455

WISCONSIN

BBB-Milwaukee
10101 W. Greenfield Ave., Suite 125
West Allis, WI 53214
(414) 847-6000

WASHINGTON

BBB-DuPont
1000 Station Dr., Suite 222
Dupont, WA 98327
(206) 431-2222

BBB-Spokane
152 S. Jefferson, Suite 200
Spokane, WA 79201
(509) 455-4200

WEST VIRGINIA

BBB-Charleston
1018 Kanawha Blvd., E, Suite 301
Charleston, WV 25301
(304) 345-7502

FREE PEN PALS

- 50 Verified Mega Church Addresses - offer free pen pals Only $10. w/ sample letter.
- 67 Churches offer a mix of free publications $6
- 200 Pen Pal Addresses off the Interweb some photos. Over half USA. Only $20
- NEW • Female Pen Pal Ads with bios & color photo

All Just Posted Only $12 each. Choices are: 100 Latina Lovers,100 Black Beauties,130 Asian Angels

NEW • 329+ Pen Pals Booklet Mixed Overseas Only $25 Now $18

NEW • 44 Verified Pen Pal Magazines who offer free pen pal ads by snail mail. Only $14

CELEBRITY ADDRESSES

Write to your favorite celeb for free photos.
Choices are:

- TV Stars: Latina, Black or White
- Athletes: NBA, NFL or Female
- Music: Top 40, Urban or Country
- Models: Mixed

$10 each / 3 for $25 EVERY LIST has 60 to 90 addresses

500 FREE MAGAZINES

500 Free Mags - Legally.
Brand new catalog of magazines order free.
Verified snail mail addresses and directions.
Huge Variety. 80 plus pages.
Only 18.99 (Add $2 s/h all orders)

Add $2 s/h on all orders

Girls and Mags Box 319, Rehoboth, MA 02769

OR Add $4 s/h with tracking

SNAIL MAIL PEN PAL ING

Over 300 New Pen Pals In Each Issue

Every issue helps you get and keep more pen pals! You get more than pen pal profiles! With articles on creating a profile that gets noticed; sending love letters, interesting topics, questions to start meaningful conversations, letters to your children and even apology letters. You deserve a copy!

$13.98

✓ Single issue
✓ We always send you the most current issue
✓ Published every quarter
✓ Free shipping
✓ Full Color Gloss

Order Today!

Send your address and payment to:

Girls and Mags
PO BOX 319
REHOBOTH, MA 02769

CHAPTER 12
TIME REVOLUTION FOR CELLPRENEURS

*"Don't start a time revolution unless you are
willing to be revolutionary."*
– Richard Koch

As a cellpreneur, most of your time should be spent doing three things. They are: reading, writing, and marketing. You read to research and get new ideas and hone your skills. You write to create new products, update your existing ones, and network with other business-minded people. You market your products to promote and make sales, get new customers, and blast your competition out of the water. These are the three areas that you should focus on. Of course, you may be wondering how you're supposed to get all this done? I have the answer that will turn you into a master of productivity. It takes self-discipline, but if will build great habits that will serve you well as your journey.

TIME MANAGEMENT: DO YOU NEED IT?

The world spends a billion dollars on "time management." But you don't need that. You're in prison so your time is already being managed for you! You need to use those few hours of "free time" to produce something valuable for others. That's how you get rich. Let me give you an example. From 2002-2007 I spent most of my time writing pen pals. The reward I sought was weekly visits, phone calls, and the here and there money orders they could (or would) send. As I look back I think how stupid I was. One year's work on one book has produced more results (mentally, spiritually, emotionally and financially) far exceeds anything else in my life ever! It eclipses every one of those pen pal years. Time is not the enemy, but your use of it is!

Another way to look at it is how productivity expert Susan Lasky (www.SusanLasky.com) describes it. She says you get 1440 minutes in a day and each minute represents a "credit" in your personal time bank. You can spend them any way you want but at the end of the day your balance always ends at zero! So, you must learn to use those credits.

> *"Don't count days, make days count!"*
> *– Muhammad Ali*

ARE YOU DOING DEAD TIME?

For cellpreneurs who want to become Millionaire Prisoners dead time is the enemy. When I say, "dead time" I mean time that is wasted. In the prison context, dead time is not yours. It's the BOP's or the State's. And when you're doing time for them, all you want to do is pass the time and mark down another day on your calendar. You sleep longer, read fiction and urban novels, and watch T.V. with no purpose except to make the hours fly by. Other prisoners play cards all day. Or chess. On my first bid I went to prison as a 17-year old. I came out three years later no better off than when I went in. I spent those three years playing cards and goofing off. That's dead time in my life that I'll never get back. Don't make that same mistake. Respect time. True ownership comes from being able to use your time wisely. Take the time the judge sentenced you to do and put it to work for you. All of us prisoners have the option to either do dead time or turn our prison into a stepping-stone to success. It's your choice.

> *"Even in prison your time is your own, if you use it for your own purposes."*
> *– Robert Greene*

TIME IS MONEY!

Because I advise in my books that you can make money by becoming a cellpreneur, you have to learn what your time is worth. Or should be worth to you if you really want to make money. I first became aware of this principal after reading Dan S. Kennedy's great book *No B.S. Time Management For Entrepreneurs, Second Edition*. He had a formula that you could use to come up with your number. When I did the math, mine had to be worth $153 an hour for me to hit my goal of

$160,000 a year. Now his formula is based on the fact that you're working for yourself and that you'll only have three or four really productive hours each day. In prison, you have a lot of distractions. There's time spent exercising on the yard, going to the chow hall, hospital and dentist trips, and a lot of other prison minutia. You'll find that you can carve out three or four hours each day where you can get things done without being interrupted. It's these precious hours that I'm talking about. For you to hit a $100,000 goal those hours have to be worth $153 an hour. (FYI: For a goal of $1 million your hours should be worth $1,530. Eye opening, isn't it?) When you have this number it's easy to see if what you're doing is worth it or not?

To further illustrate this principle allow me to share with you what Associate Professor of Economics, Emily Oster, teaches her students at the University of Chicago's Booth School of Business. Oster shows her pupils the basic economic principle of *opportunity cost*. It's really a simple question: What is the cost of my investment of time between two alternatives? For instance, I can spend two hours of my time washing clothes or I can pay another prisoner a couple bucks to do it. To figure out if I should outsource my laundry to Mr. Maytag Prisoner on the second tier, I need to decide if I can spend that time doing something profitable? For me, it's a no brainer. I can easily spend that time reading, researching, and writing. If you know that your time is worth $153 an hour, then each minute is supposed to be worth $2.55. So, if you spend 45 minutes doing laundry it costs you $114.75. That's an expensive load of laundry! Paying another prisoner two candy bars to do it for me, it actually saves me a hundred dollars. I'm only using time vs. laundry as an example. I also try to outsource my cooking, cell cleaning, and other prison tasks that I hate doing. You may like doing something that doesn't really help you out financially? Just remember this principle as you look at your time. Stop doing unprofitable things if you can. Instead, invest your time.

THE GREATEST ENEMY FOR CELLPRENEURS

Watch *LockUp* on MSNBC or other prison shows on NatGEO and HBO and you'll see tons of televisions in the prisoners' cells. If you took a survey of the prisoners and asked them what the most important item is they own, 90% of them would say their TV. At one of the prisons I was in they never had cable TV. It was whatever you could get with some homemade rabbit ears and wires stuck out the back of your cell. When the prison administration did sign up for cable, the contract said they needed it to help pacify us! Are you a baby? Do you need to be pacified? If you're going to be a successful cellpreneur you have to devalue your TV. Even if you don't have a TV, the one in the day room is still your enemy as well. A collection of non-fiction books is worth more to you than a TV. Stephen King called it the "glass teat". My grandfather called it the "idiot box." Watching TMZ and stupid reality TV shows will not get you prosperity. It will not get you healthy. *The New York Times* reported that sitting for long periods of time in front of the TV can lead to  weight gain and increase the risk of heart disease and cancer. What does that say for the prisoner who lays in the bunk all day and watches TV?

'The television has become the greatest babysitter in the world for corrections.:
– Edgar Kneiss,
former Deputy Superintendent of Corrections in Pennsylvania

In my first book *The Millionaire Prisoner* I do come across as being anti-TV. But I don't hate television. I hate TV all day long as a way of passing time. A cellpreneur should not be watching daytime soap operas unless you're writing for that genre. Nor should you watch hours of *Cops*, *Honey Boo Boo*, or *Keeping Up With the Kardashians*. Personally, I don't turn on my TV until 5 or 6pm at night. If something I'm working on isn't completed by then my TV doesn't come on. I subscribe to Channel Guide so that I can plan my TV watching for the month in advance. What shows do I watch? ABC's *Shark Tank*, CNBC's *The Profit*, *American Greed*, *The Filthy Rich Guide to Living*, and other financial shows and specials. I also like NBC's *The Blacklist* and AMC's *The Walking Dead*. I love sports, especially football. That's why I spend the day getting things done so that my reward is watching a game or my favorite TV show at night.

> *"Poor prisoners spend all day watching 15-inch flat screens. Millionaire Prisoners have subscriptions to The Wall Street Journal."*

But when I do watch TV I still find ways to make it profitable. If I'm watching *Shark Tank* I keep a pen and paper by my side and take notes. Because I write about pen pals and prison relationships in my book, Pen Pal Success, I watched shoes like *Prison Wives Club*, *The Millionaire Matchmaker*, and other relationship shows. I write stuff down that I think I can use and things people say. Also, during the commercials I read or write. I don't need to pay attention to what they're selling so I use that three minutes to read a paragraph or two in a new book. Or you can do push-ups or sit-ups, work on a crossword puzzle, or write a poem? If I was able to buy books on CD at my prison, then I would listen to audiobooks as I watched football or basketball. Whatever you do, make your TV viewing profitable and don't become a TV zombie wasting time on frivolous reality television. If you want to read more about getting rid of TV in your life, check out *Four Arguments for the Elimination of Television* by Jerry Mander.

> *"Most people would rather watch television than drag themselves out of their pit of poverty."*
> *– Richard Templar, The Rules of Wealth*

HOW TO FIND LOST TIME

As you begin to get control of your time you need to find the areas where you're losing time. One of the easiest ways to do this is to keep track of a week's worth of time. In his book Think Outside The Cell, Joseph Robinson advocates this principle. There are only 168 hours in a week. If you sleep eight hours a day that's 56 hours gone. That leaves 112 hours. Let's say you spend an average of the two hours a day exercising, eating and bathing. That's 14 hours and leaves 98 hours. You only need 28 of those hours to be productive to get ahead. Here's how you find out where you're losing time.

Get a piece of paper and start keeping track of what you do from the time you get up till the time you go to sleep. Every task that you do, put it on paper and how much time is spent on it. Do this for a whole week (or month) and you'll find tasks and times where you wasted, i.e., lost time. After you find then, then you can cut them out and replace them with other more profitable tasks that will carry you closer to your goals. The key to becoming a successful cellpreneur is to plan your days ahead of time. This is easy to do in prison because our environment is one of routine. Count is the same time every day. Yard is the same time. Chow is the same time. Prison is one big mundane time drip.

But this can be a huge bonus to the prisoner who plans his days in advance. Famous novelist Edward Bunker used to write at night after the prison was locked down. When can you script out the time to work? If you keep track of your time for a week or month, you'll find huge blocks of your time that can be used to reach your goals. Find this time.

HOW TO STEAL TIME

Scott Turow wrote his first novel sitting on the subway each morning to work. Where can you steal time like this? One of my favorite places to steal time is at the commissary while I'm waiting on them to call me to shop. All around me prisoners are gossiping, playing cards, or just sitting there doing nothing. I'm either reading or writing. Sure, it may only be 20 minutes I have to wait, but that's an extra 20 minutes I can profit from. I've had some weekly commissary trips last for over an hour. While the suckers around me are wasting time, I'm getting ahead. Maybe you can steal time at the hospital, commissary, in the chow hall, at your prison job, or somewhere else? And by stealing time you get ahead of everyone else. Don't you want to get ahead?

AN INVESTMENT THAT PAYS THE BEST INTEREST

Now that you got those things out of the way you must do the two things that all cellpreneurs do: Read and write. I'll deal with reading in this book. In my next book, I'll deal with writing. (FYI: That book is Millionaire Prisoner's Info – *Cellpreneur System: How to Make $100,000 A Year Or More Writing, Publishing*.

I can read all day. I love learning and finding one tip or tactic that I can use to make my life better. But unlike most of my carceral comrades I don't read urban novels or pornographic books. For one, when I was in the free-world I lived out both of those genres, so why do I need to read more about it? Second, I don't write urban novels or pornographic books so there's no need to read those. I write "How-To" books for prisoners. And I read what's relevant. One of the saddest things I overheard a prisoner say was that he needed a set of Harry Potter books to pass the time. He said he could occupy a whole week that way. That will be a wasted week. Nelson Mandela became a voracious reader while in prison. He didn't have a TV in his cell to pacify him. Instead, he read everything he could get his hands on. And it was in a dark, solitary cell, using the light coming under the cell door to read by that Malcolm Little recreated himself from Detroit Red – the pimp to Malcolm X – the revolutionary. If these two titans in prison lore spent their in-cell time reading and studying, why aren't you?

> *"No matter how busy you may think you are, you must*
> *find time for reading, or surrender yourself to self-chosen ignorance."*
> *– Confucius*

WHAT TO READ?

This book is about starting a business from prison. So naturally you should read other How-To business books. You need to keep up-to-date with all the latest techniques in your chosen field. You need to read about marketing, investing, and business. I would suggest subscribing to magazines such as *Inc, Entrepreneur, Wired, Success, Fast Company*, and *Business Week*. Reading *USA Today, Wall Street Journal*, and *The New York Times* will keep you abreast of the latest news. For me, since I write how to information for prisoners I read Inmate Shopper, subscribe to *Prison Legal News, The Echo, The Prison Mirror, Prison Focus* and many other prison publications. If there are trade journals or newsletters for your target audience then you need to read and study them.

*"Biographies of great, but especially of good men,
are nevertheless most instructive and useful, as helps,
guides and incentives to others."*
– Samuel Smiles

In this guide, I list a lot of books. I think you should read. It's a good place to start. When you read, books pay attention to the books they list in any bibliography or cite as a source. You may want to get a copy for yourself. Don't worry if the books are old. You'll find a wealth of helpful information in the classics. You may be thinking that this will be a lot of reading? Yes, it will be. But reading is the easiest way for a prisoner to research. And if you don't read you won't be able to come up with new ideas easily.

"First, we eat, then we beget; first we read, then we write."
– Ralph Waldo Emerson

But there are ways to speed up your research and reading times. One way is to learn how to speed read. I taught myself how to speed read using a book by Tory Buzan. I was already a fast reader, but his book helped me even more. If you have the money you should subscribe to the services

that summarize the latest business and self-help books. Success magazine has a service like this for $79 a year. There are others. The Week is a weekly magazine that provides tidbits of news from across the country and can be had for $45 a year. A lot cheaper than the $200 it costs for a year of *USA Today*. I'm not suggesting you should do this just to save money. All your magazine and newspaper subscriptions costs are tax deductible. What I'm saying is that because you're in prison and don't have access to the internet you need a system to get the latest information. These places and periodicals can help. If you have email then you should set up a Google Alerts Account for your subject matter. That way you get updated on all the latest news on your type of business. These are just some of the ways you speed things up and cut down your research time.

THE ACT OF GETTING THINGS DONE

Here are some tips and tactics that I've found to work over the years:

- Schedule your time like a movie script. Plan so every hour of the day is accounted for. Use a "Project List" and a "To Do List."

- Don't try to do everything in one hour. Take breaks. Stretch. Then come back to your work refreshed.

- Bundle your tasks so like-minded stuff gets done together. Like "clean/wash clothes & cell". "Answer mail/email." "Read newspapers/magazines."

- Outsource the mundane tasks that you hate doing so your free up time for more profitable tasks.

- Don't allow the prison time-vultures to interrupt you. Politely tell them you're busy or ignore them. Talk to them after you're done for the day.

- Besides your To Do List you need a "Stop Doing List." If it doesn't add value to your life or move you further toward your goals you shouldn't be doing it.

"Stop doing lists are more important than to do lists."
– Jim Collins, Good To Great

- Think about the past and how you can use it to better occupy your time. Think different. The masses are asses when it comes to the use of time. Do the opposite of what they do.

- Always look for ways to do stuff better, faster, easier. Try and set up systems or outsource stuff you don't like to do.

In this guide, I've listed numerous books that can help you on your cellpreneur journey. But as a prisoner you must save money anyway you can. I'm going to share my secrets on how I get books for dirt-cheap prices.

HOW TO GET THE LOWEST PRICE FOR ANY BOOK

One of my favorite places to order books from is Edward R. Hamilton Bookseller Company. But if you enlist someone in the free-world to assist you there are ways to find the same books for less. Most people use Amazon.com, BarnesandNoble.com, or Half.com when ordering books online. My favorite website is www.BookFinder4u.com. Book Finder allows you to search 130 bookstores and 60,000 individual booksellers in a single search. They also have over 90 million used and out-of-print books in their database. You can search for books by:

- Author's Name

- Book Title

- Subject Keyword

Then click on the "Compare Prices" button and you'll get the best price available. My assistant found books for $1 plus shipping, even a penny plus shipping!

Your assistant can also check out AbeBooks.com. AbeBooks has over 100 million books being sold by over 13,000 booksellers around the world. You can use it to find rare books.

Some companies tout Amazon as the best bookseller in the world. But you should always check elsewhere. Sometimes the biggest isn't always the best when it comes to price. Utilize the web to get the lowest price available. Just make sure you do the math. It could still be cheaper to order from Edward R. Hamilton once you add up all the fees.

To be honest, sometimes I just have my personal assistant do it all online because of the time saved by not having to go through the prison system's money voucher process. I pay more that way, but I can get books faster. And since I'm an info-cellpreneur, the costs are tax deductible for me. Learn to get books for the lowest price and then use the money that you saved to reinvest it back into your business. In the next section, I'll show you what to do with your books once you get them. More cellpreneur secrets!

THE ART OF READING NON-FICTION

A sign of ignorance is to take credit for ideas that aren't of our creation. I've participated in this folly every once in a while. But in my books, I've tried to give credit where credit is due. I first learned about this system of reading from Zig Ziglar and his book, Secrets of Closing the Sale. I had the opportunity to ask Zig about his system before he passed away, and he further clarified it for me. His thoughts have been incorporated into mine. Because it has been most profitable to me, and I've yet to find a better system, I include it here for your benefit. Try it out for yourself with these five steps:

1. Read through the book quickly to get the gist of the message, underlining or highlighting the things that really "grab" you. Only stop to look up words you don't know, or write them down to look up later. The first reading allows you to become familiar with the book. For those prisoners who don't have access to highlighters, I advise you to use a ruler or a bookmark with a straight edge when underlining, as this will keep your book from being sloppily marked up.

2. As you read the book the second time, keep a notebook of ideas generated by the book that you can personally use. The objective is not to see how quickly you can get out of the book, but what you can get out of the book.

3. In your third reading, invest time and patience in gleaning additional ideas you have missed in your second reading. A careful examination of each chapter is warranted. Go over what you have highlighted or underlined. Determine if you have captured the essence of the author's words, and if you can apply it to your life. Put anything you missed in your notebook.

4. The fourth reading enables the book to become an integral part of you, enhancing your effectiveness. After this reading, you can place the book in your collection, and it will be a treasure trove, ready and willing to supply you with any knowledge you may need.

5. Find people who have read the book or share it with them. Then discuss the book together to see what you get out of it. You may gain additional insights from their ideas and thoughts that you didn't see on your own.

> *"Some books are to be tasted, others to be swallowed*
> *and some few to be chewed and digested."*
> *– Francis Bacon*

A word of caution. If you're reading someone else's book, or one on loan from the library, do not dog-ear the pages, or write or highlight in the book. Nothing is more irritating than to loan a book out, only to have it come back with dog-eared pages and someone else's notes and highlights in it. That may cause someone to stop loaning you books. Respect books and their owners. That way you'll get a great education from them. By using the above system, you can make the most of your time in reading so that its most profitable in your cellpreneur journey.

> *"A reading program should be as carefully planned as a daily diet,*
> *for knowledge, too, is food, without which we cannot grow mentally."*
> *– Andrew Carnegie*

A PARTING THOUGHT ABOUT BOOKS

Some prison systems make you keep all your property in storage boxes or foot lockers. My prison does this. When he was on Death Row, Mumia Abu-Jamal could only keep seven books in his cell at a time. But he kept lots of notes. What can you do? Here's what I do.

Once a month I go through my property box to see which books I still need, which ones I can donate to the prison library (where I could still access them) or ones I don't need anymore. Some books I'm able to tear out a few pages that I need and throw away the rest. Then I file those pages with the same subject matter into another book that I'm keeping. I don't allow the prison's property rules to stop me and neither should you. Remember, excuses are the bricks that make the house of failure. Don't make them. Get busy studying and make things happen!

"The way to get started is to quit talking and begin doing."
– Walt Disney

Former cellpreneur, Michael Santos, would read books then write a report about it after he was done stating:

- The date he read the book;

- Why he decided to read that book;

- What he learned from reading it; and

- How it will help him achieve his goals

Santos is the author of seven books, including *Earning Freedom, Success After Prison!* and *Prison! My 8,344th Day*. When he got out he taught a class on corrections at San Francisco State University as an Adjunct Professor. Books helped him, and they can help you also. For more about Michael Santos, inquire about his work and books at:

Prison Professor, LLC
3333 Michelson Drive, Suite 500
Irvine, CA 92612
(949) 334-9119
Michael@MIchaelSantos.com

HOW TO TURN YOUR CELL INTO AN OFFICE

Prison isn't the ideal place to research and write. The typical prison cell is the size of a small bathroom and must be shared by two prisoners (sometimes more) in most cases. But to become a cellpreneur extraordinaire you must commit yourself to daily writing and research. Here are some tips that will aid you in creating the best environment out of your cell.

1. *Time.* Try to pick a time when you will not be interrupted by outside influences. In prison, this sometimes means staying up at night when the prison is quiet like Eddie Bunker. Or you may have to skip yard, so you can study and be alone. I have ADD and use headphones to tune out all the jailhouse jibber-jabber. Pick the time when you are mentally fresh and stick to that time. Make it a habit every day to go to work at that time.

2. *Light.* Prison can be a dreary place, but the best light to read by is daylight. So place your desk or chair by the window if you can? If that's not possible, the light should come over your shoulder opposite of your writing hand. This takes away shadows. Do not beam your desk lamp directly on your book or magazine. That creates a contrast in the cell and can be distracting. You want the light to seem natural as possible.

3. *Preparation.* Make sure that you have all of your research materials and writing tools within reach before you start. You don't want to interrupt yourself by having to stop what you're doing to search for something once you've already started. Place all your books where you can see them as a visualization tool. If you can work for a few hours in the prison library surrounded by books, do so!

4. *Posture.* Don't get too comfortable, and don't lie down to read. Your desk or table should be set up so that your thighs are parallel with the floor. Keep your feet flat on the floor, back upright. You may find it more comfortable to hold your reading material in your hands.

5. *Space*. Keep your material spread out so that you have room to work. I turn the bottom bunk in my cell into a desk. Some experts say the material you're working on should be kept approximately 20 inches away from your eyes. A lot of prisoners get headaches and strained eyes after reading for long periods of time and keeping your material at this distance should help with that problem.

By turning your cell into an office, you can rise to a level you never thought possible. Even if you aren't going to write a full-length book the above tips are useful. I follow them when I set up my cell-office. Do the same. Millionaire Prisoners learn, and learners become earners! Some prisons now have conference type quiet rooms that are supposed to be used for studying and writing. If you're so lucky to have one, use it. Of course, you'll want to pick the time when it's least occupied.

*"You are subject to your environment, therefore, select the
environment that will best develop you toward your desired objective."*
– W. Clement Stone

A PARTING THOUGHT ON YOUR USE OF TIME

This chapter is not about how much stuff you can do. Never mistake busyness for business. There's a huge difference and it's just not in the way those words are spelled. You need to focus on quality not quantity. What tasks for you produce the greatest results? Those are the objects you should spend your time on. Whatever you do, always weigh carefully someone else's demands on your time. It takes self-discipline to go against the crowd. But it's your duty to stretch as far as you can to the opposite of the masses of asses that you can without being physically hurt. Always remember that you get 1440 credits every day. How are you using them will deliver you the answer to your dreams or not? Prison time is your friend if you use it right! I know you can.

RESOURCE BOX

For more information about getting things done and better use of your time you'll want to read the following books:

- *The 80/20 Principle: The Secret To Achieving More With Less*
  by Richard Koch

- *No B.S. Time Management for Entrepreneurs, Second Edition*
  by Dan S. Kennedy

- *The Ten Natural Laws of Time and Life Management*
  by Hiram B. Smith

- *168 Hours* by Laura Vanderkam

- *Prison! My 8,344th Day* by Michael Santos

Books can be ordered from our Bookstore on page 224 or online. Contact Freebird Publishers about ordering if you don't have anyone to help you.

Freebird Publishers

Post-Conviction Relief: Secrets Exposed

Kelly Patrick Riggs

STOP - If you like prison don't read this book. This book is full of information about how to get out of prison early. Cover to cover filled with motions and secrets used by real Habeas Corpus practitioners getting real results. This book will show you the simple way to:

> - Get your case file;
> - Analyze your case;
> - Keep your records efficiently;
> - Investigate your case, see what you deserve;
> - Write simple effective motions;
> - Get out of prison; EARLY!!

1st BOOK IN SERIES OF 7 Watch For More COMING SOON!

Only $19.99 plus s/h $7

⇒ This book gives you what the courts don't want you to have, an understanding of the reason you're in prison.

⇒ You will learn the proper Habeas corpus practice that the courts follow, rather than the fairy tale that is taught in a school.

⇒ This book comes from the wisdom of real practitioners who files Habeas corpus petitions and get real relief.

⇒ You will learn in plain English how to win in a section 2255 proceeding.

⇒ This book contains real filings from real cases that have prevailed.

⇒ This book will make a good practitioner... great!

Softcover, 8x10", B&W, 190+ pages $26.99 (19.99 plus $7. s/h)

Written in simple terms for everyone to understand, it's not just for lawyers anymore.

NO ORDER FORM NEEDED CLEARLY WRITE ON PAPER & SEND PAYMENT TO:

amazon.com

Freebird Publishers Box 541, North Dighton, MA 02764
Diane@FreebirdPublishers.com   www.FreebirdPublishers.com
Toll Free: 888-712-1987   Text/Phone: 774-406-8682

PayPal
MasterCard   VISA   DISCOVER   BANK

Freebird Publishers

Post-Conviction Relief: The Appeal

Kelly Patrick Riggs

POST-CONVICTION RELIEF: **THE APPEAL**

NO FAIRY TALES, JUST APPEALS.

The appeals process taught to lawyers in layman's terms.

Step-by-Step; Rule-by-Rule, Learn the Appeal Process;

→ **Notice of Appeal;**

→ **Designation of The Record;**

→ **Certificate of Appealability;**

→ **Operational Habits of The Court Clerks;**

→ **Briefs;**

→ **Rules;**

→ **Applicable Laws; And Much More...**

2nd BOOK IN SERIES OF 7

Watch For More COMING SOON!

Only **$19.99** plus s/h $7

⇒ In this book you receive instructions, to the layman, concerning every filing individually.

⇒ Sample Letters

⇒ Sample Forms

⇒ Sample Briefs

⇒ Motions for Rehearing

⇒ En Banc

⇒ All you need to know about winning an appeal

Softcover, 8x10", B&W, 180+ pages $26.99 (19.99 plus $7. s/h)

Written in simple terms for everyone to understand, it's not just for lawyers anymore.

<u>NO ORDER FORM NEEDED</u> CLEARLY WRITE ON PAPER & SEND PAYMENT TO:

Freebird Publishers

amazon.com

Box 541, North Dighton, MA 02764
Diane@FreebirdPublishers.com www.FreebirdPublishers.com
Toll Free: 888-712-1987 Text/Phone: 774-406-8682

Freebird Publishers

Post-Conviction Relief: Advancing Your Claim

Kelly Patrick Riggs

POST-CONVICTION RELIEF: **ADVANCING YOUR CLAIM**

LEARN HOW TO THINK AND WRITE IN A STYLE THAT JUDGES WILL ADMIRE, AND LAWYERS WILL ENVY.

This third book in the Post-Conviction Relief series. This installment is written to correct the most basic problem in your case, the way you think. I have encountered hundreds of prisoners who failed to obtain post-conviction relief because they attempt to sound like a lawyer, that is a mistake. The post-conviction relief process is designed to allow prisoners to express themselves plainly without being required to know laws and rules. This book is my effort to set a standard by which a layman can measure their ability to express themselves to a court effectively. This book will teach you how to present motions and petitions that are more pleasing to judges, who in most cases want you to have what you deserve under the law. It will teach you how to refine your pleadings by understanding the importance of critical word usage and syllogistic reasoning. You will learn the importance of presenting a clear set of facts as opposed to a theory in law they already know. This book includes a full and accurate copy of the Federal Rules of Civil Procedure and other resource materials.

3rd BOOK IN SERIES OF 7

Watch For More COMING SOON!

Only $19.99

plus s/h $7

→ **Present a concise argument**
→ **Communicate clearly**
→ **Think syllogistically**
→ **Write with a clear purpose**
→ **Make a fine point**
→ **Know what judges want**
→ **Know what prosecutors hate**

→ **Present clear case citations**
→ **What claims to raise**
→ **What claims to abandon**
→ **The structure of law**
→ **Know the proper jurisdiction**
→ **Know the proper jurisdiction and so much more**

Softcover, 8" x 10", B&W, 218 pages $26.99 (19.99 plus $7. s/h)

Written in simple terms for everyone to understand, it's not just for lawyers anymore.

NO ORDER FORM NEEDED CLEARLY WRITE ON PAPER & SEND PAYMENT TO:

Freebird Publishers

Box 541, North Dighton, MA 02764
Diane@FreebirdPublishers.com   www.FreebirdPublishers.com
Toll Free: 888-712-1987   Text/Phone: 774-406-8682

amazon.com

PayPal MasterCard VISA DISC/VER BANK

CHAPTER 13
MILLIONAIRE PRISONER RESOURCE DIRECTORY

"A good general cultivates resources."
– Sun Tzu

I first learned about "The Millionaire-Dollar Rolodex" idea from Dan Kennedy's book How To Make Millions With Your Ideas. He wrote that billionaire Aristotle Onassis' secret to success was knowing something nobody else knew. Dan then listed the people and companies he used to make money and called it the Million-Dollar Rolodex. In my book *The Millionaire Prisoner*, I have an extensive list of people and resources that I think can help you succeed. But as is the case in using directories published in books, the addresses may no longer be good? Buyer beware! There are two great directories available for prisoners that you should own a copy of:

Inmate Shopper
Freebird Publishers
Box 541
North Dighton, MA 02764
$26.99 postpaid

The Best Resource Guide For Prisoners
The Cell Block
P.O. Box 1025
Rancho Cordova, CA 95741
$26.99 postpaid

Always try to get the latest edition of each book. I keep both of them close to my desk every time I sit down!

Here are a bunch of people who could help you build your cellpreneur empire

BOOKS TO PRISONERS PROJECTS – NATIONAL

Utilize these places to request free books on starting a business. FYI: Now that I have a little bit of money I no longer request free books. Instead I pay for mine. I do this because I don't want to take free books when they could go to a less fortunate prisoner than me. But if you're just starting out and have limited funds these people can help.

Books For Prisoners
c/o Groundwork Books
0323 Student Center
La Jolla, CA 92037
(free book list with SASE)

Books Through Bars – NYC
Bluestockings Bookstore
172 Allen St.
New York, NY 1009
www.abcnorio.org/affiliated/btb

Books Through Bars
4722 Baltimore Avenue
Philadelphia, PA 19143
(215) 727-8170
www.booksthroughbars.org
(No Michigan or Oregon Prisoners)

The Prison Library Project
915 West Foothill Blvd.
Suite C128
Claremont, CA 91711

Books Through Bars of Ithaca
Second Floor
Autumn Leaves Bookstore
115 The Commons
Ithaca, NY 14850
www.btbithaca.org

D.C. Books to Prisons Project
c/o The Quixote Center
P.O. Box 5206
Hyattesville, MD 20782-0206
www.quixote.org/ej/bookstoprisons

Books To Prisoners
c/o Left Banks Books
92 Pike St., Box A
Seattle, WA 98101]

Gainesville Books for Prisoners
P.O. Box 12164
Gainesville, FL 32604

Prison Book Program
1306 Hancock St., Suite 100
Quincy, MA 02169
(617) 423-3298
www.prisonbookprogram.org

Prison Book Project
c/o Food for Thought Books
P.O. Box 396
Amherst, MA 01004-0396
www.prisonbooks.org

Prisoner's Literature Project
c/o Bound Together Books
1369 Haight St.
San Francisco, CA 94117-2908
(510) 893-4648

BOOKS TO PRISONER PROJECTS – MIDWEST

Midwest Books to Prisoners
c/o Qimby's Bookstore
1573 N. Milwaukee Ave.
Chicago, IL 60622-2029
www.freewebs.com/mwbtp
(IL, MN, WI, MO, IA, KS, NE only)

Midwest Pages To Prisoners Project
c/o Boxcar Books and Community Center
310A S. Washington St.

Bloomington, IN 47401-3529
www.pagestoprisoners.org

UC Books to Prisoners
c/o Spineless Books
P.O. Box 515
Urbana, IL 61803
www.books2prisoners.org
(Illinois only)

BOOKS TO PRISONER PROJECTS – WOMEN

Chicago Books to Women in Prison
c/o Beyond Media Education
7013 N. Glenwood Ave.
Chicago, IL 60626
www.chicagobwp.org

San Diego Coalition for Women Prisoners
c/o Groundwork Books
0323 Student Center

La Jolla, CA 92037
(women only, book list for SASE)

Women's Prison Book Project
c/o Arise Bookstore
2441 Lyndale Ave. S.
Minneapolis, MN 55405
www.prisonactivist.org/wpbp

BOOKS TO PRISONER PROJECTS – SPECIFIC STATES

Books 2 Prisoners
P.O. Box 791327
New Orleans, LA 71079
(LA Prisoners Only)

Book 'Em

P.O. Box 71357
Pittsburgh, PA 15213
(PA and NY prisoners only)

Inside Books Project
c/o 12th St. Books

827 West 12th St.
Austin, TX 78701
(TX prisoners only)

Portland Books to Prisoners
P.O. Box 11222
Portland, OR 97211
(Oregon prisoners only)

DISCOUNT MAGAZINE SELLERS

Utilize these vendors to get your subscriptions to *Inc., Forbes, Fortune, Entrepreneur, Fast Company, and Small Business Opportunities*, etc.

Grant Publications
Box 28812
Greenfield, Wi 53228-0812
(SASE for Catalog)

Fort Walton Beach, FL 32549
(SASE for more info)

Inmate magazine Service
P.O. Box 2063

Tightwad Magazines
Box 1941
Buford, GA 30515
(SASE for mini-catalog)

INTERNET RESEARCH

Elite Paralegal Services (EPS)
Box 1711
Appleton, WI 54912-1711
(SASE for more info)

Jodi Van Valkenburg
23 Heller Hill Rd.
Blairstown, NJ 07825
(SASE for more info)

Help From Outside
2620 Bellevue Way NE #200
Bellevue, WA 98004
(SASE for more info)

Nurit Mittlefehldt
16251 Brookford Dr.
Houston, TX 77509
(SASE for more info)

TYPING SERVICES

Ambler Document Processing
Box 938
Norwalk, CT 06852
(SASE for prisoner rates)

Hawkeye Editing
P.O. Box 16406
St. Paul, MN 5516

Barbara Allen Writers' Services
P.O. Box 1816
Cortaro, AZ 85652-1816
www.BAwriterservices.com

Let My Fingers Do Your Typing
Box 4178
Winter Park, FL 32793
(SASE for prisoner rates)

Full House Typing and Editing
Box 361402
Decatur, GA 30036
(SASE for rates)

Sandy Coates
P.O. Box 45
Watson, MN 56295

(SASE for rates)

SMALL BUSINESS ADVICE

U.S. Small Business Administration
409 Third St., SW
Washington, DC 20416
1-800-LL-ASKSBA
www.sba.gov
(Free pamphlets on business)

PRISONER ASSISTANCE COMPANIES

Julia Capel
Help From Outside
2620 Bellevue Way NE #200
Bellevue, WA 98004
(206) 486-6042
www.helpfromoutside.com

$19.99 plus s/h

INMATE 🛒 SHOPPER

EVERY ISSUE IS ALWAYS UP-TO-DATE & NEW CONTENT

NEW ANNUAL ISSUES   MID YEAR RELEASES   JUNE 30th to JUNE 30th

1000+ Listings AMERICA'S LARGEST Resources for Inmate Services

Everything you need while in prison is available in the INMATE SHOPPER. Always Up-to-Date. Current issue, 360+ pgs. of new content, constantly adding new products, services, resources, news & more...

IN EVERY ISSUE

SEXY PHOTO SPREAD

Non Nude • Full Page Photos • Alluring Layouts

PEN PAL SECTION

NEW WHAT'S TRENDING

ENTERTAINMENT

Puzzles • Trivia • Games • Hobbies • Jokes

CRIM. JUSTICE NEWS

REENTRY SECTION

VETERANS SECTION

LGBTQ SECTION

SPORT SCHEDULES

SPECIAL FEATURE

INMATE 🛒 SHOPPER

AMERICA'S

LARGEST BOOK OF RESOURCES

FOR INMATE SERVICES

AVAILABLE JULY 2018

Freebird Publishers

ANNUAL ISSUE

RETAIL PRICE 24.99

NEW ANNUAL 2018-19

Sexy Photo Sellers
Pen Pal Resources
Magazine Sellers
Social Media
Text/Phone
Catalogs to Order
Personal Assistants
Publishing Services
Gift Shops
Typists
Business Directory
Business Ratings
LGBTQ Section
Articles, Tips & Facts
Resources
New Content Every Issue
Something for Everyone
Always Up-to-Date
Contains 360+
pages

a

CENSORED EDITION ALWAYS AVAILABLE

No Order Form Needed:
Clearly write on paper & send with payment of **$26.99** to:

Freebird Publishers

Box 541, North Dighton, MA 02764

Diane@FreebirdPublishers.com

www.FreebirdPublishers.com

Only $19.99 plus $7 S/h with tracking

► Send Me the **CURRENT ISSUE** Inmate Shopper:

► Send Me the **CENSORED ISSUE** Inmate Shopper Without Pen Pal Content & No Sexy Girls - No More Rejections

We take all forms of payments plus MoneyGram, Western Union and PayPal.me/FreebirdPublishers

CONCLUSION

*"It is the end of the action that determines who gets
the glory, the money, the prize."*
– Robert Greene

I want to commend you for reading this book. Most prisoners don't finish the books they start unless it's a simple urban novel. But your journey is not done. You must now take what you've learned and put it into action to get the results you want. I can't promise you that it will be easy. It's not. I can promise you that it will be worth it. Even if you don't make millions of dollars at first, it's still something great. You'll get pride of ownership and creation. You'll go from being a consumer to a producer. And you'll be included in the rare few of us who are cellpreneurs! I hope you turn your ideas into something alive and profitable. You can do it by using the tactics in this book and my other books. Don't let anyone tell you that you can't. I'm living proof that you can and I've been to segregation twice for my business-related activities. But I'll never stop being an info-cellpreneur. I hope you don't either. Start the process now and I may write about you in future books? Become a cellpreneur today!

THE MILLIONAIRE PRISONER NEEDS YOUR HELP

Thank you for reading *Cellpreneur*. As I hope you'll agree after using it, it's the best of its kind. If this is how you feel, I hope you won't mind if I ask you for a favor? In my attempt to get my books into every prison library in America, I'm asking my friends and comrades to do me a favor – to write their local prison librarian and recommend the purchase of my *Millionaire Prisoner* books. These librarians pay close attention to these recommendations, and I hope you'll be willing to send the letter on the next page that I've taken the liberty of writing on your behalf. All you have to do is copy it, sign it, and mail it in using your institution's mail service. Thanks for helping me and thanks for helping me bring the best in how-to carceral information to your prison's library!

LETTER TO PRISON LIBRARIAN

Dear Librarian,

I'm writing today with a recommendation that our library purchase a new book by Josh Kruger. The book is *Cellpreneur: The Millionaire Prisoner's Guide* It's $29.99 postpaid from Freebird Publishers, P.O. Box 541, North Dighton, MA 02764, also available online at www.FreebirdPublishers.com or Amazon.

Here's what George Kayer, founding editor of *Inmate Shopper*, said about *The Millionaire Prisoner*: "…this book will help thousands of prisoners focus on a more positive and profitable life." And Christopher Zoukis, author of *College For Convicts* and Federal Prison Handbook: The Definitive guide to Surviving the Federal Bureau of Prisons "…a terrific guidebook for prisoners who desire to make something more of their life, even while in custody."

I think this book would make an excellent addition to the library's collection. I would also like to bring to your attention other books by Josh Kruger for consideration. They include:

- *The Millionaire Prisoner: How To Turn Your Prison Into A Stepping-Stone To Success* (ISBN: 978-0-9906154-4-6) $26.99 plus s/h
- *Pen Pal Success: The Ultimate Guide To Getting & Keeping Pen Pals* (ISBN: 978-0-9913591-2-7) $22.99 plus s/h

I think our library's collection would be better off with these books, and I would be grateful if you'd add them.

Thank you in advance for your cooperation in this matter. I look forward to hearing your decision.

Respectfully Submitted,

s/ _____

AUTHOR REFERENCED BOOKS

All books are available for purchase through Freebird Publishers by mail:

Freebird Publishers
Box 541
North Dighton, MA 02764
or online at FreebirdPublishers.com

168 Hours by Laura Vanderkam
272 pages, $22.00 + $4 S/H
It's an unquestioned truth of modern life: we are starved for time. We tell ourselves we'd like to read more, get to the gym regularly, try new hobbies, and accomplish all kinds of goals. But then we give up because there just aren't enough hours to do it all. Or if we don't make excuses, we make sacrifices-taking time out from other things in order to fit it all in. There has to be a better way...and Laura Vanderkam has found one.

475 Tax Deductions for Businesses and Self-Employed Individuals: An A-to-Z Guide to Hundreds of Tax Write-Offs
224 pages, $24.95 + $4 S/H
Are you paying more taxes than you have to? The IRS is certainly not going to tell you about a deduction you failed to take, and your accountant is not likely to take the time to ask you about every deduction you're entitled to. As former IRS Commissioner Mark Everson admitted, "If you don't claim it, you don't get it. That's money down the drain for millions of Americans."

Attorney Responsibilities and Client Rights
256 pages, Limited copies available for price quote send SASE to Freebird Publishers
Lawyers can fail their clients in many ways. You may feel that you have been wronged by your lawyer, but do not know if you have a valid legal claim. You may want to take legal action, but do not know how to begin the process. Resolving disputes with a lawyer will require you to be well-informed and prepared to act.

Battling The Administration: An Inmate's Guide to a Successful Lawsuit
by David J. Meister
566 pages, $38.99 + $4 S/H
Inmates, know your civil rights and how to defend them in court! This self-help manual guides readers through the complex U.S. civil court system, teaches them how to pursue a lawsuit in the face of the constraints imposed by incarceration, and enables a successful outcome for the prisoner's civil rights lawsuit.

Credit After Bankruptcy: The easy-to-follow guide to a quick and lasting recovery from personal bankruptcy by Stephen Snyder
283 pages, $24.00 + $4 S/H
Whether you filed bankruptcy several years ago or last week, this book will show you how to make a dramatic and lasting recovery. Stephen Snyder and his wife, Michele, each had their Chapter 7 bankruptcy discharged in 1993. They were both so cash poor at the time that they had to borrow money from their families to file. Then, within months, obtained bank loans, major bank cards, start-up capital for a small business, and more - all using mainstream credit and without the aid of high-interest credit card companies.

Doing Business Tax Free: Perfectly Legal Techniques for Reducing or Eliminating Your Federal Business Taxes by Robert Cooke
288 pages, $30.00 + $4 S/H
Could it be possible to run your business without paying federal and state income tax for at least 36 months? What if you're not in business-how about reducing or completely wiping out your income tax? It may sound too good to be true, but the answer is YES. In this easy-to-use, plain-English book, Robert A. Cooke shows how you can legally use the tax rules to your advantage.

Finding the Right Lawyer
by Jay G. Foonberg
318 pages, $35.95 + $4 S/H
Offers advice for choosing the proper legal service, determining an appropriate fee, and evaluating a lawyer's qualifications.

Foundation Grants to Individuals by Claire Charles
1751 pages, Limited copies available for price quote send SASE to Freebird Publishers
Foundation Grants to Individuals is the most comprehensive directory available of private grant makers, public charities and corporate giving programs in the United States that provide financial assistance to individuals.

Franchising & Licensing: Two Powerful Ways to Grow Your Business in Any Economy
by Andrew J. Sherman
464 pages, $51.00 + $4 S/H
Filled with illuminating examples, stories from the field, and dozens of forms for drafting franchising agreements and licensing programs, the fourth edition of Franchising & Licensing covers all the strategic, legal, financial, and operational aspects of these complex but highly profitable business strategies.

Free Money from the Federal Government
by Laurie Blum
368 Pages, $24.95 + $4 S/H
Even in the best of times, starting and running a small business can be an uphill battle. To help make life easier, Free Money(r) guru Laurie Blum shows you how to successfully tap into the hundreds of millions of dollars in government funding available free to entrepreneurs and small business owners. Grants range from $5,000 to some in the six figures, and best of all, absolutely none of them ever have to be paid back.

From Concept to Market by Gary S. Lynn
256 pages, $31.00 + $4 S/H
 A complete guide to bringing your idea for a product or service to market. Shows you how to document your idea, start your own company, and write a business plan and get financing. Also explains the licensing and patenting processes, contract manufacturing, distribution, pricing, and marketing. This book will be invaluable as a business primer for the new entrepreneur, or as a checklist for the veteran marketer.

Getting Funded: A Complete Guide to Proposal Writing by Mary Hall
206 pages, $30.95 + $4 S/H
The definitive how-to guide covering every aspect of writing a grant proposal. Drawing on 60 years of experience in the fields of nonprofits, grant writing and grant making. The authors take the reader step by step through the entire process from planning to writing and submitting the proposal. Numerous checklists, useful websites, and other valuable tools help keep the reader informed.

Guerrilla Financing: Alternative Techniques to Finance Any Small Business
by Bruce Blechman & Jay Conrad Levinson
352 pages, $35.00 + $4 S/H
 This book offers creative financing techniques for raising money in any type of business. If you have been turned down by a bank, run out of collateral, established poor credit, or are out of money, the techniques in this book can help solve your financial problems. Non-traditional methods of achieving goals are outlined using fresh and innovative sources of financing.

How & When To Sue Your Lawyer: What You Need To Know
by Robert W. Schachner and John Phillips
248 pages, $23.95 + $4 S/H
When lawyers represent a client, they have a legal obligation to act professionally, responsibly, and ethically. Unfortunately, all too many lawyers do not live up to these standards. If you have been victimized by your attorney, How & When to Sue Your Lawyer is here to help.

How to Form

a Limited Liability Company by Mark Warda
179 pages, Limited copies available for price quote send SASE to Freebird Publishers
(Sphinx Publishing) Self-help law book covers advantages and disadvantages of an LLC, types of LLC, start-up procedures, selling interests in the company, running a LLC, amending a LLC, and dissolving a LLC. Softcover. DLC: Private companies--United States--Popular works.

Help Your Lawyer Win Your Case by Michael Hayes
176 pages, Limited copies available for price quote send SASE to Freebird Publishers
Plain English explanations of the law to help you through your legal case. Comprehensive information that will save you time and money.

How to License Technology by Robert C. Megantz
240 pages, Limited copies available for price quote send SASE to Freebird Publishers
A complete, hands-on guide to developing and implementing effective technology licensing programs How to License Technology outlines a step-by-step approach to developing and implementing effective licensing programs in technology-based companies. Written for both inventors and corporate managers, it takes readers from idea to deal in eight, concise, easy-to-follow chapters that cover all aspects of the licensing process.

How to License your Million Dollar Idea by Harvey Reese
240 pages, $22.95 + $4 S/H
The classic guide to cashing in on your million-dollar idea. Whether you've invented a great new product, or you have an idea for an app, an online business, or a reality show, How to License Your Million Dollar Idea delivers the information you need to snag a great licensing deal. Now in its third edition, this book has become the go-to source for budding inventors and entrepreneurs who have great ideas and want to cash in on them without putting themselves in financial risk.

How To Register Your Own Copyright by Mark Warda
248 pages, $24.00 + $4 S/H
How to Register Your Own Copyright gives you detailed information on everything you should know about copyrights-from whether or not your work can be copyrighted to the way to register your copyright with the government. It is important to be sure that you are taking the correct steps to protect your work.

Inc. Yourself, 11th Edition: How to Profit by Setting Up Your Own Corporation
by Judith McQuown
300 pages, $23.99 + $4 S/H
Inc. Yourself is the longest-selling business book in the history of trade publishing. In continuous print since 1977, it has sold more than 700,000 copies to date. For 37 years it has helped entrepreneurs, small-business owners, and professionals save thousands of dollars a year by incorporating.

Investors in Your Backyard: How to Raise Business Capital from the People You Know
by Asheesh Advani
448 pages, $30.99 + $4 S/H
Everything you need to create a compelling deal! Your business is your future, whether you're starting up or expanding -- but banks and other lending institutions aren't willing to invest in your "unproven" venture. The solution? Friends, family and private investors. With Investors in Your Backyard, you get the information, documents and calculators you need to create a solid agreement that works for everyone. Let it take you through the entire process of raising business capital.

Law (In Plain English) for Writers by Leonard Duboff and Bert Krages
296 pages, $38.99 + $4 S/H
The Law (In Plain English) ® for Writers describes how to take advantage of your skills and profit from your work. It looks at the business of being a writer and explains how to succeed in every area affecting a writer's livelihood

Legal Street Smarts: How To Survive in a World of Lawyers
by Dennis M. Powers
260 Pages, $25.95 + $4 S/H
Powers, a lawyer with 20 years of experience, presents an inside assessment of what to do when facing a lawsuit or solving a company's legal problems, covering cost-effective ways to hire a lawyer, proper use of insurance, and factors to consider before filing a lawsuit. He discusses estate planning, litigation cost control tips, and how to deal with excessive fees and incompetent lawyers. Includes brief case histories.

Limited Liability Companies: A State-by-State Guide to Law and Practice by Maureen Sullivan and J. William Callison
Multi-book, Limited copies available for price quote send SASE to Freebird Publishers
The complete guide for LLC formation, operation, and termination. It compares LLCs to C corporations, S corporations, general partnerships, and limited partnerships, and offers practical guidance on when LLCs should be the entity of choice

Limited Liability Companies: Law, Practice and Forms by Jeffery C. Rubenstein, et al.
Multi-book, Limited copies available for price quote send SASE to Freebird Publishers
This guide optimizes the flexibility and tax advantages of limited liability companies (LLCs), and helps analyze planning issues. It analyzes planning issues. It includes an expanded discussion comparing LLCs with other types of entities, analysis of the rights and responsibilities of LLC members and managers, and a discussion of the impact of bankruptcy and securities laws on LLCs.

Lower Your Taxes - BIG TIME by Sandy Botkin, C.P.A.
336 pages, $30.00 + $4 S/H
Whether you're a consultant, small-business owner, or independent contractor, you want to keep more of what you earn. Lower Your Taxes—Big Time! 2017 provides everything you need to know about saving money on April 15—and every other day of the year. Sandy Botkin has taught hundreds of thousands of taxpayers how to save over $300 million on their taxes with his Tax Reduction Institute seminars.

No B.S. Ruthless Management of People and Profits by Dan S. Kennedy
274 pages, $23.95 + $4 S/H
In his traditional No B.S. style, Kennedy kicks traditional leadership and management ideas squarely in the teeth with a realistic, straightforward assessment of the real relationship between business owners and their employees. Uncompromising strategies help managers gain iron-fisted control and get the results they demand.

No B.S. Time Management for Entrepreneurs, 2nd Edition by Dan S. Kennedy
240 pages, $21.95 + $4 S/H
In this latest edition, Kennedy tackles the technology of today and delivers new insights and tools for boosting personal productivity in keeping with his "less is more" approach. New material includes how to outsource, buying experts, expertise and time. Kennedy covers virtual assistants, errand-running services, and the far-reaching scope of activities and tasks people are paying others to do for them.

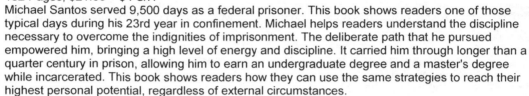

Prison! My 8,344th Day by Michael Santos
132 Pages, $21.00 + $4 S/H
Michael Santos served 9,500 days as a federal prisoner. This book shows readers one of those typical days during his 23rd year in confinement. Michael helps readers understand the discipline necessary to overcome the indignities of imprisonment. The deliberate path that he pursued empowered him, bringing a high level of energy and discipline. It carried him through longer than a quarter century in prison, allowing him to earn an undergraduate degree and a master's degree while incarcerated. This book shows readers how they can use the same strategies to reach their highest personal potential, regardless of external circumstances.

Prisoner's Self-Help Litigation Manual by John Boston and Daniel E. Manville
960 pages, $43.99 + $4 S/H
An indispensable guide for prisoners and prisoner advocates seeking to understand the rights guaranteed to prisoners by law and how to protect those rights. Clear, comprehensive, practical advice provides prisoners with everything they need to know on conditions of confinement, civil liberties in prison, procedural due process, the legal system, how to litigate, conducting effective legal research, and writing legal documents. Written by two legal and penitentiary experts with intimate knowledge of prisoner's rights.

Profit from Intellectual Property by Ron Idra
288 pages, $41.95 + $4 S/H
Licensing is a multi-billion-dollar industry. More people than ever are involved with intellectual property transactions and arrangements in everyday business. Anyone using, selling, transferring, giving, or obtaining permissions to use a product protected by intellectual property law can benefit from this book. It serves as an introduction and guide to reviewing, writing, and negotiating most of the licenses and agreements necessary to turn intellectual property into profit.

Starting Your Own Corporation by Garrett Sutton
220 Pages, $24.95 + $4 S/H
Start Your Own Corporation educates you on an action plan to protect your life's gains. Corporate attorney and best-selling author Garrett Sutton clearly explain the all too common risks of failing to protect yourself and the strategies for limiting your liability going forward. The information is timely, accessible and applicable to every citizen in every situation.

Starting Your Subchapter "S" Corporation: How to Build a Business the Right Way
by Arnold Goldstein
256 pages, Limited copies available for price quote send SASE to Freebird Publishers
This Second Edition details how to set up an S corporation and gain maximum personal benefits through tax benefits from losses, loans, salaries and wages, medical and dental plans, early retirement, etc. Describes how an S corporation functions and how to administer one. Contains forms to convert to an S corporation, maintain legal corporate records, and protect yourself, your corporation and other shareholders with essential agreements.

Starting on a Shoestring: Building a Business Without a Bankroll **by Arnold Goldstein**
306 pages, $35.95 + $4 S/H
If you've dreamed of starting your own business, but felt discouraged by a lack of start-up money, starting on a Shoestring is exactly the book you need. This authoritative, straight-talking book gives you the real-world business advice you need to start, grow, and survive. It takes you step by step

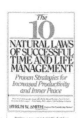

through the entire process, asking you questions, helping you plan, and giving you valuable guidance at a fraction of what consultants would charge.

The Ten Natural Laws of Time and Life Management by Hiram B. Smith
219 Pages, $22.00 + $4 S/H
Written for anyone who suffers from "time famine", this essential handbook provides simple, effective methods for successfully taking control of one's hours--and one's life. Smith shows how, by managing time better, anyone can lead a happier, more confident and fulfilled life.

The Writer's Legal Guide, 4th Edition by Kay Murray and Tad Crawford
352 Pages, $25.95 + $4
In an increasingly digitized and complex publishing world, writers need to know how to protect themselves against copyright infringement, legal trouble, and unwise concessions to publishers. Still the author's foremost advocate for copyright protection, fair contracts, and free expression, the Authors Guild has once again partnered with Allworth Press to update this invaluable reference.

Ultimate Guide to Incorporating in Any State: Everything You Need to Know by Michael Spadaccini
400 Pages, $35.95 + $4 S/H
In this authoritative handbook, business legal expert Michael Spadaccini gives the business professional all the tools necessary to plan, organize, form, operate, and maintain a basic corporation in any of the 50 states. Filled with model documents that can be easily customized using the enclosed CD-ROM, this easy-to-use kit also provides information and assistance regarding the ongoing responsibilities of running a corporation to give you a complete package.

Unlimited Business Financing by Trent Lee and Chad Lee
134 pages, $20.95 + $4 S/H
The truth about how to get up to $250,000 (or more!) in cash to invest in your business... without risking your personal credit history. Using these techniques, you can safely build a business credit history separate from your personal credit. Cash is the life-blood of every business; it fuels your business growth. Most business failures are caused not by a shortage of good ideas or know how but by a lack of operating capital. Trent makes available a much-needed resource that you can use to fund your business, finance your investments and achieve your business goals and dreams.

What Your Lawyer Doesn't Want You to Know by Douglas R. Eikermann
148 pages, $25.95 + $4 S/H
Understanding how your lawyer thinks will give you an edge! Learn how to choose the right lawyer, control your legal affairs, and know your rights and options. If you are about to hire a lawyer, chances are you are involved in a matter that is critically important to you. The information in this book will put the power in your hands and allow you to go from being a spectator in the legal process to being confidently in charge.

Who's in your Top Hive? Your Guide to Finding Your Success Mentors by Bertrand Gervais
140 pages, $25.95 + $4 S/H
These days you need more than smarts to succeed. You need a network of never-let you-fail mentors who support your growth and help you achieve your dreams. It works! All successful people have mentors in their life who help them at various stages of their development. This book will show you the five steps to pull these people towards you, every time! You will learn the 5 pillars for navigating a successful and satisfying career. Every parent, counselor, and human resource department will want to give this to a young professional they care about.

The Complete Patent Kit by James Rogers
518 pages, $45.95 + $4 S/H
Using clear language that is informative yet easy to understand, this manual provides an exhaustive wealth of information necessary for those wishing to pursue patents on their own, such as suggestions for marketing your invention in the most profitable way possible, and advice for what to do both before and after the patent process is complete. The guide even includes forms and exercises readers can use to gain a better understanding of the nuances involved.

The Licensing Handbook by Karen Raugust
275 pages, Limited copies available for price quote send SASE to Freebird Publishers
A comprehensive introduction to licensing for property owners, product manufacturers and agents.

The New Bankruptcy: Will it Work for You? by Stephen Elias & Leon Bayer
408 pages, $30.99 + $4 S/H
Is bankruptcy right for you? It's tough to know on your own. Here, you'll find clear-cut answers, worksheets and strategies to help you figure out whether bankruptcy is the best solution for your debt problems. Find out: Whether you qualify for Chapter 7 bankruptcy, which debts are wiped out, how Chapter 13 repayment plans work, how bankruptcy affects homeowners, whether you can keep cars and other property, how bankruptcy affects credit, and other ways to handle debt problems.

The Pocket Legal Companion to Copyright by Lee Wilson
329 pages, $20.95 + $4 S/H
In our age of unlimited, around-the-clock communication, copyright literacy has become a must for almost all of us, and everyone—informed or not—seems to have strong opinions about the rights of copyright owners and the rights of copyright users. This clearly written and objective book will reward readers with a more concrete understanding of our whole copyright system. This indispensable, friendly manual includes guidelines for negotiating copyrights as well as form agreements and is a must-have for anyone who wants to protect and profit from their own copyrights and use the copyrights of others—legally.

The Power Formula for LinkedIn Success by Wayne Breitbatth
232 Pages, $25.95 + $4 S/H
This book will help you create a top-notch profile AND make REAL MONEY with LinkedIn. Tens of thousands have already used Wayne Breitbarth's LinkedIn secrets to land lucrative new customers, find great new jobs, and, of course, generate more income. And most people have only scratched the surface of LinkedIn's potential.

The Power in a Link: Open Doors, Close Deals and Change the Way You Do Business Using LinkedIn by David Gowell
169 pages, $25.95 + $4 S/H
LinkedIn is not just another social media tool. It's the world's largest professional online network, with over 120 million users in over two hundred countries. The Power in a Link shows you how to employ this remarkable yet misunderstood resource to execute networking strategies and processes for your business, secure deals, and use (not abuse) your existing relationships.

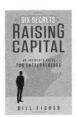

The Six Secrets of Raising Capital by Bill Fisher
144 pages, $25.95 + $4 S/H
Based on Bill Fisher's three-day seminars that regularly sell out all over the world, this book offers the kind of capital-raising street smarts no entrepreneur can do without. As a banker in Silicon Valley in the '80s and a businessman who founded a number of successful companies beginning in the '90s, Fisher has seen firsthand the kind of rookie mistakes aspiring entrepreneurs make that end up stopping them before they have a chance to get started. Fisher looks at six traditional steps in the capital-raising process and digs beneath the surface to expose subtle but critical aspects of each—knowledge that, until now, could come only with experience.

Doing Business in Arizona: A Legal Guide by Snell and Wilmer
330 pages, Limited copies available for price quote send SASE to Freebird Publishers
Doing Business in Arizona brings together in one place the essential legal information for anyone who is planning to start a business, locate a facility, or invest in Arizona. What are the differences between sole proprietorships, general and limited partnerships, and corporations? And how do you choose between them in establishing your business? What is the best form of financing for your business? What do you need to know about immigration laws, employee benefits, and intellectual property? *Doing Business in Arizona* answers these and many more essential questions for both new and veteran business owners. The book includes valuable information for the foreign investors, offering a perspective not readily available in other legal guides.

How To Form a Corporation in Florida by Mark Warda
195 pages, Limited copies available for price quote send SASE to Freebird Publishers
Each year, hundreds of thousands of corporations are registered in this country; tens of thousands in Florida alone. The corporation is the preferred way of doing business for most people as it offers many advantages over other structures. The main one being the ability to avoid personal liability. This new edition includes expanded coverage on the S-corporation and the C-corporation. Securities law as it relates to the state of Florida has also been expanded.

How To Form a Corporation in Massachusetts by Mark Warda
240 pages, Limited copies available for price quote send SASE to Freebird Publishers
Protect yourself from personal liability, without the expense and delay of hiring a lawyer, by incorporating your business on your own. How to Form a Corporation in Massachusetts contains everything you need to legally incorporate in the state of Massachusetts. This book makes incorporating your business a simple process that doesn't drain your vital time and capital.

How To Form a Corporation in Minnesota by Mark Warda
216 pages, Limited copies available for price quote send SASE to Freebird Publishers
This book takes the mystery out of creating a simple corporation. It translates difficult legal language into everyday English. It gives you practical guidance to deal with all of the State of Minnesota's legal requirements. Included are all the forms you must have and the costs to file each one.
This book has the tools you need to form your Minnesota corporation with a minimum of fuss. It has easy-to-follow instructions, addresses, phone numbers and web sites. Also, you will find tips on when you might want to consult a lawyer or other professional. This book is for people who are ready to get a corporation going quickly, correctly, and with as little time and expense as possible.

How To Form a Corporation in New York by Mark Warda
216 pages, Limited copies available for price quote send SASE to Freebird Publishers
Protect yourself from personal liability, without the expense and delay of hiring a lawyer, by incorporating your business on your own. How to Form a Corporation in New York contains everything you need to legally incorporate in the state of New York. This book makes incorporating your business a simple process that doesn't drain your vital time and capital.

How To Form a Corporation in Pennsylvania by Rebecca A. DeSimone
181 Pages, Limited copies available for price quote send SASE to Freebird Publishers
Written by an attorney in simple plain English explanation of the law. Ready to use forms with detailed instructions.

How to Form a Corporation in Texas by Karen Ann Rocick
296 pages, Limited copies available for price quote send SASE to Freebird Publishers
Incorporating your business can give you a critical competitive advantage, increasing financing potential while shielding you from personal liability. The incorporation process no longer has to be expensive or complex. Protect yourself and make the most of your business venture without the expense and delay of hiring a lawyer. How to Form a Corporation in Texas contains everything you need to legally incorporate in the state of Texas. This book helps make incorporating your business a simple process that will not drain your vital time and capital.

How To Form a Corporation, LLC or Partnership in Tennessee by W. Dean Brown
260 pages, Limited copies available for price quote send SASE to Freebird Publishers

How to Form a Limited Liability Company in Florida by Mark Warda
232 pages, Limited copies available for price quote send SASE to Freebird Publishers
The Complete Guide to Forming Your Own Limited Liability Company in Florida. Every business owner must be aware of the areas of potential risk-from violations of security laws to consumer lawsuits. Setting up an LLC is the best precaution to ensure liability protection for both individual members and the company as an entity. How to Form a Limited Liability Company in Florida teaches anyone how to protect his or her assets in an era of lawsuits and business culpability.

How to Form a Partnership in Florida by Haman
192 pages, Limited copies available for price quote send SASE to Freebird Publishers
A good partnership agreement is essential for your personal and business security. A business partnership is like a marriage--it should not be entered into lightly. How to Form a Partnership in Florida explains all the issues you need to address and takes you through the process of setting up an effective partnership.

How To Form Your Own Illinois Corporation Before the Ink Dries! by Phillip G Williams
152 pages, Limited copies available for price quote send SASE to Freebird Publishers
A step-by-step guide to incorporating a small business in the state of Illinois. Discusses pros and cons, makes entity comparisons with other forms of doing business (sole proprietorship, partnership, limited liability company). Considers federal and state tax angles. All needed forms are included in appendices and on our web site.

How to Form Your Own Michigan LLC* (*Limited Liability Company) Before the Ink Dries!
by Phillip G. Williams
152 pages, Limited copies available for price quote send SASE to Freebird Publishers
A step-by-step guide to organizing a limited liability company in the state of Michigan. Discusses pros and cons, makes entity comparisons with other forms of doing business (sole proprietorship, partnership, corporation). Considers federal and state tax angles. All needed forms are included in appendices and on our web site. Completely revised and updated second edition.

How to Start a Business in Florida by Mark Warda
264 pages, Limited copies available for price quote send SASE to Freebird Publishers
The laws, regulations and minute details of starting a business can be frustrating enough to make you wonder why you thought it was a good idea in the first place. How to Start a Business in Florida contains simple explanations of everything you need to know about federal and Florida laws to start your own enterprise. From choosing the form of your business to state and federal taxes, this book simplifies the start-up process, saving you headaches, time and money. Complete with step-by-step instructions and the forms you need, this book makes starting your own business in Florida inexpensive and hassle-free.

How to Start a Business in Georgia by Mark Warda
272 pages, Limited copies available for price quote send SASE to Freebird Publishers
Whether you are starting over in a new career or wanting to supplement your retirement, How to Start Your Own Business in Georgia can be your guide to successfully starting and running your own business.

How To Start A Business In Idaho by Entrepreneur Press
180 Pages, Limited copies available for price quote send SASE to Freebird Publishers
How to Start a Business in Idaho is your roadmap to avoid planning, legal and financial pitfalls and direct you through the bureaucratic red tape that often entangles fledgling entrepreneurs. This all-in-one resource goes a step beyond other business how-to books to give you a jump-start on planning for your business

How to Start a Business in Illinois by Mark Warda
240 Pages, Limited copies available for price quote send SASE to Freebird Publishers
The business world is brimming with new and original concepts, but few entrepreneurs possess the tools to fully realize success. How to Start a Business in Illinois is your complete guide to taking your business from concept to a full-scale, booming enterprise.

How To Start a Business in Maryland, Virginia, or DC by James E Burk and Mark Warda
272 pages, Limited copies available for price quote send SASE to Freebird Publishers
Written by attorneys in simple English explanation of the law. This book is a ready-to-use commodity with detailed forms.

How to Start a Business in Massachusetts by Mark Warda
226 pages, Limited copies available for price quote send SASE to Freebird Publishers
How to Start a Business in Massachusetts is a comprehensive aid to starting and running your own business. This book explains everything from choosing the type of business you will form to filing your state and federal taxes properly. It provides an in-depth description of how to insure your business against liability and how to draw up contracts for your transactions with both customers and vendors.

How to Start a Business in Michigan by Mark Warda
Page Count Unavailable, Limited copies available for price quote send SASE to Freebird Publishers
Written by attorneys in simple English explanation of the law. This book is a ready-to-use commodity with detailed forms.

How To Start A Business in Montana by Entrepreneur Press
288 pages, Limited copies available for price quote send SASE to Freebird Publishers
How to Start a Business in Montana is your roadmap to avoid planning, legal and financial pitfalls and direct you through the bureaucratic red tape that often entangles fledgling entrepreneurs. This all-in-one resource goes a step beyond other business how-to books to give you a jump-start on planning for your business.

How To Start A Business in New Jersey by Rebecca DeSimone
224 pages, Limited copies available for price quote send SASE to Freebird Publishers
How to Start a Business in New Jersey will guide you through successfully forming and running your own new business. This book will help you understand state laws and statutes, so you can avoid legal hassles along the way. There is an explanation of the various kinds of business you may want to form, along with an explanation of the benefits and problems that accompany each.

How To Start A Business in New York by Entrepreneur Press
250 pages, Limited copies available for price quote send SASE to Freebird Publishers
How to Start a Business in New York is your road map to avoiding operational, legal and financial pitfalls and breaking through the bureaucratic red tape that often entangles new entrepreneurs. This all-in-one resource goes a step beyond other business how-to books to give you a jump-start on planning for your business.

How To Start a Business in North Carolina or South Carolina by Stanley and DeGood
224 pages, Limited copies available for price quote send SASE to Freebird Publishers
How to Start a Business in North Carolina or South Carolina is an innovative answer to understanding the federal and state laws that accompany starting a business. From choosing your business to employment and financial matters, this book simplifies the start-up process while saving you time and money. Written by attorneys, this book uses an easy-to-understand approach to business regulations for anyone considering opening a business in North Carolina or South Carolina.

How to Start a Business in Pennsylvania by Mark Warda
264 pages, Limited copies available for price quote send SASE to Freebird Publishers
The laws, regulations, and minute details of starting a business can be frustrating enough to make you wonder why you thought it was a good idea in the first place. How to Start a Business in Pennsylvania contains simple explanations of everything you need to know about federal and Pennsylvania laws to start your own enterprise.

How to Start a Business in Texas by Mark Warda and Traci Truly
Page Count Unavailable, Limited copies available for price quote send SASE to Freebird Publishers
Written by attorneys in simple English explanation of the law. This book is a ready-to-use commodity with detailed forms.

Incorporate in Delaware from Any State by Mark Warda
304 pages, Limited copies available for price quote send SASE to Freebird Publishers
Protect yourself from personal liability without the expense and delay of hiring a lawyer, by incorporating your business on your own. Incorporate in Delaware from Any State contains everything you need to legally incorporate or start an LLC in the state of Delaware. This book makes incorporating your business a simple process that doesn't drain your vital time and capital.

Incorporate in Nevada from Any State by Mark Warda
256 pages, Limited copies available for price quote send SASE to Freebird Publishers
This title addresses several state statutes that work in favor of incorporating in Nevada. New forms, tax schedules, and a current list of companies that serve as registered agents for new corporations are included. A glossary, thorough index, blank, tear-out forms, and customized stock certificates make this title a valuable tool for financial growth.

New York Power of Attorney Handbook by William P. Coyle
144 pages, Limited copies available for price quote send SASE to Freebird Publishers
Complete step by step instructions and the forms you need, this book makes writing your own poer of attorney inexpensive and hassle free.

New York State Tax Law by CCH Tax Law Editors
1696 pages, Limited copies available for price quote send SASE to Freebird Publishers
This comprehensive reference provides full text of the statute affecting New York personal income, corporate franchise (income), estate, excise, sales and use, franchise, and other NY taxes as amended by legislative action through January 1, 2014 Key legislative changes from the previous year are described in a special Highlights section and are also incorporated in the law text. Since frequent changes are made in the New York State tax laws, each edition of this reference provides an important source for the tax laws of prior years.

Texas Business and Commerce Code: 2017 by Hopp Tech LLC
680 pages, $45.99 + $4 S/H
This edition of the Texas Business and Commerce Code has been specially edited and formatted. This formatted version is perfect for students, practicing attorneys, and for the public to use as a reference and to have access to the code at their fingertips. If you need a copy of the Texas Business and Commerce Code, then look no further. This edition is perfect anyone who needs easy access to the relevant law in an easy to read format that allows them to find what they need in quickly and easily.

Texas Corporation and Partnership Laws by Thomason West
1005 pages,
Texas Corporation and Partnership Laws includes the full text of the Texas statutes controlling corporations and partnerships. This economical volume is ideal when you need a quick answer or when annotations are not immediately required. References to law review commentaries discussing particular provisions, disposition and derivation tables, and a comprehensive index facilitate research.

The Pennsylvania Nonprofit Handbook, 10th Edition: Everything You Need to Know to Start and Run Your Nonprofit Organization by Gary M Grobman
488 Pages, $45.95 + $4
The definitive handbook on starting and running a nonprofit organization in Pennsylvania. THE PENNSYLVANIA NONPROFIT HANDBOOK, 10th Edition, includes information about current laws, court decisions, and regulations that apply to nonprofits. It also includes practical advice on running a nonprofit corporation, sample corporate bylaws, and sources of information on how to start up a new nonprofit.

All books are available for purchase through Freebird Publishers by mail:

NO ORDER FORM NEEDED CLEARLY WRITE ON PAPER & SEND PAYMENT TO:

Freebird Publishers
Box 541
North Dighton, MA 02764
or online at FreebirdPublishers.com

ABOUT THE AUTHOR

In 1999, Josh Kruger was arrested for felony murder, home invasion, and robbery. At the subsequent bench trial in 2000, he received a directed verdict of acquittal, when the state refused to participate over an evidence dispute. Kruger was released, but eventually rearrested and convicted in a 2003 jury trial and sentenced to life in prison.

After reading several of Zig Ziglar's books, Kruger reached out to the late, great motivational speaker and began corresponding with Ziglar. He adopted Zig's philosophy that you can have everything you want in life if you just help enough people get what they want.

Tired of depending on friends and family for support, the graduate of Crown Financial Ministries decided to leverage his extensive juvenile and adult prison experiences into a freelance writing career. In 2011, Kruger launched his micropublishing empire from his maximum-security prison cell by self-publishing two booklets, *How To Get Free Pen Pals* and *How To Win Your Football Pool*. Prison authorities seized his property and threw him in segregation by alleging that he was violating prison rules. Not to be dismayed, Kruger kept going and published his first book, *The Millionaire Prisoner*, to help prisoners find their cellpreneurial calling and to look for the opportunities in life instead of the obstacles. Both of his third and fourth books are based on his own personal experiences from behind the iron veil of prison. His mission is to change lives, one prisoner at a time.

Josh Kruger

WE NEED YOUR REVIEWS

Rate Us & Win!

We do monthly drawings for a FREE copy of one of our publications. Just have your loved one rate any Freebird Publishers book on Amazon and then send us a quick e-mail with your name, inmate number, and institution address and you could win a FREE book.

FREEBIRD PUBLISHERS
Box 541
North Dighton, MA 02764

www.freebirdpublishers.com
Diane@FreebirdPublishers.com

Thanks for your interest in Freebird Publishers!

We value our customers and would love to hear from you! Reviews are an important part in bringing you quality publications. We love hearing from our readers-rather it's good or bad (though we strive for the best)!

If you could take the time to review/rate any publication you've purchased with Freebird Publishers we would appreciate it!

If your loved one uses Amazon, have them post your review on the books you've read. This will help us tremendously, in providing future publications that are even more useful to our readers and growing our business.

Amazon works off of a 5 star rating system. When having your loved one rate us be sure to give them your chosen star number as well as a written review. Though written reviews aren't required, we truly appreciate hearing from you.

☆☆☆☆☆ **Everything a prisoner needs is available in this book.**

January 30, 201 June 7, 2018
Format: Paperback

A necessary reference book for anyone in prison today. This book has everything an inmate needs to keep in touch with the outside world on their own from inside their prison cell. Inmate Shopper's business directory provides complete contact information on hundreds of resources for inmate services and rates the companies listed too! The book has even more to offer, contains numerous sections that have everything from educational, criminal justice, reentry, LGBT, entertainment, sports schedules and more. The best thing is each issue has all new content and updates to keep the inmate informed on todays changes. We recommend everybody that knows anyone in prison to send them a copy, they will thank you.

* No purchase neccessary. Reviews are not required for drawing entry. Void where prohibited.
  Contest date runs July 1 - June 30, 2019.

Freebird Publishers

We Specialize in Prisoner Publications

ALL PRICES INCLUDE SHIPPING & HANDLING with TRACKING

INMATE SHOPPER, Book of Resources for Inmate Services   -2018-19 NEW ISSUE-

1000+ Listings AMERICA'S LARGEST Resources for Inmate Services. Everything you need from the outside while in prison is available in this ANNUAL ISSUE 2018-19, Split Year, June to June. All new content in each issue, constantly updated with products, services, resources, news, sport schedules, sexy non nude photo spread, pen pal section & more. Softcover, 8x10", B&W, 360+ pages... $26.99 ($19.99 plus $7 s/h)

SEXY GIRL PARADE, Non Nude Photo Book

Full color gloss non nude photos. A different photo on every page. Over $100 worth of sexy photos in one book, for one low price. Non nude prison friendly. Softcover, 8.3x6", GLOSS COLOR, 128 pages... $31.99 ($24.99 plus $7 s/h)

PEN PAL SUCCESS: The Ultimate Guide To Getting and Keeping Pen Pals

You've heard it said "The game is to be sold not told." Well, now a new book is doing all the telling about the game. In 20 information-dense chapters you'll DISCOVER the secrets. Pen Pal Success contains "insiders" wisdom especially for prisoners. You owe it to yourself to invest in this book! Softcover, 8x10", B&W, 225+ pages... $29.99 ($22.99 plus $7 s/h)

CELLPRENEUR: The Millionaire Prisoner's

Wish you could start a legitimate business from your cell? And not violate your prison rules? Do you have an idea that you wish you could license to another company and make money from it? They tell you "You can't start a business while in prison." Well the author did and book contains "insider's" wisdom especially for prisoners. You owe it to yourself to invest in this book! Softcover, 8x10", B&W, 250+ pages $29.99 (22.99 plus 7. s/h)

THE BEST 500+ NON PROFIT ORGS FOR PRISONERS and Their Families   -NEW 5th Ed.-

America's only up to date & comprehensive print resource of non profit orgs specifically for prisoners. Over 500+ Listings. All entries updated and new sections, Registry of Motor Vehicles by state, Social Security by state, Internal Revenue Service by state and region, Immigration by state and U.S. Congress by state and district. Softcover, 8x10", B&W, 160+ pages... $21.99 ($16.99 plus $5 s/h)

THE CELL CHEF Cook Book

The Cell Chef Cookbook is filled with hundreds of fantastic recipes, that can be simply made with everyday, commonly sold commissary/store foods. Every recipe has been tried and thoroughly tested. Loved by everyone. In the Cell Chef Cookbook the recipes are divided into four sections: Meals and Snacks, Sauces, Sandwich Spreads, Salsa and Dips, Drinks & Sweet Desserts. Softcover, Square 8.25X8.25"", B&W, 183 pages... $18.99 ($13.99 plus $5 s/h)

A YEAR OF THE CORCORAN SUN Book

This book filled with twelve issues of prison yard monthly newsletters compiled for hours of reading enjoyment. The book is packed full with news, entertainment, writing tips, publishing leads, resources, art, poetry, drama, and fiction by and for inmates and their loved ones. Softcover, 8x10", B&W, 240+ pages... $21.99 ($15.99 plus $6 s/h)

NO ORDER FORM NEEDED CLEARLY WRITE ON PAPER & SEND PAYMENT TO:

Freebird Publishers Box 541, North Dighton, MA 02764

DIANE@FREEBIRDPUBLISHERS.COM WWW.FREEBIRDPUBLISHERS.COM

Freebird Publishers

We Specialize in Prisoner Publications

ALL PRICES INCLUDE SHIPPING & HANDLING with TRACKING

LIFE WITH A RECORD: Reenter Society, Finish Supervision and Live Successfully

Information in this book help make sense of the major challenges facing ex-offenders today. Ten hard hitting chapters outline the purpose of making a Strategic Reentry it packs an amazing amount of material into its pages and gives you a quick, easy to follow, full spectrum of instruction. explores the most commonly confronted issues and attitudes that sabotage reentry. Addressing the whole reentry process. Softcover, 8x10", B&W, 360 pages $32.99 (25.99 plus $7 s/h)

KITTY KAT, Adult Entertainment Non Nude Resource Book

This book is jam packed with hundreds of sexy non nude photos including photo spreads. The book contains the complete info on sexy photo sellers, hot magazines, page turning bookstore, sections on strip clubs, porn stars, alluring models, thought provoking stories and must see movies. Softcover, 8x10", Color covers, B&W interior, 185+ pages $31.99 ($24.99 plus $7 s/h)

HOT GIRL SAFARI, Non Nude Photo Book

Full color gloss non nude photos. A different photo on every page. Over $100 worth of sexy photos in one book, for one low price. Non nude prison friendly. Softcover, 8.3x6", GLOSS COLOR, 128 pages... $31.99 ($24.99 plus $7 s/h)

POST-CONVICTION RELIEF: Secrets Exposed

This book is full of information about how to get out of prison early. Cover to cover filled with motions and secrets used by real Habeas Corpus practitioners getting real results. This book will show you the simple way to: Get your case file; Analyze your case; Keep your records efficiently; Investigate your case, see what you deserve; Write simple effective motions; Get out of prison; EARLY!! Softcover, 8x10", B&W, 190+ pages $26.99 (19.99 plus 7. s/h)

S.T.O.P. Start Thinking Outside Prison

Thinking is very critical to one's success, failure, and survival. Every decision requires thinking. If not, many actions will be done on impulse. And impulsive behavior tends to bring about situations from which one needs to be rescued. S.T.O.P. was written as a movement to help promote a greater thinking process - a thinking process believed to slow down the recidivism rate within our communities. Softcover, 6x9", B&W, 70 pages $18.99 ($13.99 plus $5 s/h)

SOFT SHOTS, Non Nude Photo Book

Come see our beautiful ladies dressed in the tiniest of outfits and posing in many different alluring positions. Full color gloss non nude photos. A different photo on every page. Over $100+ worth of sexy photos in one book, for one low price. Non nude prison friendly. Softcover, 8.25x5.25", GLOSS COLOR, 150 pages... $31.99 ($24.99 plus $7 s/h)

GIFT Look Book 2018-19 Plus FREE SWAROVSKI Crystal Jewelry Book   -NEW BOOK-

With Every Book Receive a $15.00 Voucher We carry hundreds of high quality gifts for every occasion to fit every budget. Our gifts are made in America! Gift Baskets, Flowers, Chocolates & Candies, Personalized Gifts and more. We offer a complete line of custom gift baskets. Our flowers are delivered fresh in bud-form to open up full bloom in front of your loved ones. Our chocolates fresh made of the finest quality. Animated singing plush gifts. Softcover, 8x10", FULL COLOR, 110 pages $15.00 (Free s/h) **2 Books for $15, Free s/h Plus Credit Voucher**

NO ORDER FORM NEEDED CLEARLY WRITE ON PAPER & SEND PAYMENT TO:

Freebird Publishers Box 541, North Dighton, MA 02764

DIANE@FREEBIRDPUBLISHERS.COM WWW.FREEBIRDPUBLISHERS.COM

Made in the USA
Middletown, DE
26 March 2023

27653013R10144